BASIL

THE SEVENTEENTH-CENTURY BACKGROUND

STUDIES IN THE THOUGHT OF THE AGE
IN RELATION TO POETRY
AND RELIGION

PENGUIN BOOKS

IN ASSOCIATION WITH

CHATTO & WINDUS

Penguin Books Ltd, Harmondsworth, Middlesex, England
Penguin Books Australia Ltd, Ringwood, Victoria, Australia

—

First published by Chatto & Windus 1934
Published in Peregrine Books 1962
Reprinted 1964, 1967
Reissued in Pelican Books 1972

—

—

Made and printed in Great Britain
by Cox & Wyman Ltd, London, Reading and Fakenham
Set in Monotype Bembo

Contents

CONTENTS

Foreword

THE following pages are the outcome of lectures on seventeenth-century life and thought given in the English School at Cambridge during recent years. The wider purpose of the book is to furnish readers of seventeenth-century literature with a sketch of the intellectual background of the period. But I have hoped to give some unity to so vast a subject by keeping steadily in view a more particular aim, that, namely, of noting how poetry, and also religion, were affected by the contemporary 'climates of opinion'. It is generally agreed that in the seventeenth century a great effort was being made, by representative thinkers, to see things 'as in themselves they really are', and the ideas of Truth and Fiction which were then evolved seem to have exerted a decisive influence upon the poetic and religious beliefs of succeeding times. It has been my aim to study this influence, and to inquire what occurred when traditional beliefs, and especially theological and poetic beliefs, were exposed to the 'touch of cold philosophy'.

I hope I need offer no apology for thus classifying poetic and religious beliefs together. Both, at any rate, seem to have been similarly affected by the 'philosophic' spirit, and those who are interested in the fate of either can hardly avoid feeling some concern for that of the other. What I do wish to make clear, however, is that this book makes no pretence to be a contribution either to the 'moral sciences' or to pure literary criticism. When speaking of philosophical matters I have supposed myself to be addressing, not professional philosophers, but students of literature, and not professed students merely, but all to whom poetry, and religion, and their relation to the business of living, are matters of importance. And as my excuse for trespassing so outrageously beyond the supposed limits of 'literary' criticism I would offer the following recent remark of Mr T. S. Eliot's, from which I have derived considerable consolation:

7

FOREWORD

In attempting to win a full understanding of the poetry of a period you are led to the consideration of subjects which at first sight appear to have little bearing upon poetry.[1]

My acknowledgements are due to the Syndics of the Cambridge University Press for permission to quote from Professor Whitehead's *Science and the Modern World*, to Messrs Kegan Paul, Trench, Trübner & Co. for allowing me to reproduce a passage from Professor Burtt's *Metaphysical Foundations of Modern Science*, and to Messrs Sheed and Ward for permission to quote from M. Maritain's *St Thomas Aquinas* and Mr Christopher Dawson's *Christianity and the New Age*.

The Postscript chapter on 'Wordsworth and the Locke Tradition' contains the greater part of an essay entitled *Wordsworth's Beliefs*, which has appeared in the *Criterion*. I am indebted to the Editor of that review for kindly allowing me to make use of this material.

B. W.

Cambridge, November 1933

1. *The Use of Poetry and the Use of Criticism*, p. 76.

CHAPTER I

The Rejection of Scholasticism

'Truth' and 'Explanation' in the Seventeenth Century

> *'I perceive'*, said the Countess, *'Philosophy is now become very Mech-anical.' 'So mechanical'*, said I, *'that I fear we shall quickly be asham'd of it; they will have the World to be in great, what a watch is in little; which is very regular, & depends only upon the just disposing of the several parts of the movement. But pray tell me, Madam, had you not formerly a more sublime idea of the Universe?'* (Fontenelle, *Plurality of Worlds*, 1686.)

To give a 'philosophical' account of matters which had formerly been explained 'unscientifically', 'popularly', or 'figuratively' – this, it would probably be agreed, has been the main intellectual concern of the last three hundred years. In a sense, no doubt, the separation of the 'true' from the 'false', the 'real' from the 'illusory', has been the task of thought at all times. But this winnowing process seems to have been carried on much more actively and consciously at certain times than at others. For us in the West two such periods are of especial importance, the period of Greek philosophy and the centuries following the Renaissance. It was in the seventeenth century that modern European thought seems first to have assumed, once more, that its appointed task was *La Recherche de la vérité*, the discovery and declaration, according to its lights, of the True Nature of Things. It is in that century that we meet once again the exhilaration which inspired Lucretius in his address to Epicurus – the sense of emancipation from inadequate notions, of new contact with reality. It was then, too, that the concepts of 'truth', 'reality', 'explanation', and the rest were being formed, which have moulded all subsequent thinking. There is some reason, then, for supposing

9

that it may be worth while to watch these concepts in process of formation.

First it may be well to inquire, not with Pilate – 'What is Truth?' but what was *felt to be* 'truth' and 'explanation' under seventeenth-century conditions. As T. E. Hulme and others have pointed out, it is almost insuperably difficult to become critically conscious of one's own habitual assumptions; 'doctrines felt as facts' can only be seen to be doctrines, and not facts, after great efforts of thought, and usually only with the aid of a first-rate metaphysician. It is, however, less difficult to detect the assumptions of an age distant from our own, especially when these have been subject to criticism. At this distance of time it should be possible, I think, to state fairly accurately what the seventeenth century felt as 'true', and what satisfied it as 'explanation'. In reading seventeenth-century writers one feels that it was as 'explanation' that they chiefly valued the 'new philosophy', and it is for this reason that I wish first to inquire, briefly, what is 'explanation'?

Dictionary definitions will not help us much here. To 'explain', we learn, means to 'make clear', to 'render intelligible'. But wherein consists the clarity, the intelligibility? The clarity of an explanation seems to depend upon the degree of satisfaction that it affords. An explanation 'explains' best when it meets some need of our nature, some deep-seated demand for assurance. 'Explanation' may perhaps be roughly defined as a restatement of something – event, theory, doctrine, etc. – in terms of the current interests and assumptions. It satisfies, as explanation, because it appeals to that particular set of assumptions, as superseding those of a past age or of a former state of mind. Thus it is necessary, if an explanation is to seem satisfactory, that its terms should seem ultimate, incapable of further analysis. Directly we allow ourselves to ask 'What, after all, does this explanation amount to?' we have really demanded an explanation of the explanation, that is to say, we have seen that the terms of the first explanation are not ultimate, but can be analysed into other terms – which perhaps for the moment do seem to us to be ultimate. Thus, for example, we may choose to accept a psychological explanation of a metaphysical proposition, or we may prefer a metaphysical explanation of a psychological proposition. All depends upon our presuppositions, which in turn depend upon our training, whereby we have come to regard (or to feel) one set of terms as ultimate, the other not. An explanation commands our assent with immediate authority, when it presupposes the 'reality', the 'truth', of what seems to us most real, most true. One cannot, therefore, define 'explanation' absolutely; one can only say that it is a statement which satisfies the demands of a particular time or place.

A general demand for restatement or explanation seems to have arisen from time to time, perhaps never more vehemently than in the period we are considering. Such a demand presumably indicates a disharmony between traditional explanations and current needs. It does not necessarily imply the 'falsehood' of the older statement; it may merely mean that men now wish to live and to act according to a different formula. This is especially evident in our period whenever a 'scientific' explanation replaces a theological one. For example, the spots on the moon's surface might be due, theologically, to the fact that it was God's will they should be there; scientifically they might be 'explained' as the craters of extinct volcanoes. The newer explanation may be said, not so much to contain 'more' truth than the older, as to supply the *kind* of truth which was now demanded. An event was 'explained' – and this, of course, may be said as much of our own time as of the seventeenth century – when its history had been traced and described. A comet, for example, or an eclipse, was explained when instead of being a disastrous omen which 'with fear of change perplexes monarchs' it could be shown to be the 'necessary' result of a demonstrable chain of causes. No one, it need hardly be said, wishes to deny that this explanation had and still has a more 'satisfying' quality than the one it superseded. But why was it more satisfying? It was more satisfying, we may suppose, because now, instead of the kind of 'truth' which is consistent with authoritative teaching, men began to desire the kind which would enable them to measure, to weigh, and to control the things around them; they desired, in Bacon's words, 'to extend more widely the limits of the power and greatness of man'.[1] Interest was

1. Quoted by Dampier-Whetham, *History of Science*, p. 137.

now directed to the *how*, the manner of causation, not its *why*, its final cause. For a scientific type of explanation to be satisfying, for it to convince us with a sense of its necessary truth, we must be in the condition of needing and desiring that type of explanation and no other.

The seventeenth century was the first of the modern centuries which, on the whole, have increasingly fulfilled these conditions. We have said that an explanation is acceptable when it satisfies certain needs and demands. What demands were met by the scientific movement in our period? To answer this question we may inquire a little into the general effects of explanation upon the minds of those who are being enlightened. Considered as a psychological event, an explanation may be described as a change in the quality of our response towards an object or an idea. This change is typically a release from some sort of tension, as in the ordinary cases of 'clearing-up' any 'mystery'. An explanation invites and – if it is in accordance with our felt or unfelt needs – produces a new attitude towards its subject-matter. Where we had formerly felt fear, pains, curiosity, dissatisfaction, anxiety, or reverence, we now experience relief, and regard the object with easy familiarity and perhaps contempt. An explained thing, except for very resolute thinkers, is almost inevitably 'explained away'. Speaking generally, it may be said that the demand for explanation is due to the desire to be rid of mystery. Such a demand will be most insistent when the current mysteries have become unusually irksome, as seems to have been the case in the time of Epicurus, and again at the Renaissance. At those turning-points men wanted 'scientific' explanations because they no longer wished to feel as they had been taught to feel about the nature of things. To be rid of fear – fear of the unknown, fear of the gods, fear of the stars or of the devil – to be released from the necessity of reverencing what was not to be understood, these were amongst the most urgent demands of the modern as of the ancient world; and it was because it satisfied these demands that scientific explanation was received as the revelation of truth. Not immediately received by everybody, we should remind ourselves. There are always those like Donne for whom new philosophy 'puts all in doubt', for whom, in fact, new explanation explains nothing, but merely causes distress and confusion; and those, like the Fathers of the Inquisition, for whom new philosophy is simply old error. But there is a deepening chorus of approval as the century wears on, and after the Restoration the unanimity is wonderful.

More was demanded than mere release from traditional hauntings. Men demanded also to feel at home in this brave new world which Columbus and Copernicus and Galileo had opened up to them, and to recognize it as 'controlled, sustained, and agitated' by laws in some way akin to those of human reason. To be no longer at the mercy of nature, no longer to be encompassed by arbitrary mystery – these benefits were to be accompanied by the great new gift of power, power to control natural forces and to turn them, in Bacon's phrases, to the 'occasions and uses of life', and 'the relief of man's estate'. All this the new thought promised and indeed performed; no wonder, then, that the types of explanation which it offered seemed the only 'true' ones. Were these promises the enticements of Mephistopheles to Faust? and has the Adversary, at any time since then, actually reappeared and demanded payment of his bond? The disturbing possibility is one which, at any rate, we shall not do ill to bear in mind as we pursue our inquiries.

We began, it will be remembered, by inquiring what was felt to be most true, most real, most explanatory, under seventeenth-century conditions. Let us guard against any implied over-simplification; no one thing answered to that description, then or at any time. Different kinds of truth were acknowledged (as we shall see later in more detail), for instance truths of faith and truths of reason; different orders of reality were recognized, and different kinds of explanation seen to be relevant in varying contexts. Nevertheless it may be said that if there was then any outstanding intellectual revolution in process of enactment, it was a general transference of interest from metaphysics to physics, from the contemplation of Being to the observation of Becoming. In Bacon's classification of the Sciences, final causes and Form are consigned to Metaphysics, while Physics deals with efficient causes and Matter. But although Metaphysics is thus given its status by the *buccinator novi temporis*, the main significance of the great instauration was to lie in the enormous extension

13

of the field of physical or 'natural' causation, the field of 'efficient causes and Matter'. In the mighty 'exantlation of truth'[1] – of which Sir Thomas Browne lamented that he should not see the end, or more, indeed, than 'that obscured Virgin half out of the pit' – no event counted for more than the realization that almost all the phenomena of the physical world could be 'explained' by the laws of motion, as movements of particles of matter in space and time. As Glanvill says, the Aristotelian philosophy had prevailed, until the present age disinterred 'the more excellent Hypotheses of Democritus and Epicurus'.[2] Although not all mysteries, by any means, had yet been reduced to mechanics, what is important for us is that now mechanico-materialistic explanations began to be 'felt as facts', felt, that is, as affording that picture of reality, of things-in-themselves, which alone would satisfy contemporary demands. It was only when you were interpreting any phenomenon – a colour, a movement, a condition, an attraction – in terms of the motion of atoms, their impingement on each other, their cohesion, collision, or eddying, that you were giving an account of how things actually and really happened. The mechanical explanation was the 'philosophical' explanation; all others were, on the one hand, vulgar, superstitious, and superficial; or, on the other hand, they were 'Aristotelian' or 'scholastic'.

Some Protests

In general it may be said that the reason why scholasticism was held to be an obstacle to truth was because it seemed to discourage further inquiry along experimental lines. All explanations of the scholastic type seemed to the new school to be merely statements of ignorance masquerading in philosophic dress, equivalent, in fact, to asserting that things are such-and-such because they are. Criticisms of scholasticism abound in our period, for instance in the writings of Bacon,

1. 'Wherein, against the tenacity of prescription and prejudice, this century now prevaileth.' *Christian Morals*, II, sect. 5.

2. *Vanity of Dogmatizing*, 1661, p. 146.

Descartes, Hobbes, Browne, Milton, Glanvill, Boyle, and many others. Most of these writers are full of the sense of having triumphed over what had hitherto seemed the ultimate limitations of human knowledge, the sense of having passed the pillars of Hercules on the intellectual voyage. And until quite recently most historians have written of them from their own standpoint, representing the intellectual history of the period as a process whereby error, fable, and superstition were finally vanquished by truth and reason. There have, however – especially of late – been voices raised in protest against the uncritical acceptance of the 'scientific' assumptions; and it should therefore be not only possible, but natural, for us to approach the seventeenth century with greater detachment. The admonitions have come to us from widely different quarters. We have the Catholics and Neo-Thomists, a group including several writers of the greatest ability, who have extolled the synthesis of St Thomas Aquinas, and expounded it with convincing brilliance. Here, for instance, is M. Maritain's version of what really took place at the Renaissance (the italics are mine):

In the sixteenth century, and more particularly in the age of Descartes, the interior hierarchies of the virtue of reason were shattered. Philosophy abandoned theology to assert its own claim to be considered the supreme science, and, *the mathematical science of the sensible world and its phenomena taking precedence at the same time over metaphysics, the human mind began to profess independence of God and Being.* Independence of God: that is to say, of the supreme Object of all intelligence, Whom it accepted only half-heartedly until it finally rejected the intimate knowledge of Him supernaturally procured by grace and revelation. Independence of being: that is to say, of the connatural object of the mind as such, against which it ceased to measure itself humbly, until it finally undertook to deduce it entirely from the seeds of geometrical clarity which it conceived to be innate in itself.[1]

Just before the war T. E. Hulme proclaimed, in language of remarkable trenchancy, the death of the humanist and scientific traditions springing from the Renaissance, and demanded what was in effect a return to the ideology of scholasticism. 'As if', he wrote in 1913, 'it were not the business of every honest man at the present

1. Maritain, *St Thomas Aquinas*, English translation, p. 91.

moment to clean the world of these sloppy dregs of the Renaissance!'[1] M. Julien Benda prefixes his *Trahison des clercs* with a motto from Renouvier: '*Le monde souffre du manque de foi en une vérité transcendante.*' Lastly, though examples could be indefinitely multiplied, I will quote from a brilliant essay by a younger representative of the Catholic school, Mr Christopher Dawson:

The Western mind has turned away from the contemplation of the absolute and eternal to the knowledge of the particular and the contingent. It has made man the measure of all things and has sought to emancipate human life from its dependence on the supernatural. Instead of the whole intellectual and social order being subordinated to spiritual principles, every activity has declared its independence, and we see politics, economics, science, and art organizing themselves as autonomous kingdoms which owe no allegiance to any higher power.[2]

Mr Dawson, and those who think with him, trace the present chaos in Western civilization to this loss of God-consciousness, the Renaissance becoming, in their view, a veritable second Fall of Man. Sentiments of this kind, it is worth remembering, can now be uttered in all soberness and with compelling force, whereas at almost any time during the past three hundred years they would have seemed a mad flouting of the dominant optimism and progress-worship. No one listened when Blake, about a hundred and thirty years ago, described Bacon's Essays as 'Good advice for Satan's Kingdom', and announced that 'Bacon's philosophy has Ruin'd England'.

But it is not only from this camp that the attacks have been launched. The most recent advances in science itself, as is well known, have had at least as unsettling an effect upon the traditional scientific 'philosophy', indeed they have perhaps contributed vitally to the recent revival of respect for scholastic ways of thought. The situation, as far as a layman can understand it, seems to be not that science has proved in any sense 'wrong' in its results, but that it has, through some of its leading contemporary writers, acknow-

1. From an article on Epstein, in *The New Age*, 25 December 1913.
2. 'Christianity and The New Age', p. 66, in *Essays in Order*, 1931.

ledged its own account of reality to be far from complete. Mechanistic determinism, the essential assumption of science, has not been 'exploded', as we are sometimes informed by persons interested in its overthrow; it has merely been shown to be a method and not a philosophy, a technique of investigation and not an account of Being. The statements of science, now seen to be abstractions, are generally recognized to be incapable of satisfying all the complex needs of the human spirit, though they are of unimpaired serviceableness within their own field of application. For some time we have been encountering, and we have now learned to expect, a changed tone from writers who treat of the origins of modern scientific thought. Though there is no diminution in the volume of praise which is bestowed on the giants of the seventeenth century – 'the century of genius' – there is no longer the old tone of expansive optimism, the glad sense of final escape from error. Though no one denies the extent of our gains, it is more often of our losses that we are now reminded. Nature, according to the mechanical philosophy, writes Professor Whitehead,

is a dull affair, soundless, scentless, colourless; merely the hurrying of material, endlessly, meaninglessly. However you disguise it, this is the practical outcome of the characteristic scientific philosophy which closed the seventeenth century. No alternative system of organizing the pursuit of scientific truth has been suggested. It is not only reigning, but it is without a rival. And yet – it is quite unbelievable. This conception of the universe is surely framed in terms of high abstractions, and the paradox only arises because we have mistaken our abstractions for concrete realities. ... The seventeenth century had finally produced a scheme of scientific thought framed by mathematicians, for the use of mathematicians. The great characteristic of the mathematical mind is its capacity for dealing with abstractions; and for eliciting from them clear-cut demonstrative trains of reasoning, entirely satisfactory so long as it is those abstractions which you want to think about. The enormous success of the scientific abstractions, yielding on the one hand *matter* with its *simple location* in space and time, on the other hand *mind*, perceiving, suffering, reasoning but not interfering, has foisted on to philosophy the task of accepting them as the most concrete rendering of fact. Thereby, modern philosophy has been ruined.[1]

1. *Science and the Modern World*, Ch. 3.

One more quotation, from a historian of scientific thought, should suffice to illustrate the prevailing attitude. Professor E. A. Burtt, writing of the emotional implications of seventeenth-century science, says:

It was of the greatest consequence for succeeding thought that now the great Newton's authority was squarely behind that view of the cosmos which saw in man a puny, irrelevant spectator (so far as a being wholly imprisoned in a dark room can be called such) of the vast mathematical system whose regular motions according to mechanical principles constituted the world of nature. . . . The world that people had thought themselves living in – a world rich with colour and sound . . . speaking everywhere of purposive harmony and creative ideals – was crowded now into minute corners in the brains of scattered organic beings. The really important world outside was a world, hard, cold, colourless, silent, and dead – a world of quantity, a world of mathematically computable motions in mechanical regularity. The world of qualities as immediately perceived by man became just a curious and quite minor effect of that infinite machine, beyond. In Newton, the Cartesian metaphysics, ambiguously interpreted and stripped of its distinctive claim for serious philosophical consideration, finally overthrew Aristotelianism, and became the predominant world-view of modern times.[1]

In approaching the question of the rejection of scholasticism, therefore, it is both our duty and our privilege today to consider the two world-views with no antecedent prejudice in favour of the modern.

St Thomas Aquinas and Galileo

Not even the briefest account of scholasticism can be attempted here. I will merely give a few examples of the way in which the scholastic mind worked, in the hope that we may then understand more clearly why the seventeenth century wished to reject its methods.

Scholastic thought was predominantly metaphysical; it was concerned, that is to say, with Being and Essence, Cause and End.

1. *The Metaphysical Foundations of Modern Science*, pp. 236–7.

It existed to give answers to the questions that children ask, but which the adult consciousness first dismisses as unanswerable and then forgets – questions taking the form of 'Why?', 'Whence?', 'What is it made of?', and 'Who made it, or put it there?' Questions so searching, it has been said, are not really questions at all, but requests for emotional assurance. This, however, does not alter their status as signs of a deep human need, the need for a formula which will express our sense of the *quality* of all things. Our first demand (in Arnold's phrases) is for 'an explanation in black and white of the mystery of existence'; then, unless our demand is met by an authoritative body of doctrine living in our time, we either grow indifferent, or fall back upon poetry, which can arouse in us a *sense* of the mystery, without 'explaining' it. Scholasticism was able to give this black-and-white explanation because it was a science of Being; its explanations were all given in terms of the forms, qualities, origins, and ends of things. This peculiarity was due to the fact that scholasticism was, in the main, a synthesis of the two great traditions inherited by the Middle Ages, those of pagan antiquity and Latin Christianity. In St Thomas Aquinas Aristotle is harmonized with Paul and Augustine, metaphysics with revelation, reason with faith. In this great synthesis theology was supreme, and the 'truth' of any proposition thus depended ultimately, not upon its correspondence with any particular 'state of affairs', but upon its being consistent with a body of *given* and of course unquestionable doctrine.[1] St Thomas sees the universe as a hierarchy of creatures ordered to the attainment of perfection in their several kinds. All things proceed from God; and God is not only the ground of their being but also the Supreme Good with which all seek to be reunited. God created the world that he might communicate himself more fully; as First Mover (the 'unmoved mover' of Aristotle) he impels all creatures to desire him. Love is thus 'the deepest spring of all causality'.[2] God not only created, but continuously sustains the world, and governs it both directly by the eternal laws, and indirectly through (for instance) the angels, and through the celestial bodies upon whose

1. Cf. I. A. Richards, *Mencius on the Mind*, p. 111 ff.
2. Gilson, *The Philosophy of St Thomas Aquinas*, trans. by E. Bullough, p. 197.

motions all terrestrial motion depends. To all creatures he has given a 'nature' or 'form' in virtue of which they are necessitated both to be what they are, and to seek that which is proper to them. Thus earth, and heavy bodies, tend downwards; fire and light bodies upwards. All motion is a striving to actualize what is as yet only potential. Though binding Nature thus fast in fate, God has in a sense left free the human will. The formal principle of man as such is the rational Soul; and virtue, for man, is therefore action conformable to reason. Whereas Nature cannot but conform to unalterable law, man, through his will, is determined to 'good', yet is capable, since the Fall, of making erroneous choices both of ends and means. He is, as it were, less perfect than the other creatures in virtue of the very gift of reason which makes him their superior. Further, his 'form' being his rational soul, he is ordered to the attainment of no limited perfection like the other creatures. Nothing short of the Supreme Good, God Himself, can be his end. Thus man by his very nature is oriented towards the supernatural world; he was created for beatitude, and he has supernatural grace to aid him in attaining it. In these affirmations we see something of the technique by which Thomism blends Aristotle with Christian theology. In scholasticism faith is indeed above reason, but not contrary to it; and the chief aim of this teaching is to show that reason, *when exercising itself upon its proper object*, must necessarily lead towards faith, or confirm its dogmas. And the 'proper object' of intelligence is Being; the proper study of mankind is God.

It may be said, then, that for the scholastics there was little or no distinction between a 'fact' and a theological or metaphysical 'truth'. For them the important consideration was not how things behave, or what their history might be, but how they were linked with Total Being, and what, in a word, was their metaphysical status. This was satisfying enough to a period in which men's interests were oriented towards a transcendental 'reality', but it was unfavourable to what, since the Renaissance, has been called 'science'. This science has achieved what it has achieved precisely by abstracting from the whole of 'reality' those aspects which are amenable to its methods. There is no point in denying that only thus can 'scientific' discovery be made. What we need to remember, however, is that we have to do here with a *transference of interests* rather than with the mere 'exantlation' of new truth or the mere rejection of error. All we can say is that at the Renaissance men began to wish for a new life-orientation, and that this involved a hitherto unthought-of degree of control over 'things'. Accordingly, the sort of knowledge which dealt with the motions of bodies came to seem the most real, the most genuine knowledge, and scientific 'truth' the only genuine 'truth'. 'Truth' of some kind cannot be denied to the knowledge on which modern civilization rests, the knowledge which enables us to construct aeroplanes and wireless-sets, to weigh the atom and chart the mysterious universe. We have merely come to see that this kind of knowledge does not exhaust reality, and that in the unreduced remainder may lie 'truths' 'belonging to our peace'. Little now, in our 'changing world', seems to matter except the quality of our living. We have to try to live, somehow, amidst the machines we have made and the debris into which they are falling; significance has somehow to be imparted to the 'unwilling dross'. There can be no return, I believe, to the specific thought-forms of scholasticism, but we are once more asking the fundamental questions. As soon as we try to live more wholly and more deeply we become aware of all that experiment and observation leave untouched. We must ask 'What?', 'Whence?', and 'Why?'; we differ from St Thomas mainly in having no direct replies to give. All we can do is to reply in terms of 'As If'; 'live according to the best hypotheses (whatever they may be)', thus runs our reply to the questioner, 'live thus, and see if you can live the hypotheses into "truths" (truths for yourself, that is).'

With these considerations in mind, let us examine an actual example of the rejection of scholasticism by a seventeenth-century scientist. The theory of motion was the keystone of seventeenth-century science: let us then compare the views of Galileo, the pioneer of scientific investigation on this subject, with those of St Thomas Aquinas.

St Thomas, following Aristotle, treats motion as a branch of metaphysics; he is interested in why it happens, not how. He discusses it in terms of 'act' and 'potency', quoting Aristotle's definition of it (8 *Phys.* v. 8) as 'the act of that which is in potentiality, as such'.[1] Motion exists, then, because things in a state of potentiality seek to actualize themselves, or because they seek the place or direction which is *proper* to them.

Everything moved, as such, tends as towards a divine likeness, to be perfect in itself; and since a thing is perfect in so far as it becomes actual, it follows that the intention of everything that is in potentiality is to tend to actuality by way of movement.[2]

To every body in respect of its 'form', is 'due' a 'proper place', towards which it tends to move in a straight line. Thus it is 'due to fire, in respect of its form, to be in a higher place',[3] or to a stone, to be in a lower.

It is unnecessary to controvert theories of this kind as if they were 'untrue'. Their 'truth' is not of the empirical kind; it consists in their being *consistent with a certain world-view*. For St Thomas the world-view with which they were consistent was a datum supplied by divine authority. For us the notion of 'revelation' may have acquired a different content, but it must be remembered that those of us who affirm the 'reality', for example, of religious or poetic experience are appealing to a principle essentially similar. Possibly the survival-value of the 'revelation' concept is due to its having symbolized our need to accept certain experiences as 'true', not because they are empirically demonstrable, but simply because they are 'given'.

Galileo typifies the direction of modern interests, in this instance, not in refuting St Thomas, but in taking no notice of him. Motion might *be* all that the angelic doctor had declared it to be; Galileo nevertheless will drop weights from the top of a tower, and down inclined planes, to see how they behave. It is undeniable that the scholastic theory of motion informs us nothing of the manner in

1. *Summa contra Gentiles*, Bk I, Ch. 13.
2. ibid., Bk III, Ch. 22.
3. ibid., Ch. 23.

which bodies move in space and time, and this was precisely what Galileo wished to determine. He is concerned with quantities, not qualities; and his energy is thus devoted not to framing theories consistent with a rational scheme, but to *measuring* the speed of falling bodies in terms of time and space. After repeated measurements, he arrives at a mathematical formula expressing the 'law' of their acceleration; he finds, for instance, that 'their speed is proportional to the time of fall' and that 'the space described increases as the square of the time'.[1]

But the contrast between St Thomas and Galileo is even more instructive when we consider their views on an empirical question, the nature and movements of the heavenly bodies. In the scholastic doctrine of the heavenly bodies we have an illustration of the strange fact that a belief can be metaphysically 'true' (in the sense of 'coherent' or 'consistent') and yet empirically false, that is, not in correspondence with what we call a 'state of affairs'. The received scholastic doctrine, for instance, taught that the heavenly bodies are unalterable and incorruptible. This belief seems to have rested on the assumption (*fact*, as it then appeared) that the motions of the heavenly bodies were circular. The 'elements' – of fire, air, water, and earth – of which all sublunary objects were compounded, moved in straight lines towards the places proper to them, fire and air 'upwards', water and earth 'downwards'. The elements thus have 'contraries', away from which they move; all straight-line movements, it was held, imply the existence of such a 'contrary'. But the heavenly bodies move in circles, thus their movement shows them to be without a 'contrary'. And that which was without a contrary must be exempt from generation and corruption, since, according to Aristotle, all generated objects proceed from their contraries and are corrupted again into contraries. It therefore follows that the heavenly bodies are incorruptible.[2] Another way of expressing the same view was in terms of 'matter' and 'form'. In all corruptible things the 'form' fails to penetrate the 'matter' completely – it does not quite inform its tenement of clay, therefore the object is in a state of potentiality,

1. Dampier-Whetham, *History of Science*, p. 144.
2. See, e.g., *Summa theologica*, Pt II, qu. 85, art. 6.

therefore it moves. But in the stars 'the form fills the whole potentiality of matter, so that the matter retains no potentiality to another form'. The stars 'consist of their entire matter'.[1] Their circular movement is the only kind of movement 'proper' to such perfectly realized creatures as the heavenly bodies; circular movement being held, it must be remembered, to be inherently 'noble', 'perfect', or, as we might say, expressive of self-completeness.

It was against these and suchlike beliefs that the early upholders of Copernicanism had to contend. The Copernican theory was unacceptable at first chiefly because it obliterated the traditional distinction between corruptible and incorruptible, placing the earth, as it were, amongst the heavenly bodies. Accordingly we find Galileo tackling the 'incorruptibility' theory at the beginning of his *System of the World*. The main purport of the First Dialogue is to refute Aristotle and the schools, and to demonstrate that the earth is one of the celestial bodies, 'and as it were place it in Heaven, whence your Philosophers have exiled it'.[2] He argues that though there may be no 'contrary' to circular motion, 'contrariety' of some kind can be found amongst the heavenly bodies; for example, 'rarity' and 'density'. But the argument upon which he, like all the anti-scholastics of the seventeenth century, really relies, is the appeal to observation. It is through his Optic Glass that the Tuscan Artist[3] views the heavens, descrying new lands, rivers, or mountains in the moon. By means of the telescope Galileo has *observed* generation and corruption going on in the heavens.

We have in our age new accidents and observations, and such, that I question not in the least, but if Aristotle were now alive, they would make him change his opinion.[4]

Comets have been observed which have been

generated and dissolved in parts higher than the Lunar Orb, besides the two new Stars, Anno 1572 and Anno 1604, without contradiction much higher

1. *Summa contra Gentiles*, Bk III, Ch. 23.
2. Galileo, *Mathematical Collections and Translations*, translated by Thomas Salusbury, 1661, p. 25.
3. *Paradise Lost*, I, 288.   4. Galileo, op. cit., p. 37.

than all the Planets; and in the face of the Sun itself, by help of the *Telescope*, certain dense and obscure substances, in substance very like to the foggs about the Earth, are seen to be produced and dissolved.[1]

Thus the metaphysical theory of the heavens is confronted by comets, new stars, and sun-spots seen through the telescope; and Salviatus, speaking for Galileo himself, makes much of an alleged saying of Aristotle that we ought to prefer sense-evidence to logic. Knowledge so gained is far more certain than any deduction from purely rational premises; it is more certain, therefore, that there are sun-spots, or mountains in the moon, than that the heavens are unalterable. This was then far from seeming the obvious 'truth' that it has appeared to most people ever since. The Professor of Philosophy at Padua refused to look through Galileo's telescope, and his colleague at Pisa tried by means of logical arguments to 'charm the new planets out of the sky'.[2] One must, however, make the effort to conceive a point of view from which the notion of lunar mountains, for example, would be abhorrent. They would be abhorrent to the Peripatetic as derogations from the moon's 'perfection', which implied her perfect sphericity (the 'sphere' being the most 'perfect' of solids).[3] Galileo makes it his affair to deny that incorruptibility, inalterability, and sphericity are necessary attributes of 'perfection'. It is more 'noble' for the earth, for example, to be as it is than to be like a lump of crystal;[4] and if for the earth, why not for the stars? The far-reaching implications of this view must not be followed out here, but we should note this as a good early example of veneration for 'things-as-they-are' rather than 'things-as-they-can-be-conceived'.

Again, scholasticism taught that the movements of the heavenly bodies implied the presence of a constant impelling force:

Now one place is not more due to a heavenly body in respect of its form than another. Therefore nature alone is not the principle of the heavenly movement: and consequently the principle of its movement must be something that moves it by apprehension;[5]

1. Galileo, op. cit., pp. 37–8. 2. Dampier-Whetham, op. cit., p. 142.
3. Galileo, op. cit., p. 69. 4. ibid., p. 45.
5. *Summa contra Gentiles* Bk III, Ch. 23.

– that is, an intellectual substance; in a word, the Unmoved Mover of Aristotle and St Thomas.

And since whatever is moved by anything *per se*, and not accidentally, is directed thereby towards the end of its movement, and since the heavenly body is moved by an intellectual substance, and the heavenly body, by its movement, causes all movement in this lower world, it follows of necessity that the heavenly body is directed to the end of its movement by an intellectual substance, and consequently all lower bodies to their respective ends.[1]

Against this comprehensive theory (indeed, it is more than a theory, it is a religious affirmation) Galileo sets the new principle of *inertia*. Constant exertion of force is *not* required to account for the incessant motions of the heavens, since motion, like immobility, once in being, will persist until affected by some force. Only the primary impulse of the First Mover, then, need be postulated; not his continual action. And it only remained for Newton to 'explain' why the motion of the heavenly bodies was circular (elliptical) and not in straight lines. Galileo admitted that he knew nothing about the ultimate nature of the forces he was measuring; nothing about the cause of gravitation, or the origin of the Universe; he deemed it better, rather than to speculate on such high matters, 'to pronounce that wise, ingenious, and modest sentence, "I know it not."'[2]

I have already hinted that I think we should cultivate the habit of looking steadily at this intellectual revolution, vigorously checking any propensity to an outrush of uncritical sympathy for either side. We have to be on our guard, I think, as much against those who represent the rejection of scholasticism as pure loss, as against those who regard it as pure gain. It is only because for three hundred years almost everybody has united to extol it as pure gain, that we may be forgiven for leaning a little (as Aristotle advises) towards the opposite side, so as to restore the true mean. With this reservation let us boldly declare that the rejection was not wholly disastrous. We are compelled to deem it no mere calamity as long as we believe that, though 'truth' has many levels, it is at each and every level prefer-

1. *Summa contra Gentiles*, Ch. 24.
2. Dampier-Whetham, op. cit., p. 146.

able to 'error'. Do we really believe this? A good way of testing our condition is to ask ourselves: do we or do we not approve the action of the Paduan professor who refused to look through Galileo's telescope? If we find that we condemn the professor, we have already decided on the main issue. To applaud him is by no means impossible for a reasonable being. But we must remember that, if we do so, we are committed to a belief which may prove inconvenient or even perilous if generally applied: the belief, namely, that truth of a lower order may be neglected in order that higher truths may be conserved. Neglect of the crudest empirical truths would cut short our frail existences very soon; observance of them, on the other hand, is what renders possible our devoting our higher energies to the metaphysical realities. The really difficult thing (the thing we have all to attempt) is to *realize* – not merely to be mentally aware – that 'Truth' (as applied to our thoughts, beliefs, or statements) is not absolute and 'One', but manifold. Whoever doubts this would be well advised to read Dr Richards's work, *Mencius on the Mind*,[1] in which the writer enumerates nine distinct types of senses of 'truth', not to mention several 'gestures' (or emotive uses) of the term. Our task then, it would seem, is to avoid the old error of neglecting one order of truth in favour of another, and, as far as possible, to cultivate the capacity to pass freely from one order to another, acknowledging the value of that saying of Sir T. Browne's (given deserved prominence by Dr Joseph Needham):

Thus is Man that great and true Amphibium whose nature is disposed to live, not only like other creatures in divers elements, but in divided and distinguished worlds.

On the other hand, as I have perhaps sufficiently suggested already, the rejection of scholasticism was not a pure gain. In so far as it led to an undue elevation of empirical 'truth', and an attribution to it of a special privilege to represent 'reality', it was a disaster. It was not the fault of the early scientists that their methods and their abstractions were mistaken for philosophies, but none the less this

1. See especially Ch. 4, pp. 111–16.

is what has tended to happen. Few today (and I believe still fewer tomorrow) can really wish to revive scholasticism *in toto*; as an account of reality it is far too exclusively intellectual and rational. But its great value must be preserved somehow: its testimony to the primacy of the 'truths' of religious experience. We may not want these 'truths' theologically and metaphysically expressed; but we do want to be able to experience reality in all its rich multiplicity, instead of being condemned by the modern consciousness to go on

> Viewing all objects, unremittingly
> In disconnection dead and spiritless.

CHAPTER 2

Bacon and the Rehabilitation of Nature

Twofold Truth

THE veneration accorded traditionally to Bacon is due in part to his having been neither a mathematician nor a metaphysician, but a master of language, so that his works have been more widely understood and admired than those of more first-hand philosophers. Bacon had the ability, and the singular good fortune, to be the *buccinator novi temporis* in England; and his oracular deliverances have seemed, to most people for the past three centuries, to embody the very charter of intellectual liberty. Even today the unwary reader of Bacon will hardly avoid according to him the kind of response which became stereotyped in the eighteenth and nineteenth centuries: 'How true,' he will find himself feeling, 'how profoundly true! A superb clearance of medieval cobwebs! Final banishment of nonsense!' and the like. Bacon's reasons for rejecting the Peripatetic-scholastic tradition, and for proposing a transference of interest from abstract speculation to observation of nature, have already been hinted at above, and are in any case so well known that I will here merely quote a few sentences of the kind to which it has been usual to respond in the manner indicated:

Being convinced, by a careful observation, that the human understanding perplexes itself, or makes not a sober and advantageous use of the real helps within its reach, whence manifold ignorance and inconveniences arise, he was determined to employ his utmost endeavours towards restoring or cultivating a just and legitimate familiarity between the mind and things.[1]

The philosophy we principally received from the Greeks must be

1. *Magna instauratio*, opening sentence.

acknowledged puerile, or rather talkative than generative – as being fruitful in controversies, but barren of effects.[1]

The understanding, left to itself, ought always to be suspected. . . . Logic . . . by no means reaches the subtilty of nature.

Our method is continually to dwell among things soberly . . . to establish for ever a true and legitimate union between the experimental and rational faculty.[2]

Those, therefore, who determine not to conjecture and guess, but to find out and know; not to invent fables and romances of worlds, but to look into, and dissect the nature of this real world, must consult only things themselves.[3]

Surely, like as many substances in nature which are solid do putrefy and corrupt into worms; so it is the property of good and sound knowledge to putrefy and dissolve into a number of subtle, idle, unwholesome, and (as I may term them) vermiculate questions, which have indeed a kind of quickness and life of spirit, but no soundness of matter or goodness of quality. This kind of degenerate learning did chiefly reign among the schoolmen: who, having sharp and strong wits, and abundance of leisure, and small variety of reading, but their wits being shut up in the cells of a few authors (chiefly Aristotle their dictator) as their persons were shut up in the cells of monasteries and colleges, and knowing little history, either of nature or time, did out of no great quantity of matter and infinite agitation of wit spin out unto us those laborious webs of learning which are extant in their books. For the wit and mind of man, *if it work upon matter, which is the contemplation of the creatures of God*, worketh according to the stuff and is limited thereby; but if it work upon itself, as the spider worketh his web, then it is endless, and brings forth indeed cobwebs of learning, admirable for the fineness of thread and work, but of no substance or profit.[4]

We can hardly, at the present day, read these noble utterances with quite the old thrill; the effects of 'continually dwelling among things' have not, in the long run, proved so exhilarating after all. Yet, although we have abandoned the contempt for scholasticism which was traditional during the eighteenth and nineteenth centuries, we must remember that Bacon's intention throughout his work was not to reject metaphysical 'truth', but to prescribe for his

1. Preface to *De augmentis*, p. 3 (Bohn ed.)   2. ibid., pp. 6–8.
3. ibid., p. 16.   4. *Advancement of Learning*, pp. 31–2 (my italics).

age a massive dose of 'truth' of another order. Given that experimental science had been neglected, and that the age needed and demanded it above all things, then Bacon's role was to indicate with fine magniloquence the path by which alone 'science' could advance. This he did, while other men, such as Galileo, Harvey, or Gilbert, in whom he took comparatively little interest, were actually achieving great discoveries on the principles which he taught. Bacon's great service to 'science' was that he gave it an incomparable advertisement, by associating with it his personal prestige, his 'Elizabethan' glamour, and his great literary power. The feeling of 'rightness' with which English and other scientists proceeded in succeeding centuries must have been due, in part, to his persuasiveness.

It was not the living core of medieval thought – its witness to other than empirical realities – that Bacon wished to kill. There was so much else to criticize in the medieval tradition – so much pseudo-science, magic, alchemy, astrology, and the like – that Bacon and his age generally cannot be blamed for feeling that their task was simply the separation of truth from error, fact from fable, reality from fiction.

The situation was that, while the central metaphysical affirmations of the schoolmen might be true, many of their deductions in the region of 'things' were false, and it was precisely in this region of 'things' that the new age wanted soberly and continually to live. There was thus a likelihood that however clearly the pioneers might see that experimental science was not a metaphysic (and Bacon and Galileo saw this), their followers might forget it. Men have never found it easy to live 'in divided and distinguished worlds'; they will have the one, or the other, exclusively, but not both at once. What was sound in the medieval tradition tended more and more to be rejected along with the quackery.

What we should doubtless have liked to get from Bacon is a classification of the meanings of such words as 'Truth', 'Reality', and a clear realization that as such meanings are multiple, not single, we need not be denying 'Truth' of one kind when we affirm 'Truth' of another. As, however, Dr I. A. Richards and Mr C. K. Ogden are still, even today, rather lonely pioneers in this field of research, it would be unreasonable to expect Bacon to have been fully alive to the linguistic aspects of the problem of 'Truth'. The remarkable thing, however, is that we get from him as much as we do, for he does provide some very significant hints in this direction. He is concerned to insist that Truth is *twofold*. There is truth of religion, and truth of science; and these different kinds of truth must be kept separate. This position is the inevitable result of any attempt to combine nominalism in philosophy with acceptance of religious dogma, and in this respect Bacon belongs with Duns Scotus and Occam. If you hold that individual 'things' are alone real, and reject universals and abstractions as 'names', mere *flatus vocis*: if you do this, and yet cling to a body of doctrine like the Christian, which implies that much else is 'real' besides 'things', you have no alternative but to accept the strange dichotomy of 'Truth', and to try, as far as possible, to keep the two kinds from contaminating each other. (It must be remembered that belief in the superior reality of 'things', or 'facts', rests on the assumptions that objectivity is the criterion of reality, and that 'things' *are* objective. Little meaning could have been attached, in the seventeenth century, except in the sense indicated by Cudworth,[1] to the theory that the mind is in some sense constitutive of reality, even a 'fact' being in part a thing made, an act of the mind. To this question we shall have to return later.)

Bacon's views on the twofold nature of Truth are summed up in the oft-quoted phrase: 'It is therefore most wise soberly to render unto faith the things that are faith's.'[2] From the 'absurd mixture of matters divine and human' proceed heresies and 'fantastical philosophy'. Science ('philosophy') has hitherto been corrupted by the admixture of theology, superstition, logic, fancy, or poetry; now we must try to have it pure. A few sentences from the *De augmentis*[3] will further illustrate Bacon's position:

Sacred theology must be drawn from the word and oracles of God, not from the light of nature, or the dictates of reason.

1. Cf. below, pp. 143 ff. 2. *Novum Organum*, I, LXV.
3. Bk IX, pp. 368 ff. (Bohn).

[To study theology] we must quit the small vessel of human reason, and put ourselves on board the ship of the Church, which alone possesses the divine needle for justly shaping the course.

We are obliged to believe the word of God, though our reason be shocked at it. For if we should believe only such things as are agreeable to our reason, we assent to the matter, and not to the author.

And therefore, the more absurd and incredible any divine mystery is, the greater honour we do to God in believing it; and so much the more noble the victory of faith.

It is a fallacy to try to confirm the truths of religion by the principles of science – this is another example of the mingling of things divine and human.[1] Neither must we try to extract scientific truth out of the Scriptures, like some, who, Bacon says, 'have endeavoured to build a system of natural philosophy on the first chapter of Genesis, the book of Job, and other parts of Scripture'.[2] The reason Bacon gives for condemning this practice is strange; it is wrong, says he, because it is 'seeking the dead amongst the living',[3] or the temporal in the eternal. It shakes one's confidence in Bacon's sincerity to find the science which he heralds classified by him amongst 'the dead'. And in fact there is something of the ceremonial and formal obeisance about many of his salutes to religion. I do not believe that he (any more than Browne, when he made a similar remark) intended any conscious irony when he wrote that 'the more absurd and incredible any divine mystery is, the greater honour we do to God in believing it'; though irony began to creep into remarks like this not long afterwards, and was perhaps always present in eighteenth-century examples. But what can be asserted with confidence, I think, is that Bacon's desire to separate religious truth and scientific truth was in the interests of science, not of religion. He wished to *keep science pure from religion*; the opposite parts of the process – keeping religion pure from science – did not interest him nearly so much. What he harps on is always how science has been hampered at every stage by the prejudice and conservatism of theologians. After three

1. Cf. *Novum Organum*, LXXXIX.   2. Cf. *Novum Organum*, LXV.
3. ibid., and *De augmentis*, Bk IX.

hundred years of science we now have writers pleading for religion in an age dominated by science;[1] Bacon was pleading for science in an age dominated by religion. Religious truth, then, must be 'skied', elevated far out of reach, not in order that so it may be more devoutly approached, but in order to keep it out of mischief. But having secured his main object, namely, to clear the universe for science, Bacon can afford to be quite orthodox (just as, in another context, he can concede poetry to human weakness). He prays eloquently that the new light, when it comes, may not make men incredulous of divine mystery. It has been objected against science that it leads to atheism, through concentration on second causes; to this Bacon replies that though science is, or should be, the study of second causes, God works in Nature only by second causes, and that thus, though natural philosophy can teach us nothing directly of God, the study of it leads us inevitably to Him in the end.

Undoubtedly a superficial tincture of philosophy may incline the mind to atheism, yet a farther knowledge brings it back to religion; for on the threshold of philosophy, where second causes appear to absorb the attention, some oblivion of the highest cause may ensue; but when the mind goes deeper, and sees the dependence of causes and the works of Providence, it will easily perceive, according to the mythology of the poets, that the upper link of Nature's chain is fastened to Jupiter's throne. [2]

These are brave words, and their tone bespeaks their sincerity. They belong to what might be called the 'heroic' stage of liberal thought, at which it is fervently declared, not only that all new knowledge can be safely embraced without fear of endangering older beliefs, but that the new knowledge in reality supplies those beliefs with their firmest support. Bacon, we may now think, was on safer ground when he was urging the separation of the spheres of religion and science than when he was trying to reconcile them.

However, the circumstances of his age were such that Bacon's plea for the Advancement of Learning necessarily assumed a theological cast. He could not proceed without first dealing with the

1. Cf Needham, *The Great Amphibium*. And D. H. Lawrence, *passim*.
2. *De augmentis*, pp. 31–2.

religious objections to science, and showing that the studies he advocated were consistent with the faith. How he treated these matters we must consider in the next section.

'Forbidden' Knowledge

The notion of a 'forbidden' knowledge is ingrained deeply in the human race; but widely different views have been held as to which kind of knowledge was the forbidden kind. Broadly it may be guessed that the knowledge which in any age is 'forbidden', is always that which presents itself as a distraction or seducement from what is then considered the main purpose of living. At the very outset of *The Advancement of Learning* Bacon is confronted with the medieval conception of natural science as the forbidden knowledge. It is objected, he says, by divines, that 'knowledge puffeth up', that it 'hath somewhat of the serpent', that (in a word) it was the original cause of the Fall of Man. Marlowe's *Faustus* had appeared not long before *The Advancement of Learning*, and the Faustus legend testifies to the strength of the fascinated dread with which the Middle Ages had thought of natural science. From the earliest days of man there had of course been evil forces in Nature to be feared and propitiated; but during the Christian centuries 'Nature' had, in quite a special sense, been consigned to the Satanic order. Both the myth-making instinct of paganism and the Stoic yearning for the Universe as the City of God were checked by the Pauline and Augustinian theology, which represented Nature (including man) as depraved since the Fall, and as groaning under the divine malediction. The divine order, the order of Grace, was felt to be wholly separate from, and in a sense opposed to, 'Nature'. The sense which above all marks the Christian consciousness, of sin in man and of imperfection in Nature, expressed itself in a virtual dualism, the Satanic forces being as real as the divine, if less powerful. The 'beggarly elements' of Nature, as St Paul calls them, were handed over to the Prince of the Air and his fallen angels, who were soon identified with the dethroned divinities of the heathen pantheons. At the Nativity of Christ, in Milton's Ode:

> Nature in awe to Him
> Had doff't her gaudy trim.

and

> woos the gentle Air
> To hide her guilty front with innocent snow,
> And on her naked shame,
> Pollute with sinful blame,
> The saintly veil of maiden white to throw;
> Confounded, that her Maker's eyes
> Should look so near upon her foul deformities.

To escape upwards from this Satan-ridden earth, and the body of this death, beyond the planetary spheres with their disastrous influences, into the divine empyrean – this was the purpose of living, this the effort of the believer; and only by divine grace supernaturally mediated was success possible. Whatever diverted attention from this supreme object would be liable to rank as 'forbidden'. Even the female sex was held by some theologians to belong to the Satanic order, Chrysostom calling woman a 'desirable calamity'.[1] How much more sinful, then, to interest oneself in Nature's ungodly secrets. Since earth, water, air, and fire were the allotted spheres of the several hierarchies of evil spirits,[2] to study nature meant to

1. Lecky, *History of Rationalism*, Vol. I, p. 78. Compare Milton's 'fair defect'.

2. Cf. Hooker, *Ecclesiastical Polity*, Bk I, sect. 4: 'For being dispersed, some in the air, some on the earth, some in the water, some among the minerals, dens, and caves that are under the earth; they have by all means laboured to effect a universal rebellion against the laws, and as far as in them lieth utter destruction of the works of God. These wicked Spirits the heathens honoured instead of gods, both generally under the name of *dii inferi*, "gods infernal"; and particularly, some in oracles, some in idols, some as household gods, some as nymphs; in a word, no foul and wicked spirit which was not one way or other honoured of men as God, till such time as light appeared in the world and dissolved the works of the Devil.'

repeat the original sin of Adam; it meant a compact with the devil and the death of the soul. Astrology, alchemy, and black magic are the (popular) medieval names for science, just as 'heresy' was the name for any trust, such as Pelagius showed, in the natural virtue of man.

On the other hand, that it had at any rate once been possible to think of science quite differently, the Prometheus myth was there to testify. The purveyor of knowledge and civilization might be the friend, and not the Adversary, of man. Bacon's task, it may be said, was to prove that natural science was Promethean and not Mephistophelean.

It is vain to assign to any particular date the waning of the theological view of nature and man, and its replacement by the more indulgent 'humanist' view. Medieval culture was to a considerable extent 'humanistic' long before the Renaissance. The process was spread over many centuries, and both views have perhaps always co-existed, down to the present day. All one can say is that at certain times the one is the dominant 'orthodoxy', at other times the other. It was likely that as the prosperity and stability of civilization gradually increased, the distinction between nature and supernature would become less and less harsh. The doctrines of 'grace' and 'original sin' may, as has been suggested, have arisen out of the despair accompanying the disintegration of the ancient world; 'but as life became more secure man became less otherworldly'.[1] For practical purposes, however, in spite of such harbingers as Petrarch, we may perhaps take the later fifteenth and the sixteenth centuries as the epoch of the rebirth of confidence in 'Nature'. In encountering such men as More, Montaigne, and Bacon we find ourselves at the beginning of a process which continues for about three centuries, and culminates in what we may perhaps call the age of Wordsworth (meaning by that term the age of Wordsworthian influence as well). In Montaigne, for example, one can discover almost all the attitudes usually associated with the naturalism of the later eighteenth century. He continually exalts Nature over conventions, codes, and systems:

1. Babbitt, *Rousseau and Romanticism*, p. 116.

Whoever contemplates our mother Nature in her full majesty and lustre is alone able to value things in their true estimate.[1]

Although wisdom is what he craves for, he believes health and cheerfulness to be even more important, or rather, to be necessary ingredients of wisdom. At the beginning of the nineteenth century it was not extravagant to speak of

> Spontaneous wisdom breathed by health,
> Truth breathed by cheerfulness;

but in a learned and pedantic age like the sixteenth century it was startlingly original to write:

This book employment is as painful as any other, and as great an enemy to health, which ought to be the first thing considered. . . . If, by being over-studious, we impair our health and spoil our good-humour, the best pieces we have, let us give it over.[2]

Montaigne had himself been brought up as a sort of sixteenth-century Émile, and in his famous essay, *Of the Education of Children*, he expresses the naturalistic view of childhood:

How much more fitting to strew their classrooms with flowers and leaves than with stumps of blood-stained willows! I would portray there Joy, Sprightliness, Flora, and the Graces.

Sainte-Beuve, commenting on this passage, remarks that here '*il passe les bornes, comme un enfant d'Aristippe qui oublie le mal d'Adam*'. He was '*tout simplement la Nature . . . la Nature au complet sans la Grâce*'.

This recrudescence of confidence in Nature was immensely strengthened by the scientific movement of the Renaissance, which reclaimed the physical world from its traditional association with Satan. In the *Utopia* of Sir Thomas More, natural philosophy is considered, not as 'conjuring', involving a pact like that of Faust and Mephistopheles, but as something acceptable to God, and even as part of religious duty. The strength of the 'Faust' tradition is

1. Montaigne, *Of the Education of Children*.   2. Montaigne, *Of Solitude*.

attested by the fact that Bacon concerns himself, at the outset of his great work, to show that whatever the forbidden knowledge may be, it is not natural science. Bacon's argument is of great importance, because it furnished the scientists of the following two centuries with a technique for reconciling science with religion, and gave a first impulse to the movement towards scientific deism. Bacon's purpose requires that Nature should be established as divine instead of Satanic, and this he secures by arguing that God has revealed himself to man by means of *two* scriptures: first, of course, through the written word, but also, secondly, through his handiwork, the created universe. To study nature, therefore, cannot be contrary to religion; indeed, it is part of the duty we owe to the great Artificer of the world. 'It was not', he says,

the pure knowledge of nature and universality, a knowledge by the light whereof man did give names unto other creatures in Paradise, as they were brought before him, according to their proprieties, which gave the occasion to the fall;[1]

it was not, that is to say, natural science. It was

the proud knowledge of good and evil, with an intent in man to give law unto himself, and to depend no more on God's commandments, which was the form of the temptation.

To Bacon the logic-spinning of the schoolmen was a kind of forbidden knowledge; it was a presumptuous attempt to read the secret purposes of God, and to force his works into conformity with the laws of the human mind. This was for him the real *hubris*, this metaphysical arrogance, which 'disdains to dwell upon particulars', and confidently explains all things by syllogism. The true humility is the attribute of the Baconian scientist, who is content to come forth into the light of things, and let nature be his teacher. 'Nor could we hope to succeed, if we arrogantly searched for the sciences in the narrow cells of the human understanding, and not submissively in the wider world.'[2] Access to the kingdom of man, which is

1. *Advancement of Learning*, Bk 1, i, 3.
2. *De augmentis*, p. 10 (Bohn ed.).

founded on the sciences, resembles 'that to the kingdom of heaven, where no admission is conceded except to children'.[1]

The 'anti-rational' tendency of this part of Bacon's programme has been pointed out by Professor Whitehead. Nothing is more characteristic of Bacon than his distrust of the 'meddling intellect', which interposes too soon with its abstractions and distorts nature instead of explaining her. The Idol of the Tribe, that most deeply ingrained of our tendencies to error, is the spirit of over-hasty generalization: 'The human understanding is, by its own nature, prone to abstraction, and supposes that which is fluctuating to be fixed.'[2] Man despises

the light of experiment, from arrogance and pride, lest his mind should appear to be occupied with common and varying objects.[3]

If he had had the ordonnance of the stars, he would have arranged them

into some beautiful and elegant order, as we see in the vaulted roofs of palaces ... so great a difference is there betwixt the spirit of man, and the spirit of the universe.[4]

This campaign of Bacon's against excessive rationalism is perhaps, to us, the most interesting aspect of his work. For it raises him above all mere pleaders for 'science' or 'freedom' of thought, and associates him with those poets and prophets who have urged that 'wise passiveness' is the attitude most favourable to fine living and creating.

> Wisdom oft
> Is nearer when we stoop than when we soar.

With the spirit of this, and of other similar utterances of Wordsworth, Bacon would have been in agreement; and indeed he owes much of his impressiveness to the fact that it is something covered by the term 'wisdom' that he often seems to be inculcating, not

1. *Novum Organum*, LXVIII. Cf. *De augmentis*, Bk v, Ch. 2 (p. 186).
2. ibid., LI.   3. ibid., XLIX.
4. *De augmentis*, Bk v, Ch. 4 (p. 209).

merely a new technique of scientific research. The humility, the submission of the whole self to 'things', which Bacon desiderates for science, is precisely what is emphasized by Keats as the condition of healthy growth for the poet. Keats calls this 'negative capability, that is, when a man is capable of being in uncertainties, mysteries, doubts, without any irritable reaching after fact and reason'; and declares that this is the quality which goes to make 'a man of achievement, especially in literature, and which Shakespeare possessed so enormously'.[1] There is, of course, plenty of evidence that a lying-fallow of the mind in a kind of fruitful indolence is a state which often precedes successful imaginative creation. These intervals of wise passiveness seem to be times when our ordinary consciousness is almost suspended and the subconscious is free to incubate and to shape what is afterwards delivered into consciousness. Keats speaks more than once of such moments.[2] Wordsworth's period of 'tranquillity' seems to have meant much the same to him; and we know from Mrs Carswell that when Lawrence said he was doing nothing and did not care, a new work was often in process of gestation.

Anything worth having is *growth*: and to have growth, one must be able to let be.[3]

It is, I think, not fanciful to apply the experience of poets to the elucidation of Bacon, for Bacon was in truth the seer, almost the poet, of the scientific movement in England. His very detachment from the actual work of experimentation protected him from all 'irritable reaching after fact and reason', and left him free to contemplate a new intimacy of union between the mind and the external world, and to prophesy of the creation which they, 'with blended might', could accomplish.[4] This was Bacon's, as well as Wordsworth's, 'high argument'. At the beginning of the seventeenth century science could still be humble, for it was now to be the study

1. Keats, Letter to Geo. and Thos. Keats, 28 December 1817.
2. Cf. Letter to G. and Georgina Keats, 19 March 1819.
3. D. H. Lawrence, Letter to Rolf Gardiner, 7 January 1928.
4. Cf. Wordsworth's *Recluse*.

of God's Work as a supplement to his Word. Moreover, the natural philosopher, pitting himself against the assertive and dogmatic schoolman, could excusably feel that he excelled him in humility.

Man should not dispute and assert, but whisper results to his neighbour.[1]

The words are Keats's, but they well express the aspiration which was in Bacon.

It is significant that Bacon's charge against scholasticism is almost identical with that of M. Maritain and Mr Dawson against the very movement of which Bacon was the herald; both parties accuse their opponents of pride, and of making man the measure of all things; and both claim to be on the side of true humility. Perhaps there may be in truth more than one kind of humility; a humility of religion, and a humility of science. The man of religion humbles himself before Being; the man of science, before Becoming. And as long as religion is whispering results, as long as science is whispering results, so long each is showing its own proper humility. The greatest results in each sphere have been won through humility. But as 'results' accumulate, both begin to dispute and assert; religion ceases to be *scientifically* humble, and science ceases to be *metaphysically* humble. The humility of each consists largely in keeping to its own sphere, and recognizing the independent validity of the other. On the whole, I think, science was still in this condition in Bacon's time; the results were still scanty, and the whisperers few. If only Bacon's exposure of the Idols had been remembered, all might have been well. But

naturam expellas furca tamen usque recurret

and the Idol of the Tribe returned with increasing vigour as the Baconian method hardened into a dogmatism as assertive as scholasticism itself. It seems almost impossible to prevent both religion and science from becoming assertive in each other's sphere, even while they remain (as they must) humble within their own. If, swallowing this unpleasant truth as inevitable, we next inquire which is to be preferred: religion with its by-product of 'scientifi-

1. Keats, Letter, 19 February 1818.

cally false' assertions, or science with its by-product of 'metaphysically false' assertions? only one reply, I think, is possible: that alternative is to be preferred which best satisfies the needs, or best counteracts the defects, of each age. Science was undoubtedly what was most needed at the beginning of the seventeenth century; and, if one's own opinion is to be given, religion (but not scholasticism) is what is most needed now. And we may gladly grant to the neo-Catholics that St Thomas had more, and a more important kind of humility than Bacon. 'To extend more widely the limits of the power and greatness of man' is not the ambition of the humble; and a certain magnificent arrogance, born of the Renaissance, appears in what we know of Bacon's life, and – still more revealingly – in the rhythm of his sentences.

CHAPTER 3

Sir Thomas Browne

The 'Metaphysical'

BACON was pleading for science in an age dominated by 'religion';[1] Browne is already – at least in the *Religio medici* – pleading for religion in an age which was beginning to be dominated by science. This is partly what makes him so interesting to us now. He has been represented[2] as a type of the scientific man who yet retains a religious faith. And indeed he did combine in rare fashion an enthusiasm for verified truth with a constantly 'marvelling temper'. He was himself his own 'great amphibium', living simultaneously in divided and distinguished worlds; or perhaps we may say his own Janus, the double-faced divinity he so often uses as a symbol of paradox. Perhaps no writer is more truly representative of the double-faced age in which he lived, an age half scientific and half magical, half sceptical and half credulous, looking back in one direction to Maundeville, and forward to Newton. At one moment a Baconian experimentalist and herald of the new world, at another Browne is discoursing of cockatrices and unicorns and mermaids in a tone which implies that though part of him is incredulous, the world is still incalculable enough to contain such marvels. At one moment he professes himself a follower of Hermes Trismegistus, and feels, pantheistically, 'the warm gale and gentle ventilation' of the world-soul; at another, he accounts the world 'not an Inn, but an Hospital; a place not to live, but to Dye in'.[3] He exhorts us now to 'live by old Ethicks, and the classical rules of Honesty',[4] and now to 'Look be-

1. Cf. the subtitle of Dr J. Needham's *The Great Amphibium*.
2. ibid.
3. *Religio medici*, II, sect. xi.   4. *Christian Morals*, I, sect. xii.

yond Antoninus, and terminate not thy morals in Seneca or Epic-
tetus. Be a moralist of the Mount, and Christianize thy Notions.'[1] He
had, in fact, what Mr T. S. Eliot has called the 'unified sensibility' of
the 'metaphysicals', which was the offspring – perhaps unrepro-
ducible in different circumstances – of a scholastic training blended
with the expansive curiosity of the Renaissance. It meant the capacity
to live in divided and distinguished worlds, and to pass freely to and
fro between one and another, to be capable of many and varied
responses to experience, instead of being confined to a few stereotyped ones. Many different worlds or countries of the mind then
lay close together – the world of scholastic learning, the world of
scientific experiment, the worlds of classical mythology and of
Biblical history, of fable and of fact, of theology and demonology,
of sacred and profane love, of pagan and Christian morals, of activity
and contemplation; and a cultivated man had the freedom of them
all. They were divided and distinguished, perhaps, but not, as later,
by such high barriers that a man was shut up for life in one or other
of them. The distinctions were only beginning to be made which for
later ages shut off poetry from science, metaphor from fact, fancy
from judgement. The point about these different worlds was not
that they were divided, but that they were simultaneously available.
The major interests of life had not as yet been mechanically appor-
tioned to specialists, so that one must dedicate oneself wholly to fact,
or wholly to value. Bishops and Deans could still write excellent
poetry, and an essay by a provincial doctor on cinerary urns – which
today would be a dull paper read to a local archaeological society –
could also be, in De Quincey's words, an 'impassioned requiem
breathing from the pomps of earth and from the sanctities of the
grave'. I think that something of the peculiar quality of the 'metaphysical' mind is due to this fact of its not being *finally committed* to
any one world. Instead, it could hold them all in a loose synthesis
together, yielding itself, as only a mind in free poise can, to the
passion of detecting analogies and correspondences between them.
Scholastic philosophy, Christianity, the Classics, these (apart from
first-hand emotion) supplied most of the material upon which

1. *Christian Morals*, III, sect. xxi.

metaphysical wit played; it was between these worlds that its comparisons are chiefly made. The quality of these comparisons, their naïveté, their surprise, comes from their being made by men to whom each world matters much, but not everything.

Let us take a few examples. One of the commonest juxtapositions in Browne is the use of a classical image to enforce a Christian moral (a piece of hybridization which has its obvious analogies in baroque architecture and much else that is typical of the age).

> Weapons for such combats are not to be forged at *Lipara*: *Vulcan's* Art doth nothing in this internal Militia; wherein not the armour of *Achilles*, but the Armature of *St Paul*, gives the Glorious day, and Triumphs not leading up to Capitols, but up into the highest Heavens.[1]

This, I suggest, is the work of a man to whom classical learning meant much, but not all – for there was also Christianity; and conversely, to whom Christianity meant much, but not so much as to exclude classical culture. The 'divided worlds' are so equipollent that they are almost interchangeable. While Browne is writing as a Christian, his experience as a scholar is also available to him; while writing as an archaeologist, his experience as a mystic is available; as a naturalist, his experience as poet, scholar, or seer. Like the metaphysicals, he seems to us to get his thrill rather out of the actual process of fusing disparates than from any 'truth' that may emerge from the process. The next example shows him using the resources of the scholar and poet to describe what to a specialist of later days would have been a 'mere fact' of petrology: Crystal, he writes, is a mineral body.

> transparent and resembling Glass or Ice, made of a lentous percolation of earth, drawn from the most pure and limpid juice thereof, owing unto the coldness of the earth some concurrence or coadjuvancy, but not immediate determination and efficiency, which are *wrought by the hand of its concretive spirit, the seeds of petrifaction and Gorgon of itself.*[2]

A 'fact' to Browne, it is evident, was no mere item from the 'inanimate cold world'; it was something to be felt as well as thought

1. *Christian Morals*, I, sect. xxiv.
2. *Pseudodoxia epidemica*, Bk II, Ch. I (my italics, here and below).

about; it 'lay in glory in his mind'.[1] It is this which makes Browne's science so 'unscientific', if by 'scientific' we mean 'chemically pure' from feeling. To the same cause, the inter-availability of all his worlds of experience, is due the famous (but largely unanalysed) quality of 'quaintness' in Browne. As in Mr Eliot's celebrated instance of Spinoza and the smell of cooking,[2] Browne thinks of Gorgons when he is discoursing of crystal, and fuses them into a whole. It will be noticed in Browne's 'scientific' writings that the impression he conveys of 'feeling' his thought is due to his explanations being often fundamentally scholastic. Scholasticism normally 'explains' a physical event by describing it in terms of imputed human reactions – antipathy, sympathy, *fuga vacui*, or the operation of some innate 'quality' or 'spirit'. Browne wonders

whether all *Coral* were first woody substance and afterwards converted; or rather some thereof were never such, but *from the sprouting spirit of salt*, were able even in their stony natures to ramifie and send forth branches.[3]

His free use of terms such as 'temperamental contrariety', 'occult form', 'elemental repugnancy' is significant. Mr Eliot has rightly pointed out that 'a thought to Donne was an experience; it modified his sensibility'; this is largely true of Browne as well, and both owe it, I believe, to the scholastic tradition, in which 'fact' and 'value' had not yet been sundered by the mechanical 'philosophy'. On almost every page of Browne one can see how his 'thought' proceeds *pari passu* with his 'feeling'; the forces of his erudition are constantly mobilized to support his emotion. He can introduce, without incongruity, a mathematical image into a passage of profound musing:

Pyramids, Arches, Obelisks, were but the irregularities of vain-glory, and wild enormities of ancient magnanimity. But the most magnanimous resolution rests in the Christian Religion, which trampleth upon pride and sets on the neck of ambition, humbly pursuing that infallible perpetuity, unto which all others must diminish their diameters and be poorly seen in Angles of contingency.[4]

1. Emerson said this of Thoreau. 2. *Homage to J. Dryden*, p. 30.
3. *Pseudodoxia epidemica*, Bk II, Ch. 5. 4. *Urn Burial*, Ch. 5.

Or his emotion can fuse into a strange amalgam (as it inevitably seems to modern readers) materials from many mental countries – Bible story, Greek legend, Egyptian embalming, together with a certain mathematical exactness of computation:

But in this latter Scene of time we cannot expect such Mummies unto our memories, when ambition may fear the Prophecy of *Elias*, and *Charles* the fifth can never hope to live within two *Methusela's* of *Hector*.[1]

The peculiar irony of Browne, his wistfulness, the air of compassion with which he ponders all time and all existence, proceed from his detachment from each and all of the worlds he contemplates; so that he can indulge his whim in fitting together what patterns he pleases with their fragments.

The world that I regard is my self; it is the Microcosm of my own frame that I cast mine eye on; for the other (i.e. the Macrocosm), *I use it but like my Globe, and turn it round sometimes for my recreation.*[2]

It is a romantic falsification to 'relish' Browne for his 'quaintness'. It is more valuable, in reading him, to try to recover something of his own inclusiveness, in virtue of which his juxtapositions are *not* quaint, but symbols of his complex vision.

Browne's 'style' is the incarnation of his sensibility, and we can trace, I think, even in some of its details, his sense of the proximity of the different worlds of thought and feeling, and his desire to exploit the resources of them all. For instance, there is his trick of the *reduplicated phrase*, of which a few examples may be worth examining (the italics are mine):

While they lay obscure in *the Chaos of preordination, and night of their fore-beings*[3]

The America and untravelled parts of truth.[4]

This *funambulatory Track and narrow Path* of Goodness. . . . The *Hill and asperous way* which leadeth unto the House of Sanity.[5]

1. *Urn Burial.*   2. *Religio medici*, II, sect. xi (my italics).
3. *Urn Burial*, Ch. 5, end.   4. *Pseudodoxia epidemica*, 'To the Reader'.
5. *Christian Morals*, beginning.

To well manage our *Affections and wild Horses of Plato*, are the highest Circenses.[1]

The *circinations and spherical rounds* of onions.[2]

Conscience only, that can see without light, sits in *the Areopagy and dark Tribunal* of our Hearts, surveying our Thoughts and condemning their obliquities.[3]

It is more than likely that Browne was sensitive to the Janus-like quality of the English language itself, half Latin and half Saxon; and that in feeling for the most significant phrases he was impelled to tap each reservoir of meaning in turn. For it will be noticed that in each of the italicized pairs a Latin (or Greek) member is balanced against a Saxon, or a rarer term against a more homely one. Nothing, he seems to feel, has been completely *said* until it has been given richness and intellectual content by the far-sought word, and then 'proved upon our pulses' with the simpler one.[4] Sometimes after a passage bristling with Latin abstracts, he will suddenly right the balance with a concrete image, as in the familiar passage from *Urn Burial*:

We whose generations are ordained in this setting part of time, are providentially taken off from such imaginations; and being necessitated to eye the remaining particle of futurity, are naturally constituted unto thoughts of the next world, and cannot excusably decline the consideration of that duration, which maketh pyramids pillars of snow, and all that's past a moment.

1. *Christian Morals*, I, sect. xxiv.   2. *Garden of Cyrus*, Ch. 4.
3. *Christian Morals*, III, sect. xv.
4. That Browne understood the linguistic situation of his time is indicated by the following passage from the foreword to the *Pseudodoxia*: 'Our first intentions considering the common interest of Truth, resolved to propose it unto the Latine republique and equal Judges of Europe, but owing in the first place this service to our Country, and therein especially to its ingenuous Gentry, we have declared ourselves in a language best conceived. Although I confess *the quality of the Subject will sometimes carry us into expressions beyond meer English apprehensions*. And indeed, if elegancy still proceedeth, and English pens maintain that stream, we have of late observed to flow from many; we shall within few years be fain to learn Latine to understand English, and a work will prove of equal facility in either.'

Only an inclusive sensibility like Browne's, to whom the world of homely feeling is not remote even while he is being learnedly homiletic, could have saved that passage from pedantry, and dissolved its massiveness in a kind of sweet irony. The peculiar lightning-flicker of Browne is traceable to this, that just when we think him most deeply engaged in one world of thought or feeling, he surprises us with a proof of his freedom; he remembers another (to us far-distant) world, and hangs pensively over them both, 'turning them round for his recreation'.

The Baconian

In thinking of Browne as a 'metaphysical' we must not forget that he had in him a large infusion of the Baconian experimentalist. In the *Pseudodoxia epidemica* he makes as it were an amateur contribution to what I have called the main intellectual problem of the seventeenth century, the separation of the 'true' from the 'false'. It is true that much of the literary attractiveness of this book is due, as I have suggested, to its scholastic tincture, and to the 'marvelling temper' in which Browne so often explodes his marvels. Nevertheless its conscious intention, and often its real drift, is to clear away the vast deposit of pseudo-science and fantastic lore left over from the unscientific centuries. Browne, on this side of him, is an ardent modernist (in the seventeenth century sense of the term); he believes that a great new advance towards truth is being made in his time, and wishes to feel that he is in the forefront of the movement. Rather unexpectedly it is in *Christian Morals* that we find one of Browne's most enthusiastic salutes to the brave new world. He is exhorting his reader to study and to speculate, but to 'fly not only upon the wings of Imagination' like the Peripatetics; he must 'joyn Sense unto Reason, and Experiment unto Speculation', so as not to 'swell the leaves of learning by fruitless repetitions'. Then he continues:

There is nothing more acceptable unto the ingenious World, than this noble Eluctation of Truth; wherein, against the tenacity of Prejudice and

Prescription, this Century now prevaileth. What Libraries of new Volumes aftertimes will behold, and in what a new World of Knowledge the eyes of our Posterity may be happy, a few Ages may joyfully declare; and is but a cold thought unto those who cannot hope to behold this Exantlation of Truth, or that obscured Virgin half out of the Pit.[1]

Just as Descartes strips himself of all but his own 'clear and distinct ideas', and proceeds to test reality by those, so Browne, in less rigorously logical fashion, will be another David of the new age, setting out to meet 'the Goliath and Giant of Authority', armed only with 'contemptible pibbles' drawn from the 'scrip and slender stock' of himself.[2] For Browne's appeal is not only to the Baconian experimental test, though he applies this constantly; he has also an Ithuriel's spear with which he sometimes directly probes a vulgar error. Is this belief, he asks, consonant with reason and sound sense? And by that he means, is it consistent with what by now has come to seem the nature of things, with what we feel we know of the way things hang together? As I have hinted above, what then seemed 'truest' about the nature of things was that God worked in nature only by second causes, that is, that throughout the universe we must expect to meet nothing but order, uniformity, and strict (and probably mechanical) causation. Our tendency to ascribe a natural event to a supernatural cause is with Browne one of the temptations of Satan, luring us away from genuine knowledge. Doubtless scholasticism admitted the universality of second causes in nature, but the language with which it had described them was coming to seem 'supernaturalist', now that 'affinities', 'antipathies', 'substantial forms', and the like were being 'explained' in mechanical terms. It was not so much to *establish* the principle of strict causation that Bacon and Browne were working, as to drive home its truth upon their readers' imagination, to compel more of their generation to feel it as fact. For at that time, just as many sincere Christians believed in the existence of a 'supernatural' which was certainly not the official supernature of religion, so many could be well-versed in Aristotle, and the schoolmen, and yet believe in magic. Browne

1. II, sect. v.　　　　2. Foreword to *Pseudodoxia epidemica*.

himself, as we have seen, sometimes uses highly 'unscientific' language, yet he is a firm believer in what he calls 'the settled and determined order of the world',[1] and it is this, the fundamental principle of science, that most of his inquiries are supposed to illustrate.

> To behold a Rainbow in the night, is no prodigy unto a Philosopher. Than Eclipses of the Sun or Moon, nothing is more natural. Yet with what superstition they have been beheld since the Tragedy of Nicias and his Army, many examples declare.[2]

It is God that we shall meet in Nature, not Satan; that is to say, we shall everywhere encounter law, not arbitrary mystery or capricious exertions of power. For God keeps his own laws, or only breaks them on extraordinary occasions.

> There is no liberty for causes to operate in a loose and straggling way; nor any effect whatsoever, but hath its warrant from some universal or superiour Cause ... even in *sortilegies* and matters of greatest uncertainty, there is a settled and pre-ordered course of effects.[3]

Browne is as eager as Bacon to rescue Nature and natural science from their traditional association with witchcraft and sorcery. Not that he disbelieves in witchcraft; on the contrary, he even admits that 'at first a great part of Philosophy was Witchcraft'. The secrets once extorted from the devil, at the price of their souls, by self-sacrificing sorcerers, have now 'proved but Philosophy', and 'no more than the honest effects of Nature: what, invented by us, is Philosophy, learned from him [i.e. Satan] is Magick'.[4] What Satan taught the magicians was after all only 'the principles of Nature', the important thing is that we now should learn these from Nature itself and not from him. Browne joins with Bacon in scouting the notion that there is risk of damnation in exploring the secrets of Nature:

> There is no danger to profound these mysteries, no *sanctum sanctorum* in Philosophy. The World was made to be inhabited by Beasts, but studied

1. *Pseudodoxia epidemica*, Bk I, Ch. 2, end.   2. ibid., Bk I, Ch. 2.
3. *Religio medici*, I, sect. xviii.   4. ibid., I, sect. xxxi.

and contemplated by Man: 'tis the Debt of our Reason we owe unto God, and the homage we pay for not being Beasts. ... The Wisdom of God receives small honour from those vulgar Heads that rudely stare about, and with a gross rusticity admire His works: those highly magnifie Him, whose judicious inquiry into His Acts, and deliberate research into His Creatures, return the duty of a devout and learned admiration.[1]

'Nature is the Art of God'; and Browne uses the Baconian technique again in also calling Nature a Scripture:

There are two Books from whence I collect my Divinity, besides that written one of God, another of His servant Nature, that universal and publick Manuscript, that lies expans'd unto the Eyes of all: those that never saw Him in the one, have discovered Him in the other. This was the Scripture and Theology of the Heathens:

and Browne even has the courage to commend the heathens for

knowing better how to joyn and read these mystical Letters than we Christians, who cast a more careless Eye on these common Hieroglyphicks, and *disdain to suck Divinity from the flowers of Nature*.[2]

Nearly two hundred years after Browne, Wordsworth exclaimed:

> Great God! I'd rather be
> A pagan, suckled in a creed outworn;
> So might I, standing on this pleasant lea
> Have glimpses that would make me less forlorn;

and only yesterday Lawrence was telling us that the human race is 'like a great up-rooted tree, with its roots in the air. We must plant ourselves again in the universe.'[3] It is significant to reflect that Wordsworth and Lawrence were making their protest against some of the effects of the very science which Browne was trying to vindicate. Browne wanted to plant us in the universe so that we might have science; Wordsworth and Lawrence, that we might forget it.

1. *Religio medici*, I, sect. xiii.
2. ibid., I, sect. xvi.
3. *À Propos of Lady Chatterley's Lover*, p. 52.

Browne's account of the sources of the Common Errors is to some extent parallel to Bacon's Confutation of Idols. Corresponding to the Idols of the Tribe, though different in so far as Browne means rather a moral than an intellectual defect, is the imperfection of our fallen nature, whereby we are radically prone to err. The second source is in the 'erroneous disposition of the people', the 'democratical enemies of truth', and corresponds roughly to Bacon's Idols of the Market. We must not be surprised to find the tolerant and charitable Browne exclaiming upon 'that great enemy of reason, virtue, and religion, the Multitude'. The culture of the Renaissance was essentially aristocratic, and Browne wishes to preserve it from the contamination of the vulgar, who are taken in by 'saltimbancoes', 'quacksalvers', and charlatans of every description. Browne was neither the first nor the last champion of sweetness and light who has disliked the *profanum vulgus*.

The third class of errors is of the opposite kind, and may be connected with Bacon's Idols of the Theatre. These are the errors or distempers to which learned men are prone. As would be expected, it is at this point that Browne affirms his own 'rejection of scholasticism', and associates himself with the Moderns against the Ancients. He notes a number of logical errors, and censures the credulity of the erudite, and their 'supinity', which consists either in 'rather believing than going to see' or in 'rather doubting with ease and gratis than believing with difficulty and purchase'. But if there are some who have failed through 'supinity', there are others, he observes, 'who have sweat to little purpose, and rolled the stone in vain'; and with such, he adds, our Universities are often filled.[1] But the chief error in this division is slavish adherence to antiquity, and especially to Aristotle. We dishonour that pioneer by failing to carry forward the work so auspiciously begun by him. 'Ancient knowledge was imperfect in many things, and we have enlarged the bounds of knowledge beyond their conception.' We must emancipate ourselves from 'testimonial engagements', and 'erect upon the

---

1. *Pseudodoxia epidemica*, Bk I, Ch. 5. 'And this is one reason why, though Universities be full of men, they are oftentimes empty of learning.' Cf. Bacon's censure of the Universities.

surer base of reason'.[1] In its effort to throw off authority, the seventeenth century discovered, in each sphere of interest, an Ancient still
older than the Ancients; in theology, the Ancient of Days, in science,
Nature herself; in ethics, and in literary theory, 'nature and reason'.
Browne gives us the names of the main authorities from whom most
of the pseudodoxies of his day proceeded – Herodotus, Ctesias,
Pliny the Younger, Claudius Aelianus, Basil and Ambrose, Albertus
Magnus, Cardan, and many more – and it is to the exposure of the
errors derived from such as these that most of the book is devoted.
Browne deplores that so many of the moderns think that to follow
nature is to follow them, and that when they have a treatise to com-
pose, instead of studying their subject experimentally, they 'prom-
iscuously amass all that makes for their subject' and then 'break
forth at last in trite and fruitless Rhapsodies'.[2]

But Truth has another and still more powerful enemy. Besides
all these sources of error in the general infirmity of human nature,
there is the ubiquitous Satan, whose activities are so widespread that
Browne, in enumerating them, seems almost to fall into that mani-
chaean heresy which, he says, is one of Satan's own deceits. In spite
of his Baconian enthusiasms, and his trust in the settled and determined order of nature, Browne was far indeed from conceiving the
world as the Great Machine. He would not be so representative of
his Janus-age were it otherwise. Behind the gauze curtain of science
the old supernatural drama was still proceeding as before. Browne's
Satan is very unlike the kind of domestic demon or poltergeist who
pestered Luther or Bunyan; he is akin to Milton's in the breadth of
his views and the scope of his strategy. As the century wore on there
was certainly a remarkable waning in Satan's prestige; Nature had
been rescued from him, and human nature was following suit as
quickly as might be. The gradual evaporation in the later years of
the century of the belief in witchcraft – that commonest of all the
modes of Satanic interference with human affairs – bears witness to
the final triumph of the new philosophy. But during the greater
part of the century Satan remained the most living figure in the

1. *Pseudodoxia epidemica*, Bk 1, Ch. 7.
2. ibid., Bk 1, Ch. 8.

current mythology. 'God' had been rationalized through centuries of theology, and was now receding still further into the inconceivable as the frontiers of natural causation were pushed back and back. But Satan, symbol of how much! of the endless indignation of the subconscious against the mind-forged manacles of fear, and pride, and rebelliousness – Satan was still far more than an allegory which could be explained in conceptual language. The century was in fetters when it wrote of Angels and God, and at liberty when of Devils and Hell.[1] When 'God' becomes a scientific hypothesis, almost identifiable with absolute space,[2] it is not surprising that the religious consciousness should express itself through 'Satan'. It is probably for this reason that those who, as the scientific philosophy strengthened its hold, adhered tenaciously to a supernatural world-view, felt that they must cling to Satan in order to keep God. The idea that to abandon belief in witches was to begin on the slippery slope to atheism was a common one at this time. It is seen well developed in Glanvill's *Sadducismus Triumphatus*, and survives in the eighteenth century in Wesley. Browne's views on witchcraft are well known, and may be best read in the *Religio medici*:

For my part I have ever believed, and do now know, that there are Witches: they that doubt of these, do not only deny *them*, but Spirits; and are obliquely and upon consequence a sort not of Infidels, but Atheists.[3]

But Browne, like Glanvill, has felt the change in the 'climate of opinion' which showed itself in an increasing scepticism about the devil and his witches. Accordingly he adopts a device highly characteristic of him and of his time: the subtlest of all Satan's stratagems, he tells us, is to *pretend his own non-existence* in general; and in particular the non-existence of witches.[4] Not only is it to Satan that we owe the disposition not to believe in Satan, but Browne can even ascribe to him all the superstitious and unscientific learning, the vain pseudo-science, which attributes natural phenomena to supernatural causes. Browne described himself accurately when he wrote 'in Philosophy, where Truth seems double-faced, there is no man more

1. Blake, *Marriage of Heaven and Hell*. 2. See pp. 152 and 252 below.
3. I, sect. xxx. 4. *Pseudodoxia epidemica*, Bk I, Ch. 10.

Paradoxical than myself'.[1] For Browne will have it both ways: Satan is accountable for both our scepticism and our credulity.

Browne's description of Satan's other activities follows more usual lines. Amongst the errors which the devil tries to disseminate are, for instance, that there is no God, or at least no Providence; that God 'looks not below the Moon', or that all things hang on Fate, Destiny, Necessity, and so forth. Or, alternatively, that there are many Gods. He also pretends to be God, as in the Oracles and other assumed attributes of Deity. But of the remaining Satanic deceits the most interesting are those referring to the interpretation of Scripture, and this is the topic of the following Chapter.

1. *Religio medici*, 1, sect. vi.

CHAPTER 4

On Scriptural Interpretation

Browne

THE question of scriptural interpretation was bound to be a vital one for many seventeenth-century English writers, since they were not only Protestants, and therefore committed to the authority of holy writ, but beginning to be 'philosophic' as well, and therefore eager for 'the truth'. How to fit a supernaturalist and poetic scripture into the new world-scheme, how to reconcile Jehovah with the ontologically-certified *Dieu* of Descartes, and the whole miraculous structure of Christianity with the new 'philosophical' principles, this was a major problem confronting the critical intelligence of the age. The difficulty of writing *Paradise Lost* in the seventeenth century was even greater than is generally supposed.[1]

Browne attributes to Satan all the errors and misgivings about Scripture which prevailed in his time, and of which he personally had had his full share. 'More of these no man hath known than myself, which I confess I conquered, not in a martial posture, but on my knees.' Amongst these are such questions as, How did the creatures from the Ark, starting as they did from Mount Ararat, get disseminated over all the countries of the world, in spite of the estranging seas? Gold does not turn to powder under high temperatures, so how can Moses have calcined the Golden Calf? Manna is an actual plant, flourishing in Calabria and formerly gathered in Arabia; 'where then was the miracle in the days of Moses?' Similarly, there is such a thing as 'Secret Sympathy', and may not the Brazen Serpent of Moses have healed the people thus, without a miracle? and might not Elijah have kindled the fire on God's altar by means of naphtha? – 'for that inflammable substance yields not easily unto

1. Cf. pp. 197 ff. below.

Water, but flames in the Arms of its Antagonist'. In this manner Satan 'takes a hint of Infidelity from our Studies, and by demonstrating a naturality in one way, makes us mistrust a miracle in another'.

> Thus the Devil played at Chess with me, and yielding a Pawn, thought to gain a Queen of me, taking advantage of my honest endeavours; and whilst I laboured to raise the structure of my Reason, he strived to undermine the edifice of my Faith.[1]

Browne has more than one way of meeting these difficulties. One is the Baconian method of assigning Scripture to the region of Faith, and so rendering it immune from the questionings of Reason. 'It is no vulgar part of Faith', he says, 'to believe a thing not only above but contrary to Reason, and against the arguments of our proper senses.'[2]

> To believe only possibilities is not Faith, but meer Philosophy. Many things are true in Divinity, which are neither inducible by reason, nor confirmable by sense.[3]

In 'Philosophy', as we have seen, Browne delighted to be 'paradoxical', but in 'Divinity' he loved to 'keep the Road; and though not in an implicite, yet an humble faith, follow the great wheel of the Church'.[4] To classify every scriptural statement as 'divinity' and to rebut all critical questionings as temptations of Satan was indeed a short way with biblical problems. Browne is not afraid of stating the extreme position:

> I can answer all the Objections of Satan and my rebellious reason with that odd resolution I learned of Tertullian, *certum est quia impossibile est.*[5]

It was one of the privileges of the seventeenth century to be able to believe, without any effort or striving, that 'truth' was not all of one order. It would be more accurate to say that this was unconsciously assumed, or felt, rather than consciously 'believed'. Thus, however eager one might be for the 'exantlation' of one kind of

1. *Religio medici*, I, sect. xix ff.   2. ibid., I, sect. x.
3. ibid., I, sect. xlviii.   4. ibid., I, sect. vi.   5. ibid., I, sect. ix.

truth, the new kind, the old order of numinous truth was still secure in its inviolate separateness. The feeling that there was a divine meaning, an *otherness*, in the universe, as well as a mechanical order, was still natural and inevitable; it had not, as so often since, to be deliberately worked up or simulated. At the same time one could of course be more interested in one order or the other. Bacon, as we have seen, desired their separation chiefly for the sake of science. As for Browne, it is difficult to say which he valued most; indeed it is precisely the capacity for living in both worlds that distinguishes him. But when he is actually speaking of the separation of the worlds, it is nearly always for religion that he is pleading. He had – what Bacon probably had in much smaller measure, and Hobbes and most succeeding 'philosophers' of the enlightenment lacked – a positive *goût* for the numinous. To lose himself in an *o altitudo!* was an experience he highly valued; he loved 'to teach his haggard and unreclaimed reason to stoop unto the lure of faith'. And Scripture (to return to our immediate point) was a numinous book, and horror must be felt towards any attempt to apply to it the usual scientific tests. The part that the Bible has played, as a storehouse of numinous values, has of course been immense. Since the scientific movement began, and numinous experience has become less and less accessible, Scripture and the liturgies have preserved a range of experiences which have been increasingly threatened by modernity in its various manifestations, and might have been altogether lost. Perhaps it is a sense of the importance of these experiences that is expressing itself when the Bible is reverenced as 'holy', and when reluctance is shown to 'revising' or 'modernizing' the Prayer Book. At all costs (so the plea might run) let us not cut the last thread that links us with a lost world of feeling.

But it would be quite a mistake to suppose that the 'holiness' of the Bible meant anything like this in the seventeenth century. For us, let us say, its 'holiness' means first, that it contains, together with a mass of historical material, certain records of religious experience. These, like other such records, are capable of reproducing some degree of the religious experience in us, not by reasoning, but by communication, as in poetry. The Bible is holy, then, in so far as it is an aid to religious experience. Secondly, its efficacy in this kind is reinforced by the feelings traditionally associated with it; it evokes, in fact, a 'stock response' of a special kind. And those who wish now to conserve this holiness believe that the aid to religious experience, and even the stock response, are more than ever valuable in the modern world. We may perhaps argue that already in the seventeenth century its unconscious meaning was beginning to be something like this. But its conscious meaning was very different. The Scripture, that is, the whole contents of the biblical canon, belonged to Divinity, not to Philosophy; its Truth was truth of faith, not truth of fact. But further (and this is what more especially differentiates that century from ours), every statement in Scripture, whether narrative, psalm, prophecy, parable, vision, or exhortation, had a 'spiritual' meaning; that is to say, it was pointing, through its literal 'sense', to a 'Truth' beyond sense. This must necessarily be so for two complementary reasons: first, because Scripture was divinely inspired, 'given', and secondly, because so much of Scripture could only be regarded as 'divine' if it *had* a multiple meaning. We are thus brought face to face with the main crux of scriptural interpretation from the earliest down to quite recent times. The position may be expressed thus: you begin with a preconception about the divine inspiration of Scripture; you immediately find that a great part of Scripture does not fit your preconception; therefore, you conclude, the words must mean something other than they say. As St Augustine puts it:

Quidquid in sermone divino neque ad morum honestatem neque ad fidei veritatem proprie referri potest figuratum esse cognoscas.[1]

1. 'Whatsoever in holy writ cannot be properly said to be concerned either with morality or with the faith must be recognized as allegorical.' Quoted by Farrar, *History of Scriptural Interpretation*, 1886, p. 237, to which I am indebted for the references in the ensuing paragraphs.

The Allegorists

The allegorical method of interpreting Scripture, as this quotation will suggest, had already had a long and illustrious history before our period. It first arose (as far as the Hebrew and Christian Scriptures are concerned) out of the conjunction of Judaism with Hellenism in Alexandria. The Alexandrian culture of the first and second centuries A.D. is indeed in some ways parallel to that of seventeenth-century Europe. In both, 'philosophy' and 'religion' confronted each other; and in both, efforts were made to harmonize them, to be philosophical while remaining faithful to the letter of Scripture. The name of Philo Judaeus (*c.* 20 B.C. to *c.* A.D. 45) is usually associated with the early use of the allegorical method. It was natural that this should originate with an Alexandrian Jew, for, after all, the Western reverence for 'scriptures' is of Hebrew derivation, and Philo, being an Alexandrian, was also a Hellenist. The Jewish Rabbis had, of course, already evolved a vast apparatus of scriptural interpretation, but for them 'the Pentateuch was the germ of all ritualism', whereas 'to the Hellenists it was the veil of all gnosis'.[1] The crossing of Hebraic scripturalism with Platonic and neo-Platonic speculation produced the allegorical interpretation.[2] I think it may also be said that philosophic 'realism', either Platonic or Christian, is usually present by implication in most Western allegorical writings; for it is of the essence of allegory to assume that the *most real thing*, that which is to be demonstrated, illustrated, or inculcated, is something abstract, while the image, the personification, is created for the sake of the abstraction, and points only thither. Now, the assumption behind the interpretations of the scriptural allegorists is, not only

1. Farrar, op. cit., p. 131.
2. It is noteworthy that Homer, whose status amongst the Greeks bore some analogy to that of Scripture amongst the Jews, had already been subjected to allegorical interpretation by, e.g., Theagenes, Metrodorus, Stesimbrotus, Glaucon, and the early Stoics. Philo merely applied their methods to Scripture. Cf. Farrar, op. cit., pp. 131ff.

that the structure of the universe is neo-Platonic, but that God himself allegorizes. He cannot create a stone without a sermon in it; in His own words, then, how manifold must be the depths of meaning! Thus, according to Philo, it would be a sign of great simplicity to suppose, after reading Genesis, that the world was 'really' created in six days, or in 'time' at all. To take literally the words 'God planted a Paradise in Eden' is impiety; 'let not such fabulous nonsense ever enter our minds'. The true meaning is, that God implants terrestrial virtue in the human race. In the biblical description of the Promised Land, says Philo, 'cities' mean general virtues, 'wells' mean noble dispositions towards wisdom, 'vineyards and olive-trees', cheerfulness and light, or the products of a contemplative life. The 'five cities of the plain' are the five senses. All the Old Testament characters are personifications. The sacred books were written by persons in a state of ecstasy, during which all their human powers were exploited by the divine afflatus. If, at first, we are inclined to applaud Philo for some of his rationalizations, we must remember that his 'enlightenment' is purchased dearly, at the price of believing that God *intends* the abstract meaning which is alleged to underlie the literal sense. In practice, as can be seen from some of the quoted examples, the result was that almost any 'interpretation', however wildly fantastic, could be confidently recommended as the 'real' meaning of any passage. One may welcome Philo's emancipation from the bonds of 'literalism', but his enslavement to the belief in allegorical intention involves him in such distortions of historical narrative that it is doubtful which 'error' is the worse. To the modern mind it is, of course, just the complete absence of all historical sense that is so remarkable in early biblical criticism. The whole of Scripture is treated as homogeneous, and any passage can be connected with any other for the extraction of further meanings.[1]

Just as the Alexandrian Jews had allegorized the Old Testament,

1. For instance, the belief, current in Browne's time, that the world was to last six thousand years, was 'proved' by the author of the *Epistle of Barnabas*, by the Six Days of Genesis, coupled with the phrase in the Psalm: 'one day with the Lord is as a thousand years'.

so the Apostolic Fathers, before the full formation of the New Testament Canon, allegorized it in order to make it a witness for Christian truth. The Gnostics, furthermore, dissolved into abstractions all the 'positive truths of historical Christianity', and this provoked the 'literalist' or 'realistic' reaction of Irenaeus and Tertullian. Dean Farrar's comment on the 'odd paradox' which Browne learned from Tertullian reveals the gulf between the seventeenth century and the nineteenth, or at any rate between the theology of a seventeenth-century *savant* and that of a Victorian liberal divine. The views of Browne, and of Bacon, about the 'absurd' or 'impossible' in matters of faith will be remembered.[1] Dean Farrar is horrified at this attitude. Tertullian, says he, 'adopted the paradox *credo quia absurdum est*, and the wild conclusion that the more repugnant to sound reason a statement was, it ought so much the more to be deemed worthy of God'.[2] Alas, we are not quite so sure as Farrar (or Matthew Arnold) that we know what 'sound reason' is, or what the limits of its truth-value may be; neither do we feel so certain as to what precisely is 'worthy of God'. Of what God? Yahweh, the First Person of the Trinity, the Supreme Being, the Absolute, Quetzalcoatl? What is unworthy of a God who is Sound Reason deified, may not unfitly represent the God who created Behemoth, Leviathan, and the spiral nebulae; the God who is, in Pascal's phrase, *Deus absconditus*.

While Tertullian blames the Gnostics for their use of allegory, and repudiates all attempts to philosophize the faith (though using allegory himself when he so desires), the Alexandrian Fathers anticipated the effort of the Cambridge Platonists to unite revelation with a platonic philosophy. For Tertullian, as for all since who have dwelt upon the *otherness* of God, philosophy was suspect; for Clement and Origen, it was of divine origin. Accordingly, for Clement all Scripture is allegorical, even the Decalogue. The New Testament miracles he treats as if they were parables.[3] He does not deny the literal sense, but considers that this is not for the philosophic Christian. It was Origen, however, who formulated the famous 'threefold sense' of Scripture – which later became the 'fourfold

1. See above, pp. 33 and 59.   2. op. cit., p. 164.   3. op. cit., p. 165.

sense'[1] of the Scholastics (and of Dante) – the literal, the moral, and the mystical. The division corresponded to Plato's tripartite division of Man, into body, soul, and spirit,[2] and as might therefore be supposed, the 'literal' was for him the least of all the meanings. One appreciates the insight of these cultivated and philosophic theologians, and prefers their view, in many ways, to the narrow protestantism of a Tertullian. The theory of multiple senses was also, in itself, a remarkable first step towards the science of meaning which we are still desiderating at the present day. And yet all the wisdom of the allegorists is vitiated by two assumptions, first that 'Scripture' is homogeneous throughout; and secondly, that this homogeneous Scripture is *deliberately intended*, either by its 'inspired' writers or by God himself, as a figurative expression of spiritual truths. It is hard to say which is the more misleading – the 'fundamentalist' reading which mistakes mythology for history, or the Alexandrian, which sees allegory where none was intended. In both there is a lack of capacity to distinguish between what is 'statement' and what is emotive speech, a deficiency which not only affected scriptural interpretation, but rendered impossible any satisfactory theory of poetry or the imagination for very many centuries. It is probable that literalism, through its greater closeness to the intention of the authors, may have caused less distortion than allegorism, with its excessively intellectual presuppositions. Some such feeling was certainly present in the mind of Luther, who, in rejecting the fourfold sense, proclaimed a return to '*unum simplicem germanum et certum sensum literalem*'.[3]

The Rabbinic and Alexandrian doctrine of a *multiplex sensus* in every verse of Scripture prevailed throughout the 'Dark' and Middle Ages. Augustine, for example, tells us that Eden can be understood in a spiritual sense; that its four rivers may be taken to signify the cardinal virtues, or even the four gospels. He adds, however, that

1. See below, p. 66.
2. And apparently he based it also on a (mistranslated) passage in the Septuagint and Vulgate: '*Ecce descripsi tibi tripliciter*' (Prov. 22: 20), which he characteristically applies to the whole Bible.
3. Farrar, op. cit., p. 327.

these interpretations are quite consistent with belief in the strict truth of the history. His general rule (which I have quoted above) is that whatever in Scripture is not directly profitable or edifying must be figurative. The characteristic medieval doctrine of the quadruple sense, familiar to students of St Thomas and of Dante, is summed up in an epigram attributed to Nicholas of Lyra (d. 1340):

> Littera gesta docet, quae credas Allegoria,
> Mora lis quid agas, quo tendas Anagogia.[1]

It is well known that Dante intended his *Divina Commedia* to carry the same fourfold meaning which he attributed to Scripture. Dante may thus be said to be the only great poet to whom the method of fourfold interpretation both may and must be applied. The view, common in the seventeenth century, that much of Scripture is 'language of accommodation', is also clearly stated by him in the *Paradiso* – the divine mysteries surmount the reach of human understanding, 'and therefore doth the Scripture condescend to your capacity, assigning foot and hand to God', etc.[2]

Two other points must be indicated before we return to the seventeenth century. The first is that a tendency had already shown itself, in certain medieval mystics, to emphasize a moral rather than a metaphysical approach to 'truth'. From Hugo of St Victor (d. 1141) we have the saying: '*Tantum de veritate quisque potest videre, quantum ipse est*'; and from Richard of St Victor (d. 1173): '*In tantum Deus cognoscitur in quantum amatur*'. The attitude here implied is an obvious corrective to excessive intellectualism in any form, and has bearings on issues wider than those of scriptural interpretation. The other point is that at the time of the Renaissance scholars and critics had begun to apply historical analysis to the text of Scripture, and to distinguish between its various ingredients. Erasmus produced the first critical edition of the Greek Testament (1516), and is reckoned the chief founder of textual criticism. Luther and Hooker may both be credited with the capacity to discriminate between the different portions of the Bible, and both believed that the 'Word of God' was *contained* in it, rather than present in its every syllable. Much of

1. op. cit., p. 277.   2. Cf. *Paradiso*, IV, 43.

Hooker's *Ecclesiastical Polity* is devoted to showing that although the Bible contained what was necessary for salvation, *all* that it contained was not necessary. God had only revealed in it what was undiscoverable by the light of Reason; the rest he had left to our discretion. He had not, for example, prescribed one fixed form of government for the Church, and that the Presbyterian, as Hooker's Calvinist opponents were then asserting. The ritual and ceremonial injunctions of the Old Testament were relevant only to the time and place for which they were originally intended.

Browne (concluded)

Browne's reactions to Scripture are as manifold as his character, and reflect most of the attitudes to be found in his century. As we have seen, when he is in the mood to pursue his reason to an *o altitudo*, he feels that 'there be not impossibilities enough in Religion for an active faith'. But there are occasions when he does not see fit to force his haggard and unreclaimed reason to stoop unto the lure of faith, and these arise when scriptural statements conflict with scientific truths which he cannot surrender. At such times he falls back in the usual way upon allegorical interpretation, and the theory of 'language of accommodation'. For instance, he allows himself to wonder whether the first chapters of Genesis are not an allegory illustrating the seduction of Reason by the Passions:

though Divines have to the power of humane reason endeavoured to make all go in a literal meaning, yet those allegorical interpretations are also probable, and perhaps the mystical method of Moses bred up in the Hieroglyphical Schools of the Egyptians.[1]

The Scripture speaks of the sun and the moon as the two great lights of heaven, but Browne hopes he 'shall not offend Divinity' if he denies that the moon is therefore the second largest heavenly body, and adheres rather to 'the demonstration of Ptolemy than the popular description of Moses'. The Book of Chronicles describes

1. *Religio medici*, I, sect. xxxiv.

Solomon making a circle of which the diameter was to the circumference as 7 to 21, whereas Archimedes has demonstrated that the true proportions are 7 to nearly 22. Here too, Browne will 'adhere unto Archimedes who speaketh exactly, rather than the sacred Text which speaketh largely'.[1] In fact, Divinity may and often does make use of 'language of accommodation', whereas Philosophy requires 'strict and definitive expressions'. The Scriptures, in a word, were written to be understood by all men, and so often use popular rather than scientific and technical descriptions. Browne cannot think that God took six days to create the world; the six days must rather symbolize the conception of the work in the mind of God. Neither can he think that at the Last Day there will be any actual judicial proceeding, or calling to the bar, as Scripture implies, and the literalists believe.

For unspeakable mysteries in the Scriptures are often delivered in a vulgar and illustrative way; and being written unto man, are delivered, not as they truly are, but as they may be understood; wherein, notwithstanding, the different interpretations according to different capacities may stand firm with our devotion, nor be any way prejudicial to each single edification.'[2]

This causes Browne no uneasiness so long as it is 'unspeakable mysteries' that are being delivered. The trouble arises when Scripture appears to state incorrectly what science was demonstrating to be neither mysterious nor unspeakable. It is clear that Browne shared Bacon's anxiety that Scripture should not be allowed to be an obstacle to science. And it is significant of the times that Browne should not only feel Scripture as a potential obstacle, but should couple it as such with poetry.

Milton

The fuller discussion of Milton's thought must be deferred to a later section,[3] but it may be convenient, for purposes of comparison, to

1. *Pseudodoxia epidemica*, Bk I, Ch. 9.   2. *Religio medici*, I, sect. xlv.
3. See below, pp. 197 ff.

indicate here his attitude to Scripture. The very existence and nature of his *De doctrina christiana* serves to show that however boldly Milton may have re-interpreted Scripture for himself, its authority for him, as indeed for almost every seventeenth-century English writer, was axiomatic. So great a labour of collation and compilation could have proceeded from no other source than reverence for a book of unique holiness, and a conviction that it must be 'searched' unweariedly by the intelligent believer. It cannot be denied that in assembling what seem to him relevant texts under each heading Milton has often treated the Bible in the old uncritical way as if it were of one homogeneous texture throughout. That Milton should have felt it necessary to undertake such a heavy task, in order to free his mind from the misinterpretations of others, illustrates forcibly what a burden was laid upon the conscience of Protestants by the doctrine of biblical inspiration and authority.

Two questions especially concern us at this point: What kind or kinds of Truth did Milton find in Scripture? and, Did he ever, like others of his century, feel Scripture to be an obstacle to anything which he highly valued? First, then, Milton believed, with Browne and the allegorists generally, that in Scripture truth was often conveyed figuratively. He knew quite well that the Absolute which his intelligence acknowledged could not be equated with Jehovah, or with the 'School Divine' of his own *Paradise Lost*. But by means of the 'language of accommodation' theory, and the neo-Platonic doctrine that earthly things correspond shadow-wise to their heavenly patterns, he is able to overcome both the scriptural difficulty, and one of the main intellectual difficulties of his own great poem. Speaking of God, in the second chapter of the *De doctrina christiana*, he says:

Our safest way is to form in our minds such a conception of God as shall correspond with his own delineation and representation of himself in the sacred writings. For granting that both in the literal and figurative descriptions of God, he is exhibited not as he really is, but in such a manner as may be within the scope of our comprehension, yet we ought to entertain such a conception of him, as he, in condescending to accommodate himself to our capacities, has shown that he desires we should conceive. . . .

For instance, if the text says that 'it repented Jehovah that he had made man',

let us believe that it did really repent him, only taking care to remember that what is called repentance when applied to God does not arise from inadvertency, as in men.

And the theory underlying the supernatural portions of *Paradise Lost*, it will be recalled, is summarized by Raphael in one of his speeches to Adam:

> What surmounts the reach
> Of human sense, I shall delineate so,
> By lik'ning spiritual to corporal forms
> As may express them best; though what if Earth
> Be but the shadow of Heaven, and things therein
> Each to other like, more than on earth is thought?[1]

Secondly, if Milton ever felt Scripture as an obstacle, it was not, as with Bacon or Browne, as an obstacle to scientific truth. This, though he admired Galileo, was never the prime object of his search.[2] What he sought above all was moral guidance; the truth he valued was the truth that makes us free – free from the bondage to sin and to external tyrannies. Scripture itself could be a hindrance if it were allowed to tyrannize over the free choice of a responsible moral agent. And so Milton argues that the moral sense, which is the law of God written upon the heart, is the final tribunal – superior even to Scripture itself. Through that, the Spirit which inspired the sacred writers speaks, here and now, to the individual believer. We possess, he says, a twofold Scripture: not, significantly, the twofold Scripture of the scientific writers, the Bible and Nature, but one 'external' (the Bible), and the other 'internal', which is the Holy Spirit speaking in the heart. Although

the external ground which we possess for our belief at the present day is highly important, . . . that which is internal, and the peculiar possession of each believer, is far superior to all, namely the Spirit itself.[3]

1. *Paradise Lost*, v, 571.
2. Cf. his indifference about the Ptolemaic-Copernican controversy.
3. *De doctrina christiana*, Ch. 30.

The text of Scripture has come down to us through the hands of many redactors and editors and translators; and

it is difficult to conjecture the purpose of Providence in committing the writings of the New Testament to such uncertain and variable guardianship, unless it were to teach us by this very circumstance that the Spirit which is given to us is a more certain guide than Scripture, whom therefore it is our duty to follow.[1]

Thus Milton, with a lofty self-reliance worthy of his own Satan, frees himself from that last infirmity of noble Protestants – subservience to holy writ. In appealing to an inner principle of certainty, Milton shows himself to be in the main current of seventeenth-century thought, which in all directions was seeking by this very means to liberate itself from the authority of tradition. For philosophers, divines, and critics alike, as the century proceeded, 'what is most true' came increasingly to mean (in addition to 'what is mechanically explicable')[2] 'what can be clearly and distinctly conceived; what is innate or inscribed upon the minds of all men in common; what is inwardly approved by the moral sense; what is consonant with nature and reason'. For making a fresh start such as this century was everywhere attempting, nothing was more essential than to discover a principle which would set men free from the accumulations of the past, and provide a basis of (as it seemed) unquestionable and verifiable truth for the erection of new systems.

In this, as in other directions, Milton is seen to be one of the rationalizing theologians of the century; and it is therefore not surprising to find that his view of Scripture is substantially at one with that of the Cambridge Platonists, whose attitude is summed up in the phrase of John Smith: 'To follow Reason is to follow God.' Reason (used in a sense to be discussed later) was for the Platonists the ultimate source of authority in matters of faith; and the function of Scripture was to illuminate and confirm its dictates, never to contradict them. Revelation is not confined to the pages of holy writ, nor to the age of the prophets and apostles, for Reason, a 'seed of deiform nature', is 'natural revelation'. 'The written word of God',

1. *De doctrina christiana*, Ch. 30.   2. See above, p. 14.

says Whichcote, 'is not the first or only discovery of the duty of Man'. 'Clear principles of truth and light, affirmed by the natural reason and confirmed by the law and purpose of the Gospel, are above all particular examples and texts of Scripture.' The same tendency is seen in George Fox, who, as is well known, liberated himself from the letter of Scripture in like manner, and claimed access to the original source of all illumination. The 'inner light' of the Quakers ranks with the 'Reason' of the Platonists, the 'clear and distinct ideas' of Descartes, or the 'common notions' of Lord Herbert of Cherbury, as another of the inward certitudes by means of which the century was testing the legacies of antiquity and declaring its spiritual independence. So potent was the change in the climate of opinion after the middle of the century that even a Puritan like Baxter, who was prepared to endure persecution for nonconformity throughout the Restoration period, is affected by it. In one of the interesting passages of self-analysis to be found in his *Autobiography*, he tells us that as he grew older he became more and more convinced of the supreme need for the 'witness of the indwelling Spirit'. Whereas in youth all his concern had been for the correctness of his doctrinal position, now it was centred upon 'internal experience'. In spite of the excesses of Ranters and Illuminists who find their 'witness' in 'a certain internal assertion or enthusiastic inspiration', he feels that in another manner 'the Holy Ghost is the witness of Christ . . . the Spirit by renovation, sanctification, illumination, and consolation, assimilating the soul to Christ and to heaven'.[1] The degree of relief which this change brought with it can best be appreciated by the perusal of such a document as *Grace Abounding*, in which Bunyan describes the agonized years during which he was at the mercy of conflicting texts of Scripture, which seemed alternately to smile upon him and then to condemn him to everlasting perdition.

For all their detestation of Hobbes, those who were moving in the direction indicated by Milton, the Platonists, Fox, or Baxter, might have found themselves in accord with this observation of his:

1. Baxter's *Autobiography*, ed. J. M. Lloyd Thomas, p. 110.

Newton of

For it is not the bare words, but the scope of a writer, that giveth the true light by which any writing is to be interpreted, and they that insist upon single texts, without considering the main design, can derive nothing from them clearly; but rather by casting atoms of Scripture, as dust before men's eyes, make everything more obscure than it is.[1]

Hobbes, indeed, must be accounted one of the pioneers of destructive biblical criticism. For him, as we shall see later, the Bible, together with the Church and the clergy, formed one of the strongholds of a way of thinking and feeling which he considered pernicious; and, while appearing to preserve a decorous orthodoxy, he analyses away most of the keywords and phrases – 'Word of God', 'spirit', 'prophecy', 'authority of Scripture', 'revelation', and the rest – connected with the current beliefs. To him the only question is, Why do we believe that certain books are of God, and contain the rule of faith? and his reply is that, as we personally have no 'supernatural' evidence for this, we must believe it because we are so commanded by the only competent authority, the civil sovereign.

Towards the close of the seventeenth century the prestige of Scripture, though outwardly unchanged, had actually diminished appreciably. It was not so much that men had rejected it as 'false'; it was rather that as 'natural religion' came more and more to seem all-sufficient, 'revelation' began to appear, if not superfluous, at least secondary, and perhaps even slightly inconvenient. An age which discovered God effortlessly in the starry heavens above, and in the moral law within, could not but be embarrassed by having to acknowledge dependence upon the annals and legends of an unenlightened Semitic tribe. Shaftesbury, the philosopher of the Augustan *Aufklärung*, censures the orthodox for proving the necessity of Revelation by denying man's natural goodness, 'as if Good-nature and religion were enemies'.[2] And by the time we reach Joseph Butler,[3] Nature, instead of being a valuable supplement to Revelation as it was with Bacon, has virtually become the standard against which Revelation itself is to be tested.

1. *Leviathan*, Ch. 43, end.
2. Cf. his Preface to *Select Sermons of Dr Whichcot*, 1698.
3. *Analogy of Religion*, 1736.

CHAPTER 5

The Philosophical Quest for Truth: Descartes

Descartes' 'Method' and *Meditations*

WE are beginning to see, then, that in its quest for truth the seventeenth century discovered two main kinds of certainty, one objective or external, the other subjective or internal. In respect of the external world, that account was 'truest' which explained the mechanics of causation; and the most 'real' of the properties of things were those which could be mathematically expressed. The internal certainties, as we have seen, were chiefly relevant in the regions of faith and of ethics, where truth came to mean that which is vouched for by the 'inner light', by 'Reason' and the 'moral sense', or by 'nature and good sense'.

These two orders of certainty, objective and subjective, correspond to Descartes' division of reality into Extension (matter) and Thought (mind, soul), and it is now desirable to consider some of the relevant problems arising from the work of that thinker, who is generally recognized as the 'father of modern philosophy', and certainly exerted a major influence on the intellectual history of our period.

The philosophic quest for truth in the seventeenth century was typically concerned with the epistemological problem. The besetting questions were, Can I know anything of 'reality'? and if so, how, and what? Why, we may ask, was this the central preoccupation of seventeenth-century philosophy? The problem of knowledge had not greatly troubled the schoolmen, since they had assumed that the mind was in contact with real things in sense-perception. 'Things' were, for them, entities having certain qualities or accidents which they regarded as being 'in' the objects, somewhat as we do in the ordinary common-sense view. The process of knowledge was that by which the mind in a sense *becomes* its object, by catching from it its visible, audible, or tangible 'species'. But since the advent of the Copernican theory and the mechanical philosophy, it had been brought home with increasing emphasis that *things are not what they seem*, neither are they what they have been said to be. Sense-data, as well as authoritative teaching, were found to be misleading. This disturbing result was due above all to Galileo's analysis of bodies into 'matter in motion', and his analysis of the properties of 'matter' into 'primary' and 'secondary'. At the beginning of our period the question 'What are the characteristics of real things?' had been answered by mathematicians and physicists. The reply had been that the 'real' (as far as the physical world is concerned) is that which is extended and movable in space and time. The mathematical properties which alone were relevant to the science of dynamics founded by Galileo – the properties of figure, position, motion, and the rest – were for him the primary qualities of matter; that is, they were the qualities which could be said to be *in* things, and which were measurable, and expressible in mathematical formulae. Galileo was the heir of the atomists of the ancient world, for he revived the conception of bodies as composed of particles or atoms of matter. All bodies whatsoever are so composed; the differences between them are in reality only differences in the figure, density, and motion of these particles. Our senses, however, report the presence of other qualities, which seem, equally with mass, figure, motion, etc., to be 'in' objects around us – colour, temperature, and sound, for example. These are the 'secondary' qualities – secondary because irrelevant for the purposes of mechanics, and because they are mental phenomena, not objective entities. The 'reality' behind each one of them is a certain configuration or motion of the atoms; the 'colour' or the 'sound', etc., is merely a sign in consciousness of the existence of this reality outside us. Thus the senses do not give us knowledge of the thing-in-itself. Only the abstracting intellect can approach such knowledge; and it does so by filtering sense-impressions as clear as possible of subjective ingredients. True knowledge would be knowledge to which the mind itself had contributed nothing. Thus the analysis of the properties of matter into primary and secondary may be said to be the philosophical aspect of the general seventeenth-century effort to separate the true from the false: 'primary' being more or less equivalent to 'true' and 'secondary' to 'false', or 'fictitious'. It was not given to the seventeenth century to perceive that the 'primary' qualities were as much dependent upon sense-perception as the 'secondary'. It was still felt that what could be weighed, measured, and expressed mathematically must be wholly independent of the mind, and therefore must possess a reality-status of a unique kind.

The celebrated 'method' of Descartes[1] is at once the outcome of the unsettling effect of the new thought, and the type of the way in which a fresh winnowing of truth from error was being attempted. Descartes' starting-point is a scepticism, as complete as he can make it, about the truth, first, of commonly received opinions and beliefs, and, secondly, of sense-data. The schools, he says, and my senses tell me that the sun moves round the earth; I now learn that schools and senses have alike deceived me. As for the schools,

I had become aware, even so early as during my college days, that no opinion, however absurd and incredible, can be imagined, which has not been maintained by some one of the philosophers.[2]

Accordingly, first amongst the rules of method which he lays down appears this significant one:

Never to accept anything for true which I did not clearly know to be such; that is to say, carefully to avoid precipitancy and prejudice, and to comprise nothing more in my judgement than what was presented to my mind so clearly and distinctly as to exclude all ground of doubt.[3]

He begins, then, in his *First Meditation*, by announcing his intention to doubt all his former beliefs and the evidence of his senses, and to continue doubting until he arrives, if at all, at something indubitable. He will even suppose

that some malignant demon who is at once exceedingly potent and deceitful

1. *Discours de la méthode*, written 1636, published 1637.
2. *Discours de la méthode*, Pt 2.   Cicero had made the same observation.
3. ibid.

has employed all his artifice to deceive me; I will suppose that the sky, the air, the earth, colours, figures, sounds, and all external things, are nothing better than the illusions of dreams.

But then, in the *Second Meditation*, he discovers the thing that cannot be doubted, his own existence. I must exist, in order to doubt, or to be deceived. And what, essentially, is this 'I'? A *thinking* thing; *cogito, ergo sum*. That is to say, not only is this consciousness of self-existence the first and most indubitable of all truths, but I, as a *thinking* being, must be of a non-material nature. But now, what of external objects, which I have assumed to exist also? My perceptions of external objects may be deceptive; they may not be true copies of the objects themselves; nevertheless it is certain that I have these perceptions, and moreover I habitually assume that I know 'things' better than I know 'myself'. In order to illustrate the nature of our knowledge of external objects Descartes performs a little experiment. Take a piece of beeswax, he says, and note its attributes; it has sweetness, and odour; it has a certain colour, figure, and size; it is hard and cold, and easily handled; and when struck it emits a certain sound. Then place it near the fire, and what happens? its taste and smell vanish, its colour changes, its figure is destroyed, its size increases, it becomes liquid and hot, it cannot be handled, and although struck it emits no sound. In short, all the attributes by which we recognized it as a piece of wax have been changed to their opposite, and yet we judge that it is still wax. 'What, then, was it that I knew with so much distinctness in the piece of wax?' None of the things I observed by the senses, none of the attributes, but only 'a body' that appeared first under one set of attributes, and then under another. 'Retrenching all that does not belong to the wax, let us see what remains. There certainly remains nothing except something extended, flexible, and movable.' I cannot imagine what the wax is in itself; I can only perceive it by an intuition (*inspectio*) of the mind. Bodies, themselves, then, are not perceived by the senses, but by the intellect. And the discovery that when the wax is 'stripped of its vestments' and considered 'quite naked' it is the *mind* that apprehends it, not the senses – this confirms his assertion that there is nothing we can apprehend so clearly as our own mind.

Having doubted of all things, and found nothing, as yet, more certainly true than his own existence as a thinking being, it is the philosopher's next concern to rebuild the world he has demolished, by discovering, if he can, more certainties. What is to be thought, then, of the world of external objects, earth, sky, stars, and the rest, of which he had hitherto not questioned the existence? He decides that *whatever is clearly and distinctly apprehended is true*.[1] But the ideas our senses offer us of objects are not clear and distinct, as the experiment with the beeswax has shown. All that is true about these ideas is that we perceive them; and the error to which we are so prone is that of judging that these are the exact 'likenesses' of the real things. Granting for the moment that our ideas do proceed from real objects, and are not all modes of consciousness in us (as they yet may be), it does not follow that they are 'like' those objects. The eye tells me that the sun is a very small object, but on astronomical grounds I hold it to be immense. Can I discover any object, amongst those of which I have ideas, which must needs exist apart from me? In order to determine this point, Descartes searches himself for some clear and distinct idea which could not have been derived from his own ideas of himself. For even what seemed most clear and distinct about the piece of wax – its mathematical aspects – might have been taken by analogy from various parts of his self-awareness (consciousness of himself as a substance, having duration, position and so forth).

There only remains, therefore, the idea of God, in which I must consider whether there is anything that cannot be supposed to originate with myself.

The idea of God cannot so originate, he continues, for the attributes of omniscience, eternity, immutability, omnipotence, and perfection which made up that idea, could not be derived from my idea of myself.

And thus it is absolutely necessary to conclude, from all that I have before said, that God exists.

Indeed, it may be said that my perception of God's existence is presupposed in my perception of myself, for how could I know myself

1. *Third Meditation.*

as a limited, imperfect, doubting being unless I previously had the idea of a being more perfect than myself? Thus Descartes is able to satisfy himself that

the idea of a being more perfect that myself must of necessity have proceeded from a being in reality more perfect.

All clear and distinct ideas have the attribute of 'truth', that is, they 'contain reality'; now this idea of God is more clear and distinct than any other, clearer even than my idea of 'substance'; therefore it contains more reality than any other; therefore God exists.

If, after pondering this celebrated 'ontological proof', we attempt to express our feeling about it, we shall very likely echo Keats's remark, 'I can never understand how anything can be *known for truth* by a process of abstract reasoning.' The difficulty we chiefly feel, I think, is that the statements, 'The idea of God contains more reality than any other' and 'God exists', so far from being identical, appear to have very little connexion with each other. For us, 'God exists' is simply the central affirmation of *religious* experience, and no alleged meaning for the phrase in abstraction from that experience can have any significance. The ontological proof, one feels, attempts to prove by an intellectual process what is in reality 'given' (if at all) by other than intellectual means. Why did Descartes find the idea of a perfect being innate within him? Because centuries of Christian discipline, based upon the religious experience of Christ and the apostles, had written it upon the hearts of Europeans, so that it seemed to be 'naturally' there. The possession of the idea of God in the heart, like the revelation of God through Nature, only proves his existence to those who believe it already on other grounds.

However, having satisfied himself in this way that God exists, Descartes feels that he can now deduce from this the existence of material things. If God exists and possesses, as he must, all the perfections I attribute to him, he cannot be a deceiver, so that my ineradicable conviction that there is a world of objects distinct from myself cannot be a delusion. I must still, however, guard against the erroneous supposition that my 'ideas' are necessarily 'like' their originals. But that there is something extended and movable, which is the substratum for all the sensible qualities, and the cause of my 'ideas', Descartes considers as certain. Although objects may not be in themselves what we apprehend them to be by the senses,

It is at least necessary to admit that all which I clearly and distinctly conceive as in them, *that is, generally speaking, all that is comprehended in the object of speculative geometry*, really exists external to me.[1]

The mathematical properties are *true* (i.e. clear and distinct, and therefore guaranteeing objective reality); other 'properties' are confused and obscure, and must be carefully distinguished from the true and the real. 'For I will assuredly reach truth if I only fix my attention sufficiently on all the things I conceive perfectly, and separate these from others which I conceive more confusedly and obscurely: to which for the future I shall give diligent heed.'[2]

My certainty of my own existence, then, and my certainty of God's existence, are the two first certainties; from these we can also derive certainty that the objects of mathematical thought are real.

But there is another aspect of the Cartesian thought which must be emphasized, namely, its dualism – that is, its division of reality into two substances – thought and extension. Outside, extended throughout infinite space, there is the world of mathematical objects strictly controlled by mechanical law; and that this is real we have seen. Within, there is the thinking substance which is the true 'I', unextended, distinct from the body, and not subject to mechanical laws; and the reality of this is intuitively certain. Within the human individual, then, these divided and distinguished worlds mysteriously met and blended; soul and body, thought and extension being somehow inexplicably found in union. Descartes is as sure as Plato that 'I' am not my body or any part of it, that my thinking self can be conceived apart altogether from the body, and that thus my soul may be immortal. This fundamental dualism greatly complicated the epistemological problem, for if the soul were totally distinct from the body, how could it have that contact with matter which is implied in knowledge? Whatever theory of sense-perception one

1. *Sixth Meditation* (my italics).   2. *Fourth Meditation* (last sentence).

adopted, there was always a point at which one arrived at the gulf, which must somehow be bridged, between matter-in-motion and Mind or Soul. The difficulty of conceiving how this junction could be made haunted and hampered philosophical speculation for another century and a half. The problem is admirably expressed by Joseph Glanvill, a fervent Cartesian, in his *Vanity of Dogmatizing*, in the course of an enumeration of the limitations of human knowledge. 'How the purer Spirit', he writes,

is united to this Clod, is a knot too hard for fallen Humanity to unty. . . . How should a thought be united to a marble-statue, or a sun-beam to a lump of clay! The freezing of the words in the air in the northern climes, is as conceivable, as this strange union. . . . And to hang weights on the wings of the winde seems far more intelligible.[1]

And if we are unable to conceive how matter can act upon mind, neither can we conceive how mind can agitate matter – how the soul can move its tenement of clay. We can do this, Glanvill continues, by material analogies, but if we consider the soul

under the notion of the ingenious Sir K. Digby as a pure Mind and Knowledge, or as the admir'd Descartes expresses it, *une chose qui pense*, as a *thinking substance*; it will be as hard to apprehend as that an empty wish should remove Mountains: a supposition which if realized, would relieve *Sisyphus*.

Strange devices had to be resorted to in order to link together what God had joined and philosophers had put asunder. It was widely held, as by Descartes himself, that the liaison was effected by the 'animal spirits', which though material, were sufficiently rarefied to be able to communicate directly with spirit. But although

> Our blood labours to beget
>   Spirits, as like soules as it can,
> Because such fingers need to knit
>   That subtile knot, which makes us man:[2]

the knot was really still untied, for in the last analysis there yet remained a point at which matter set in motion that which was not

1. p. 20 (1661). Cf. below, p. 159.   2. Donne, *The Extasie*.

matter, and conversely, at which mind actuated matter. There was also the theory known as Occasionalism (Arnold Geulincx,1625–69), according to which there is no interaction between mind and matter except through the dependence of both upon God. When I perceive a tree, for example, a motion is caused in my nerves. This motion is not mechanically transferred to my soul, since that is inconceivable. What happens is that God miraculously causes a corresponding effect to take place in my soul 'on the occasion' of my perceiving the tree. Or conversely, when I will anything, for instance to move my hand, God causes the matter of my body to conform to the intention of my mind. Here then was a queer outcome of the new search for truth: miraculous interventions had been banished from the physical universe only to reappear within the narrow compass of the individual human being. God had made the world in such a way that it could run 'of itself', but he had made man so fearfully and wonderfully that he could not act or perceive without God's continuous intervention. God was indeed a necessary hypothesis in seventeenth-century philosophy.

Poetry and the Cartesian Spirit

What seemed, to Descartes' contemporaries, an outstanding merit of his system was that although it represented a complete break with the scholastic tradition it left unchallenged the main fabric of the faith. Indeed, Descartes had shown that the new thought, so far from being hostile to theism, presupposed it, and must therefore be a powerful support to it. It was partly for this reason that the Cambridge Platonists, whose great desire was to amalgamate religion with the best philosophy of their time, were attracted to Cartesianism. Yet it is probable that Descartes' influence told against religion in the long run, just as it told against poetry; and Henry More's ultimate reaction against it may have been due to his realization of this. At first sight it may seem inexplicable that a philosophy in which God and the soul are the first certainties should prove an enemy of religion and poetry. And yet this should cause no surprise if we remember that the 'God' and the 'I' of Descartes are both intellectual abstractions; his 'God', as we saw, having no kinship to the God of genuine religious experience, and his 'I' being merely the 'thinking part of me'. To be certain of these realities meant, in the end, to be certain only of mathematics. The feeling that whatever can be clearly and distinctly conceived is 'true' means that the very structure of things is assumed to conform with the laws of the human mind – a capital instance of the Idols of the Tribe. The converse of this feeling is, as I have indicated, that whatever cannot be clearly and distinctly (i.e. mathematically) conceived is 'not true'. In this way Cartesian thought reinforced the growing disposition to accept the scientific world-picture as the only 'true' one. The criterion of truth which it set up, according to which the only real properties of objects were the mathematical properties, implied a depreciation of all kinds of knowing other than that of the 'philosopher'. And as both religion and poetry (whatever may be our conception of them) spring from quite other modes of knowing, the Cartesian spirit, in so far as it prevailed, was really hostile to them both. Descartes himself is perhaps only the most conspicuous representative of a way of thought which was irresistibly gaining ground as the century proceeded, and we must not, therefore, ascribe to him all the consequences of that thought. But the fact remains that by the beginning of the eighteenth century religion had sunk to deism, while poetry had been reduced to catering for 'delight' – to providing embellishments which might be agreeable to the fancy, but which were recognized by the judgement as having no relation to 'reality'. As Dryden wrote in his *Apology for Heroic Poetry and Poetic Licence*, we were to be 'pleased with the image, without being cozened by the fiction'. The Cartesian spirit made for the sharper separation of the spheres of prose and poetry, and thereby hastened that 'dissociation of sensibility'[1] which Mr Eliot has remarked as having set in after the time of the Metaphysical poets. The cleavage then began to appear, which has become so troublesomely familiar to us since, between 'values' and 'facts'; between what you *felt* as a human being or as a poet, and what you

1. *Homage to J. Dryden*, p. 30.

thought as a man of sense, judgement, and enlightenment. Instead of being able, like Donne or Browne, to think and feel simultaneously either in verse or in prose, you were now expected to think prosaically and to feel poetically. Prose was for conveying what was felt to be true, and was addressed to the judgement; poetry was for conveying pleasure, and was addressed to the fancy.

These developments could not fail to result in a lowering of the status of poetry, as an activity which by its very nature forswore the only methods by which, it was now felt, truth could be reached. 'Philosophy' has indeed proved itself more than once the natural enemy of poetry. It was not only from the Cartesian universe, but also from Plato's Republic, that poetry was banished. From the Augustan world poets themselves were, of course, so far from being literally banished that they were highly honoured; it was poetry itself which suffered from the intellectual climate. After Descartes, poets were inevitably writing with the sense that their constructions were *not true*, and this feeling robbed their work of essential seriousness. It was felt, as Locke said, that poetry offers 'pleasant pictures and agreeable visions', but that these consist in 'something that is not perfectly conformable' to truth and reason.[1] All that one could do, then, was either to make one's verse as conformable to truth and reason as possible (e.g. the *Essay on Man*), or to indulge in agreeable visions in the full consciousness that they were fiction. It is the sense that their material is only agreeable fiction which gives the peculiar hollowness to much of the mythological and other 'machinery' employed by eighteenth-century poets. Even in the seventeenth century, as we have seen, even in that most biblical of centuries, the very Scriptures were coming to seem a potential obstacle to truth on account of the 'vulgar and illustrative' manner often adopted by the inspired writers – who wrote, said John Smith the Platonist, for the 'most Idiotical sort of men in the most Idiotical way'. No wonder, then, that other poetry should still more decisively be felt as misrepresentation, or at least as fiction. The effect upon poetry of the Cartesian identification of truth with 'clear and distinct ideas' is

1. *Essay Concerning Human Understanding*, Bk II, Ch. 2, sect. 3. Cf. below pp. 261 ff.

thus summed up by Jean-Baptiste Rousseau, in a letter to Brossette (24 July 1715):

J'ai souvent oui dire à Despréaux que la philosophie de Descartes avait coupé la gorge à la poésie, et il est certain que ce qu'elle emprunte des mathématiques dessèche l'esprit et l'accoutume à une justesse matérielle qui n'a aucun rapport avec la justesse metaphysique, si cela se peut dire, des poètes et des orateurs.

It would be rash to suggest that Descartes had a direct influence upon the thought or style of any particular writers (other than professed philosophers), but the intellectual movement of which he is the representative product undoubtedly had. Literary developments in England after the middle of the seventeenth century show a marked analogy with his thought. His insistence upon sound and plain Reason, and clear and distinct ideas, and, in general, the mathematical lucidity of his spirit and writings, find their counterpart in the general set of that time towards prose and good sense, and in the reaction against the metaphysical tradition in poetry. The difference between Dryden and Donne is largely due to the fact that in the interval which separates them the Cartesian world-picture had replaced the Scholastic. The order, precision, and correctness of post-Restoration art echo the methodical regularity of Descartes' thinking and the perfection of his mechanized universe. Thus Descartes' influence counted strongly for neo-classicism of the later type which looked for authority less to the ancients than to Nature and Reason. Nature herself, as the Great Machine, hardly needed any methodizing to yield the 'rules' of art. And Nature and Homer were, they found, the same.

Above all, Descartes' influence was decisive in effecting that break with the past which started the modern world on its career. After him it became natural to appeal to 'reason', the inner tribunal, instead, as hitherto, to external authority. In thus encouraging his age to shake off its awe for antiquity Descartes was contributing an essential ingredient to the growth of the idea of 'progress'. The revolutionary philosophy of the next century, with its contempt for history and its confident perfectibilism, owes its initial impulse largely to him. For Descartes' thought, like all thought which is purely rational and intellectual, was fundamentally unhistorical. When we can construct the world from the inner certainties, what need of history to tell us how things have come to be as they are? We have that within which passes history. In this way Descartes' *cogito ergo sum* not only fostered intellectualistic views, but increased man's sense of his own dignity and importance. Man must be little lower than the angels if, from the thinking principle within him, he can evolve the world and God himself. The glamour of Renaissance magnificence hangs over Descartes, as over Bacon, as he prophesies the entry of Man into the promised land:

I perceived it to be possible to arrive at a knowledge highly useful in life; and in room of the speculative philosophy usually taught in the schools, to discover a practical, by means of which, knowing the force and action of fire, water, air, the stars, the heavens, and all the other bodies that surround us, as distinctly as we know the various crafts of our artisans, we might also apply them in the same way to all the uses to which they are adapted, *and thus render ourselves the lords and possessors of nature.*[1]

To this sense of having made a proud step forward towards the conquest of Nature, can be traced, I think, much of the contempt for the Middle Ages which abounds in the next century. And to *cogito ergo sum* can also be ascribed the remarkable prevalence of satire in the same period. For the identification of man's nature with the thinking principle within – the feeling that we *are* that part of us which cogitates – must produce the concurrent realization that there is a vast discrepancy between man's ideal and his actual nature. The temper which views all things in their theory rather than in their historical setting must also see little, as it gazes upon human institutions, but failure and futility, and as it contemplates human actions, little but departures from the rational norm. It is just in the comparison between actual things and their theory that satire consists, and the dry light of Cartesianism threw upon the deformities of actual humanity just the kind of illumination which is necessary to evoke the satiric comparison.

One further consideration may serve to bring out, by way of

1. *Discours de la méthode*, Pt 6 (my italics).

contrast, the quality of Cartesian thought. As might be expected of a philosophy which sets its face so resolutely towards the future, Cartesianism despises not only history, but also the past of the individual human being. A comparison may usefully be suggested between the estimates of childhood in, say, Wordsworth's *Immortality Ode* and that in section lxxi of Descartes *Principles of Philosophy*. Wordsworth, it will be remembered, sees childhood as a period of life and illumination from which the later course of existence is but one long decline. Recollections of childhood are cherished as mitigations of the heavy and the weary weight of the adult consciousness; and the child is addressed as

> Mighty Prophet! Seer blest!
> On whom those truths do rest
> Which we are toiling all our lives to find.

For Wordsworth, in full revolt against the eighteenth-century consequences of Cartesianism, it is precisely the 'meddling intellect', the cogitating principle, which 'misshapes the beauteous forms of things'; the adult consciousness, schooled by custom and an arid philosophy, distorts reality instead of apprehending it. For Descartes, eager only for what was clear and distinct, that is, for mathematical truth, childhood was a period of error and prejudice from which we could and must emerge, though only by steady and prolonged effort. The Section in question is entitled 'That the chief cause of our errors is to be found in the prejudices of our childhood'. After an enumeration of childish errors (which all consist in mistaking sense-impressions for real things) he continues:

And our mind has been imbued from our infancy with a thousand other prejudices of the same sort, which afterwards in our youth we forgot we had accepted without sufficient examination. . . . And although now in our mature years,' he adds in the following section, 'when the mind, being no longer wholly subject to the body, is not in the habit of referring all things to it, but also seeks to discover the truth of things considered in themselves, we observe the falsehood of a great many of the judgements we had before formed; yet *we experience a difficulty in expunging them from our memory, and, so long as they remain there, they give rise to various errors.*[1]

1. Descartes, *Principles of Philosophy*, sects. lxxi and lxxii (my italics).

CHAPTER 6

The Philosophical Quest for Truth: Hobbes

'Body'

The universe, that is, the whole mass of all things that are, is corporeal, that is to say, body, and hath the dimensions of magnitude, namely length, breadth, and depth; also, every part of body is likewise body, and hath the like dimensions, and consequently every part of the universe is body, and that which is not body is no part of the universe: and because the universe is all, that which is no part of it is nothing, and consequently nowhere. (Leviathan, Ch. 46.)

ATTENTION has recently been drawn by Dr I. A. Richards to the fact that the works of Mencius and other Chinese thinkers are not disinterested inquiries into 'truth' (as we have understood that phrase since the Renaissance) but are 'designed to give intellectual support to a system whose basis is social'.[1] They are 'dominated by a suasive purpose'. And Dr Richards reminds us that 'this dependence of conceptions upon social purposes is not a peculiarity of Chinese thinking, though possibly more evident there than in our own thinking'. What we have to look out for, in reading the philosophers of Western Europe, is the emotional or social determinant which makes their work what it is, and this is usually implicit rather than explicit. As I have attempted to suggest above, what will seem 'true' or 'explanatory' to any age or individual is what satisfies current demands and interests. What has this writer most urgently demanded from life? is the question we must constantly ask ourselves. The original impulse, towards, say, 'materialism', or 'idealism', is usually something sublogical; not, that is, a 'conviction' resulting from an intellectual process, but a quite simple set of the whole being towards a particular way of life. The direction once

1. *Mencius on the Mind*, p. 56.

given, the subconscious affirmation once made, the character of the metaphysical superstructure is determined accordingly. It would be well if it were more generally realized that metaphysical utterances which appear to be statements of 'fact' are disguised imperatives, or at least disguised optatives; and our studies of the philosophers would be more remunerative if we went to them, not for 'truth', but in order to discover what particular *fiat* or *utinam* their teaching implies.

Few of our modern classical philosophers illustrate these considerations more clearly than Thomas Hobbes. And this is so not merely because in his best known book, the *Leviathan*, he avowedly mobilizes his 'philosophy' for the purpose of political suasion. This certainly makes it much easier to detect his fundamental preferences and aversions, but these can also, I think, be divined in his 'purely speculative' passages, and in the quality of his prose style. Consider, for instance, the utterance quoted at the head of this chapter – perhaps Hobbes's most typical affirmation about the nature of things. It represents what, to Hobbes, was Truth; nothing, probably, was felt by him to be truer than this: 'The universe is corporeal; all that is real is material, and what is not material is not real.' What does this statement 'mean'? Is it 'true'? If, in asking these questions, our desire is to know whether the statement correctly represents a real state of affairs, we shall find ourselves involved in the further questions, What is 'matter'? what is a 'state of affairs'? And it is doubtful whether any reply to such questions can be more than suasion, that is, a recommendation or an exhortation to feel in a certain way, and to act accordingly. 'The universe is material' loses its efficacy as 'statement' when we call to mind that we have no conception what 'matter' in itself may be; but it retains none the less a powerful latent meaning as incantation, and as a pointer indicating a particular state of mind in its author. Its 'meaning', then, is the emotion in Hobbes which it symbolizes, and which it may also communicate to us. The contents which it disguises are too varied to catalogue, but they probably include some of the following injunctions: 'Fear and reverence Nature no longer; she is no mystery, for she "worketh by motion", and Geometry, which is the mother of the sciences, and indeed the *only* science God has yet vouchsafed to us – Geometry can chart these motions. Feel, then, as if you lived in a world which can be measured, weighed, and mastered; and confront it with due audacity. Do not trust those who will tell you of "substantial forms" or "separated essences", for these figments are part of a vast system of imposture, and if once you come under the influence of such men, your sense of political obligation will be impaired. . . .' Very nearly every statement of Hobbes can be reduced either to hatred and contempt of schoolmen and clerics, or to fear of civil war and love of ordered living in a stable commonwealth. A certain belief is of the kind which discourages inquiry, or weakens the authority of kings, therefore it is false and pernicious. Another belief, on the contrary, favours 'speculation of bodies natural', the favourite pursuit in which Hobbes had been interrupted by the civil commotions; or it buttresses the lawful authority of sovereigns – therefore it is true. Contempt is one of the commonest of Hobbes's emotions: contempt for all upholders of what he calls 'Aristotelity', and for their doctrines. He is unable to conceive – and scarcely can we, as we read him – that schoolmen and theologians can be anything but madmen or knaves. This contempt gets into his prose-rhythm, and flashes out in many a 'brutally telling' image:

For the proper (i.e. 'literal') use of the word 'infused', in speaking of the graces of God, is an abuse of it; for those graces are virtues, not bodies to be carried hither and thither, and to be *poured into men as into barrels.*[1]

For, from the time that the Bishop of Rome had gotten to be acknowledged for bishop universal, by pretence of succession to St Peter, their whole hierarchy, or kingdom of darkness, *may be compared not unfitly to the 'Kingdom of fairies'*; that is, to the *old wives' fables in England concerning 'ghosts' and 'spirits'*, and the feats they play in the night. And if a man consider the original of this great ecclesiastical dominion, he will easily perceive that the Papacy is no other than the *'ghost' of the deceased 'Roman Empire', sitting crowned upon the grave thereof.*[2]

[Reason is] not to be *folded in the napkin* of an implicit faith, but employed in the purchase of justice, peace, and true religion.

For it is with the mysteries of our religion as with *wholesome pills for the*

1. *Leviathan*, Ch. 34 (my italics).   2. ibid., Ch. 47.

sick, which, swallowed whole, have the virtue to cure; but chewed, are for the most part cast up again without effect.[1]

In the grim homeliness of these similitudes, as in the sledge-hammer thudding of the clauses in the motto-extract above, we can hear the voice of a man to whom only one kind of truth – his own – is conceivable, but whose scorn for his deluded or deceiving foes is mingled with fear of their power. A comparison between the prose styles of Hobbes and Browne would reveal, almost without considering their thoughts, the difference between a simple and a complex sensibility. Hobbes, though the elder by seventeen years, writes as one for whom Truth, that 'obscured Virgin', is now wholly 'exantlated' from the well in which she had been hidden. Browne lives, amphibiously, in divided and distinguished worlds, and the richness of his prose betokens the range of his explorations and the rapidity of his transits. With Hobbes there is but one real world, that in which all is 'body'; all else belongs to the 'kingdom of darkness' inhabited only by fairies, ghosts, and 'surds'; and this is what gives his style its singleness and force, while making it, in the long run, monotonous and unsatisfying.

Hobbes belongs to that class of thinkers, usual in periods of rapid scientific advance, to whom a 'naturalistic' type of explanation seems completely satisfying. In Hobbes's age this meant the acceptance of mechanico-materialism as an exhaustive account of reality. Hobbes is a specially significant figure for the purpose of this study, for he illustrates perhaps better than any other seventeenth-century writer the immediate results of the whole-hearted adoption of the new philosophy, and its application in every field of inquiry. A consideration of some of his views, we may therefore hope, should help us to answer the questions with which we are mainly concerned, namely, what affirmations were involved in the acceptance of mechanical 'truth' in our period? and what, in consequence, had to be rejected as 'error'?

We have already seen that the philosophy of the schoolmen was first and chief amongst the hindrances to the new 'truth'. As an

1. *Leviathan*, Ch. 32.

enemy of the Aristotelian tradition Hobbes may be classed with Galileo, Bacon, or Descartes. His reasons for rejecting it are much the same as theirs, and for the most part he merely adds to the usual arguments his characteristic bluffness of tone. 'When men write whole volumes of such stuff, are they not mad, or intend to make others so?'[1] Hobbes was an extreme nominalist, and the metaphysics of the schools, with its 'entities' and 'quiddities', seemed to him simply sound and fury, signifying literally 'nothing'. Words are names, and names may be used to signify (1) the bodies that work on the senses, (2) the sense-impressions themselves ('imaginations'), (3) the parts of speech ('names of names'), or (4) the relations between names (e.g. the verb 'to be'). 'All other names are but insignificant sounds;'[2] 'and words whereby we conceive nothing but the sound, are those we call "absurd", "insignificant", and "nonsense"'. When we say, he writes,

that 'a man is a living body', we mean not that the 'man' is one thing, the 'living body' another, and the 'is' or 'being' a third; but that the 'man' and the 'living body' is the same thing; because the consequence, 'if he be a man, he is a living body', is a true consequence, signified by that word 'is'. Therefore 'to be a body', 'to walk', 'to be speaking', 'to live', 'to see', and the like infinitives; also 'corporeity', 'walking', 'speaking', 'life', 'sight', and the like, that signify just the same, are the names of 'nothing' . . .

Hobbes may not have taken more than the first steps towards the analysis of the meaning of 'meaning', but he must be allowed to have been unusually aware of what Dr Richards calls the 'symbol-situation'.[3] His constant endeavour to think behind words to the objects or mental images which they symbolize makes him, for his period, exceptionally astute in the detection of 'bogus entities'. Bogus, that is, according to his criterion of 'reality'. For in reading Hobbes, or any other thinker, we have to try, as far as we can, to remain constantly on the alert for his unquestioned assumptions –

1. *Leviathan*, Ch. 8, end. Said with reference to Suarez' chapter on the 'Concourse, motion, and help of God'.
2. ibid., Ch. 4. Cf. the *'flatus vocis'* of William of Occam.
3. *Mencius*, p. 111, and *The Meaning of Meaning*, Ch. 1.

for the doctrines, that is, which he *feels to be facts*, and therefore leaves unanalysed. With Hobbes this underlying trust is in the sole reality of 'body'. He has an inward assurance of the materiality of the universe, that is, of all 'real things'. A 'material' or 'real' thing, or a 'body natural', was one which occupied space, was divisible, movable, and in sum, behaved geometrically. What Hobbes seems to leave unquestioned is *that he knows the meaning of 'matter' or 'body'*. It is as certain, for him, that 'body' means what is real as that 'entity' or 'being' means nothing. Following Hobbes's own method of analysis, we might say that words like 'body' and 'real' were names referring to all that interested him, all that seemed to him worthy of the attention of himself or any other sane being. These words stand, then, in the last resort, for a state or disposition of mind; and the reason why Hobbes did not regard 'body' as a name signifying nothing was because it symbolized a sense of certainty in himself which he never criticized. It ought, perhaps, to be added that we are not entitled to reproach Hobbes for failing to criticize his fundamental assumptions, unless we ourselves are in the habit of watching, as well as using, our own. Probably those who today most resemble Hobbes are interested in psychology rather than in geometry, in 'mind' rather than in 'body', and it is likely that to the modern consciousness generally what is felt to be most 'explanatory' is one or other of the current accounts of our mental processes and habits. To appreciate Hobbes's position it is necessary to remember how difficult we find it not only to *regard*, but to *feel* these accounts as largely fictional and metaphorical. Our difficulty is far less than his, for we have been warned, and he had not.

If the metaphysics of the schoolmen were madness, what should be said of their 'physics'? Hobbes makes the usual complaint, that the scholastic explanations not only explain nothing, but discourage further research. They were the explanations of men who felt that all really important truth was already known, and were therefore not eager to fill in the picture with physical detail. It was enough, to explain a phenomenon, to say, in different words, that it happened because it was its nature so to do. Probably this is the only *ultimate* explanation that can be given of anything; but the new age did not want ultimate explanations: it wanted descriptions of intermediate processes.

If you desire to know why some kind of bodies sink naturally downwards towards the earth, and others go naturally from it, the schools will tell you out of Aristotle, that the bodies that sink downwards are 'heavy', and that this heaviness is it that causes them to descend. But if you ask what they mean by 'heaviness' they will define it to be an endeavour to go to the centre of the earth. So that the cause why things sink downward, is an endeavour to be below; which is as much as to say, that bodies descend, or ascend, because they do. Or they will tell you the centre of the earth is the place of rest, and conservation for heavy things; and therefore they endeavour to be there: as if stones and metals had a desire, or could discern the place they would be at, as man does; or loved rest, as man does not; or that a piece of glass were less safe in the window than falling into the street. . . .

And in many occasions they put for cause of natural events their own ignorance, but disguised in other words: . . . as when they attribute many effects to 'occult qualities'; that is, to qualities not known to them; and therefore also, as they think, to no man else. And to 'sympathy', 'antipathy', 'antiperistasis', 'specified qualities', and other like terms, which signify neither the agent that produceth them, or the operation by which they are produced.

'If such "metaphysics" and "physics" as this be not "vain philosophy",' he concludes, 'there never was any; nor needed St Paul to give us warning to avoid it.'[1]

The Soul

But Hobbes rejected much more than the mere 'Aristotelity' of which he, like Milton, had had his fill at the University. He rejected also much that his contemporaries retained. We have seen that Descartes, the representative philosopher of the seventeenth-century enlightenment, had recognized two substances as real, matter and soul; and that he had taken as his starting-point the thinking 'ego' conceived as immaterial, that is, not extended and not subject to

1. *Leviathan*, Ch. 46.

the laws of motion. From this, which was to him the primary certainty, Descartes had derived his certainty of God and his certainty of the world. I have tried above to indicate some of the inconveniences involved in this dualism. Probably any system which dichotomizes reality in this kind of way is likely to invite attempts to resolve the divided worlds into one, and the uncomfortable antithesis of matter and mind in the Cartesian scheme seems to have made inevitable both the materialist and the idealist solutions. Either all is 'really' matter, or all is 'really' mind. Hobbes chose the first alternative: 'soul' as an 'immaterial substance' having no location or motion, was one of the 'insignificant sounds', and must consequently go. Thus the last stronghold of a once all-powerful system of thought falls before the attack of mechanico-materialism. The accepted tradition of centuries past, blended out of Platonic, Aristotelian, neo-Platonic, Stoic, and Christian elements, spoke with seemingly overwhelming authority for the soul as a spiritual and even divine essence, informing the body, but existing in its own right, separable, and consequently immortal. And if the authority of this teaching had needed any reinforcement, which it hardly did, the revival of Platonic studies at the Renaissance had served to give it renewed sanction for the philosophically-minded. If any doctrine has ever been felt as a fact, it was this, as held throughout the Christian centuries. No wonder Descartes, and most others, found it first among their certainties. To deny it, in the seventeenth century, was no light matter of academic debate; it was the worst of atheisms, for it set man amongst the brutes.

Hobbes denied it; but the manner of his denial must be a little examined, for it throws light on the mentality of the age. For Hobbes, 'thought' was no alien substance unaccountably subsisting in an otherwise material world, and 'perception' no exception to the universal mechanical rule. Thought was itself a form of motion in matter; my 'ideas' are vibrations in the matter of my brain or nerves. There is no gulf to bridge between the world and the soul or between the soul and the body; no question of hanging weights on the wings of the wind, or uniting a sunbeam to a lump of clay. The cause of 'sense' (perception), Hobbes explains, is the motions in external bodies acting directly or indirectly upon the 'organ' of perception. All external bodies are 'really' composed, it will be remembered, of particles of matter in a state of motion. These motions are mechanically transferred, either by contact with the object as in touch or taste, or through some medium as in sight or sound, to the organs of sense, and thence conveyed to the brain, where the corresponding motions give rise to the seemings which are our 'ideas'. I have already drawn attention to the importance, in the formation of seventeenth-century notions of the 'true' and the 'real', of the separation of the 'primary' from the 'secondary' qualities of things. Hobbes, though he does not use these terms, will have us clearly to understand that

whatsoever accidents or qualities our senses make us think there be in the world, they be not there, but are seemings and apparitions only: *the things that really are in the world without us, are those motions by which these seemings are caused.*[1]

Similarly, all that 'really' takes place in us when we perceive anything is 'divers motions', for 'motion produceth nothing but motion'.[2] These motions appear in our consciousness as colour, sound, temperature, and so on. Hobbes does not seem to have troubled himself to ask the further question, How do these 'real things', these motions, get turned into 'seemings'? True, he tells us that the 'pressure' from bodies outside us is carried inwards by the 'nerves' and 'membranes' to the brain and heart, and 'causeth there a resistance, or counter-pressure, or endeavour of the heart to deliver itself, which endeavour, because "outward", seemeth to be some matter without'.[3] But this highly metaphysical account is only intended to explain why, although the object is one thing and our image of it another, the image appears to be 'outside' us. It does not explain *to what* the image 'appears'; what it is in us which is 'conscious' of the seemings. Every particle of matter in the universe is supposed capable of receiving motion from the impact of another,

1. *Human Nature*, Ch. 2 (Molesworth ed. of Works, Vol. IV, pp. 8–9, my italics).
2. *Leviathan*, Ch. 1.   3. ibid., Ch. 1.

but it is not therefore held to be 'conscious' of it. However, all I am now concerned to point out is that Hobbes did not feel the need to postulate a separate entity or 'soul' in order to account for the phenomena of consciousness. He felt quite sure that he knew what was real, namely the abstract geometrical world of matter in motion, and that this world extended without a break into ourselves. The relative unreality of our 'ideas' need not trouble us, since they are at any rate produced by real things, and the only mode in which we can perceive them. We are safe as long as we do not confuse these 'ideas' with the 'things' they represent. He even (inconsistently?) calls 'sense' 'absolute knowledge' or 'knowledge of fact'.[1]

The received doctrine of the soul occupied a central position in the vast corpus of traditional teaching which Hobbes wished to set aside as 'error'. It was the grand example of the deluded scholastic belief in 'substantial forms' and 'real essences'. It is salutary to remind ourselves once again that in the *Leviathan* Hobbes has a 'suasive' purpose, and that almost in Chinese fashion, he is there bringing doctrines to a *pragmatic test*. Do they or do they not make for the maintenance of lawful authority? he is asking. Full of loathing for the civil war which is going on around him, he heaps together into one compendious amalgam all the beliefs which he dislikes, and sees in every one of them an element in the vast conspiracy against lawful civil government. This is quite explicitly recognized by him in an interesting passage towards the close of the book:

But to what purpose, may some men say, is such subtlety in a work of this nature, where I pretend to nothing but what is necessary to the doctrine of government and obedience? It is to this purpose, that men may no longer suffer themselves to be abused by them that by this doctrine of 'separated essences', built on the vain philosophy of Aristotle, would fright them from obeying the laws of their country, with empty names; as men fright birds from the corn with an empty doublet, a hat, and a crooked stick. For it is upon this ground that when a man is dead and buried, they say *his soul, that is his life*, can walk separated from his body, and is seen by night among the graves. Upon the same ground they say that the figure, and colour, and taste of a piece of bread has a being there where they say there is no bread.

1. See *Leviathan*, Ch. 7 and Ch. 9.

And upon the same ground they say that faith, and wisdom, and other virtues, are sometimes 'poured' into a man, sometimes 'blown' into him from heaven, as if the virtuous and their virtues could be asunder; and a great many other *things that serve to lessen the dependence of subjects on the sovereign power of their country.* For who will endeavour to obey the laws, if he expect obedience to be poured or blown into him? Or who will not obey a priest that can make God, rather than his sovereign, nay, than God himself? Or who, that is in fear of ghosts, will not bear great respect to those that can make the holy water that drives them from him? And this shall suffice for an example of the errors which are brought into the Church from the 'entities' and 'essences' of Aristotle, *which it may be he knew to be false philosophy, but writ it as a thing consonant to & corroborative of their religion,* and fearing the fate of Socrates.[1]

One further consequence of Hobbes's denial of the separate immaterial soul may be noted before we pass to the next topic. And that is, that Hobbes (it is one of his several points of contact with Milton) is a 'mortalist'. He believes, as he logically must, that the death of the body is the death of the man, since 'soul' for him simply means 'life'.

That the soul of man is in its own nature eternal, and a living creature independent of the body, or that any mere man is immortal otherwise than by the resurrection in the last day except Enoch and Elias, is a doctrine not apparent in Scripture.[2]

How Hobbes deals in general with Scripture must shortly be considered; for the moment let us merely observe that he saves appearances in this connexion by means of the 'resurrection in the last day'. That far-off divine event was sufficiently distant and hypothetical to be safely admissible into Hobbes's scheme. To say that dead men wake on the Day of Judgement is, for him, as good as to say that they wake up never, only it has the advantage of sounding much more orthodox. The traditional view has been the source of many most undesirable superstitions, in particular the belief in

1. *Leviathan*, Ch. 46 (my italics). Aristotle, it will be noticed, is here accused by Hobbes of the 'Chinese' pragmatism of which he himself, in another manner, is an exponent.
2. ibid., Ch. 38.

purgatory and in ghosts. Hobbes lays the blame for all this upon the Greeks and the Fathers.

For men being generally possessed before the time of our Saviour, by contagion of the demonology of the Greeks, or an opinion that the souls of men were substances distinct from their bodies, and therefore that when the body was dead, the soul of every man, whether godly or wicked, must subsist somewhere by virtue of its own nature, without acknowledging therein any supernatural gift of God; the doctors of the Church doubted a long time, what was the place which they were to abide in, till they should be reunited to their bodies in the resurrection; supposing for awhile, they lay under the altars; but afterwards the *Church of Rome found it more profitable to build for them this place of purgatory*; which by some other Churches in this latter age has been demolished.[1]

In fact, the doctrine of the soul's immortality has been a source of revenue to the ecclesiastical government through the sale of indulgences and pardons; and similarly the belief in 'walking ghosts' has been either deliberately taught or not confuted, 'to keep in credit the use of exorcism, of crosses, of holy water, and other such inventions of ghostly men'.[2] Hobbes cannot, of course, deny the reality of 'eternal life' and the torments of hell. But he gives them a twist of his own. In the first place, he will not accept the 'dark doctrine' of 'eternal torments'. The fires of hell may be unquenchable, but that does not mean that those who are cast into it will suffer endless torture. There is for them a 'second death', which being everlasting, mercifully ends their woes sooner or later. But further, the Scriptural accounts of both heaven and hell are for the most part to be understood 'metaphorically', they are states of felicity or of misery, and what is more startling, their probable location is on this earth. Hobbes can find texts which prove to his own satisfaction that 'after the coming again of our Saviour in His majesty and glory, to reign actually and eternally, the kingdom of God is to be on earth';[3] and the scene of the torments of hell, he infers, is also terrestrial. Even today the reader has a queer sense of lost bearings as he beholds all the splendours and glooms of Christian eschatology being thus given, by this prosaic intellect, a local habitation and a name.

1. *Leviathan*, Ch. 44.   2. ibid., Ch. 2.   3. ibid., Ch. 38.

The Will

Bound up with the traditional belief in the Soul was the belief in Free Will as one of the Soul's 'faculties'; and rejection of the one meant rejection of the other also. Hobbes unhesitatingly takes the step into determinism. 'Free will' he classes amongst the meaningless terms 'whereby we conceive nothing but the sound';

> And therefore if a man should talk to me of 'a round quadrangle', or 'accidents of bread in cheese'; or, 'immaterial substances'; or of a 'free subject'; a 'free will', or any 'free', but free from being hindered by opposition, I should not say he were in an error, but that his words were without meaning, that is to say, absurd.[1]

Hobbes's account of the Will forms part of his theory of perception:

> External objects cause conceptions, and conceptions appetite and fear, *which are the first unperceived beginnings of our actions*.[2]

The motion set up in the organs of perception by the 'pressure' of external objects is conveyed, as we saw, to the heart. Here it either helps, or hinders, a new principle which looks suspiciously like a disguised 'entity', but which Hobbes employs with no misgivings – the 'vital motion'. If the vital motion is 'corroborated' by this new motion, we have the sensation of 'delight', which implies 'appetite' or an impulse to advance towards the pleasing object. If it is thwarted, we experience 'aversion', which implies an impulse to withdraw. In either the 'real effect' in the heart is only a form of motion; the feelings of delight or aversion, like the sensations of colour or sound, are but the 'appearance' or 'sense' (consciousness) of that motion. That which causes 'delight' or 'appetite' we call Good, and strive to obtain it; that which causes 'aversion' we call Evil, and strive to avoid it.

> Nor is there any such thing as absolute goodness, considered without relation. Seeing all delight is appetite, and presupposeth a further end, there

1. *Leviathan*, Ch. 5.   2. *Human Nature*, Works, Vol. IV, p. 67.

can be no contentment but in proceeding. . . . Felicity, therefore, by which we mean continual delight, consisteth not in having prospered, but in prospering.[1]

The life of man is characteristically figured by Hobbes under the similitude of a race, in which all are contending against all for the most choiceworthy things – power and glory:

> In it to endeavour is appetite; to be remiss is sensuality: to consider them behind is glory: to consider them before is humility: . . . to fall on a sudden is disposition to weep: to see another fall is disposition to laugh:[2] to see one outgone whom we would not, is pity: to see one outgo whom we would not, is indignation: to hold fast by another is love: to carry him on that so holdeth is charity: to hurt oneself for haste is shame: . . . continually to be outgone is misery: continually to outgo the next before is felicity: and to forsake the course is to die.[3]

Happiness lies, not in the repose of achievement, but in the excitement of pursuit, and for the eternal felicity proposed to us by theologians as the ultimate goal of our striving Hobbes has only a contemptuous remark in passing:

> What kind of felicity God hath ordained to them that devoutly honour him, a man shall no sooner know, than enjoy; being joys that now are as incomprehensible as the word of the schoolmen 'beatifical vision' is unintelligible.[4]

The final outcome, then, of the complicated processes by which we respond to external stimuli is some kind of *action*, whether it takes the form of choosing some 'good' or of avoiding some 'evil'. It may happen that appetency and aversion jostle with each other, and that the victory hangs for a while uncertain between them. This is the state called 'deliberation'. But in the end one of them wins, and we make our 'choice'. This final choice, or as Hobbes calls it, 'last appetite', *is* the 'Will'. Thus the Will itself is not 'free' or 'voluntary', in the sense of 'self-originating'. It seems to be so because we are conscious of the act of choice, but unconscious of the

1. *Human Nature*, Works, Vol. IV, pp. 32–3.
2. He defines laughter as 'sudden glory' in *Leviathan*, Ch. 6.
3. *Human Nature*, Works, Vol. IV, pp. 52–3.   4. *Leviathan*, Ch. 6, end.

obscure processes which led up to it and really determined it. Nevertheless Hobbes finds a sense for 'voluntary action'; it is action determined by this 'last appetite' only, and not by external compulsion. In no other sense can there be 'freedom' of will:

> But if by freedom we understand the faculty or power, not of willing, but of doing what they (i.e. men or animals) will, then certainly that liberty is to be allowed to both.[1]

This result, that man is really an automaton, was of course implicit already in the account of 'sense' as being itself a form of motion in matter. It was that classification of 'mind' with 'matter' which rendered it, along with every other part of the universe, subject to all the rigour of strict causation. If the 'will' is part of 'Nature', then it too must be bound fast in Fate. It must be remembered that the fast binding of Nature herself, though by no means a new thought, had been brought home to the thinkers of that time with unexampled force by the new mechanics. It had perhaps been 'held', but it had hardly before been so deeply *felt*, that 'Nature could move only along one road to a pre-destined end', and that 'in brief, the act of creation had created not only the universe but its whole future history. . . . The final establishment of this law as the primary guiding principle in Nature was the triumph of the seventeenth century. . . .'[2] It is not surprising, if this was so, that the seventeenth century should have witnessed an attempt to subdue the stubborn human will to the same great law. There was also a clear analogy between this scientific determinism and the current predestinarian theology; God's 'foreknowledge absolute' included, and his 'immutable decrees' controlled, both the course of each atom and the destiny of each soul. It was for this reason that those who, like Milton and the Platonists, were concerned above all for the moral life of man, clung passionately to the doctrine of Free Will.

Dr Johnson's 'Sir, we *know* our will is free, and there's an end on't!' may or may not be the last word on the question of deter-

---

1. *De corpore*, English Works, Vol. I, p. 409.
2. The phrases are those of Jeans, *Mysterious Universe*, p. 16. (Cf. above, p. 49.)

minism, but at any rate it expresses what seems to be proved by experience, namely that however essential determinism may be to science, it is also essential for man to feel and to act *as if* he were 'able to affect the course of events by his own volition'.[1] Hobbes's *Leviathan* is an admirable illustration of this point; for in that work the determinist philosopher uses all his powers to urge that man can and must so affect the course of events. That he can do so is shown in the Social Contract, which converted the life of man at one blow from a welter of mutual rapine into an ordered commonwealth. That he must at all costs continue to do so, by supporting in every way the authority of the Leviathan, is the purport of the whole argument, and is illustrated by many a despairing reference to the contemporary chaos. But the Contract, the authority of the Leviathan and the Civil War are all alike products of determinism? True, but the point is that Hobbes writes throughout *as if* these issues were for men to decide. In strict determinism there should, I suppose, be no passion for values which may be lost or preserved by taking thought, for nothing is contingent upon human volitions. But Hobbes's book, as we have seen, is nothing if not suasive; he cares supremely for strong government, and blames his opponents quite as lavishly as if they were completely answerable for their own actions. Hobbes sees the need for determinism as a scientific hypothesis, and also finds it most useful as a solvent for views he dislikes, but where his own interests are deeply engaged he leaves it out of account. It is noteworthy that throughout the *Leviathan*, although it is of course implicit, he hardly makes more than one direct reference to it.[2]

1. Cf. Jeans, loc. cit.
2. *Leviathan*, Ch. 21: '"Liberty" and "necessity" are consistent, as in the water that hath not only "liberty", but a "necessity" of descending by the channel; so likewise in the actions which men voluntarily do: which, because they proceed from their will, proceed from "liberty"; and yet, because every act of man's will, and every desire and inclination proceedeth from some cause, and that from another cause, in a continual chain, whose first link is in the hand of God the first of all causes, proceed from "necessity". So that to him that could see the connexions of those causes, the "necessity" of all men's voluntary actions would appear manifest.'

The Christian Commonwealth

It was one of the characteristics of the seventeenth century that no
English writer of that time, whatever his philosophical views might
be, could explicitly abandon the assumption that the universe rested
upon a basis of divine meaning. Further, all thinkers of that century,
with but one or two exceptions, assumed the truth in some sense of
the specifically Christian doctrines, and the supernatural status of the
Bible. It can hardly fail to strike a modern reader that there is a
radical incompatibility between the principles of Hobbes's philosophy and those of any sort of Christianity, if not of any sort of
religion. One would have supposed that of all the forms of 'error'
which he was trying to expel from men's minds, the beliefs com-
prised under the general heading 'religion' – including Christian
doctrine, Bible, and Church – would for him have been the first and
the most formidable. And I shall suggest, in a moment, that it was
indeed so in reality, yet the pages of the *Leviathan* are thick-sown
with Scriptural citations, and the appearance, at least, of orthodoxy
is somehow preserved. The fact is that in the seventeenth century one
did not make frontal attacks upon the religious tradition; particularly if, like Hobbes, one happened to be constitutionally timorous.
Hobbes was born in 1588, the Armada year, and he used to say that
the alarms of that time had affected his nativity. He certainly had no
inclination for the glories of any kind of martyrdom; moreover, the
lawful religion claimed his loyalty as part of his duty as a subject. To
believe as one is bidden by the sovereign is, according to him, a
political obligation; thus to venture all for 'truth', if that truth happened to conflict with the established creed, would not be courage
but sedition. But indeed the very notion of truth conflicting with
what is lawfully established involves a contradiction, for in these
matters 'truth' *is* what is established. We have no means of verifying
the 'truths' of religion: neither can we therefore be said to 'know'
them – unless God vouchsafes us some direct supernatural proof.
And as this is not to be expected to occur in these days, we must

trust the ruling of the sovereign, who, until the final inauguration of God's kingdom at doomsday, is God's earthly lieutenant. No Chinese sage, not the Vicar of Bray himself, could more decisively subordinate speculative truth to pragmatic considerations than Hobbes when, after venturing some conjectures about the geographical position of the kingdom of God, he adds:

> But because this doctrine, though proved out of places of Scripture not few nor obscure, will appear to most men a novelty, I do but propound it; maintaining nothing in this, or any other paradox of religion; but attending the end of that dispute of the sword, concerning the authority, not yet amongst my countrymen decided, by which all sorts of doctrine are to be approved or rejected; and whose commands, both in speech and writing, whatsoever be the opinions of private men, must by all men, that mean to be protected by their laws, be obeyed. For the points of doctrine concerning the kingdom of God have so great influence on the kingdom of man, as not to be determined but by them that under God have the sovereign power.[1]

What is important for us, however, is to notice how, holding the views that he does, Hobbes comports himself towards that vast complex of dogmas, traditions, institutions, and attitudes based upon principles diametrically opposite to his own – the 'Christian Commonwealth'. The matter is important, because the study of it brings before us with unusual distinctness one of the main issues in seventeenth-century thought, the problem, that is, of reconciling two inconsistent world-views. Two principal orders of Truth were present to the consciousness of the time: one, represented by Christianity, which men could not but reverence, and the other, represented by science, which they could not but accept. We have seen how Bacon and Browne dealt with the difficulty; let us now watch the behaviour of one who, much more fully than either of these, accepted all the implications of the 'new philosophy'. We shall find, as might have been expected, that while leaving the outer shell of the orthodox structure to all appearance unaltered, he is really at work rebuilding the interior with entirely new materials.

RELIGION. Hobbes's account of the origin of religion does not suggest that he had a very high opinion of it. In four things, he tells

1. *Leviathan*, Ch. 38.

us, 'consisteth the natural seed of religion: opinion of ghosts, ignorance of second causes, devotion towards what men fear, and taking of things casual for prognostics'.[1] The gods were at first the creation of human fear; for 'this perpetual fear, always accompanying mankind in the ignorance of second causes, as it were in the dark, must needs have for object something'. Surrounded by unknown and largely hostile forces, and continually anxious for the future, man supposed himself to be at the mercy of invisible agents; and ignorant of natural causation, he supposed these spiritual powers to be the cause of his good or evil fortune. In his natural desire to propitiate the gods, he used towards them the same sort of obsequious behaviour as he would towards a man who had power over him. And in his anxiety to probe the unknown and the future he mistook coincidences for omens and prophecies. These seeds of religion have been carefully nurtured by rulers and priests, who saw that it was to their interest to keep men superstitious. With the 'Gentiles' religion was thus 'part of human policy'. It will be noticed that in this account the existence of religion is attributed to causes which must needs tend to disappear as enlightenment increases. Does Hobbes, one asks, recognize any other and better kind of religion, which is not dependent for its existence upon superstition, the arts of priests and politicians, or 'juggling and confederate knavery'? The reply is, I think, that he does recognize it – distantly; but takes very little interest in it. We are to distinguish, he tells us, between the Gentile Gods, who are the product of fear, and the One God, who is a necessary postulate of science. No one can think much about causation without seeing that there cannot be an infinite regress; there must be, 'as even the heathen philosophers confessed, one first mover; that is, a first and an eternal cause of all things, which is that which men mean by the name of God'.[2] So also 'by the visible things in this world, and their admirable order, a man may conceive there is a cause of them, which men call God.' It is, then, the God of deism – first mover and designer of the world-machine – that Hobbes offers as substitute for Zeus or Jehovah. But even to say that he 'offers' this is an overstatement. For him the

1. *Leviathan*, Ch. 12.   2. ibid., Ch. 12.

word God is really little but a symbol of the philosopher's fatigue. In his quest for truth the investigator at last reaches the limits of human capacity; then, in sheer weariness, he gives over, and says 'God'. But what inspires Hobbes is not the moment of the *o altitudo*, but the discovery that we need not reach this point in our researches anything like so soon as had been supposed. And it is noticeable that in speaking of God his main endeavour is to empty this conception of all content. Of that which has not reached us through the senses we can have no 'image', thus we can have no 'idea' or 'conception' of God. We can only speak of him in a series of negatives, such as 'infinite', 'immutable', 'incomprehensible', or in terms signifying his remoteness from our mortal state, such as 'omnipotent', 'most high', and the like. All these 'attributes' are really 'pseudo-statements', that is to say, the reality to which they point is just simply our own pious disposition:

for in the attributes which we give to God, we are not to consider the signification of philosophical truth, but the signification of pious intention, to do him the greatest honour we are able.[1]

And from this account of God's attributes as 'signs of honour' Hobbes is quick to deduce the principle of uniformity of worship in a commonwealth. The 'attributes' are words signifying, and evoking, certain *attitudes and actions* on our part, in particular the acts of public worship. Now all that relates to *how we are to behave* is within the province of the sovereign, hence it follows

that those attributes which the sovereign ordaineth, in the worship of God, for signs of honour, ought to be taken and used for such, by private men in their public worship.[2]

This discovery of a social and political reference in the most soaring terms of theology illustrates Hobbes's technique in the explanation of meanings, and the kind of use to which he put it. What he is virtually saying is that as we can have no *knowledge* of these high matters, we must regard our religious affirmations as signs that we intend to behave properly as subjects and citizens. They are, indeed,

1. *Leviathan*, Ch. 31.   2. ibid.

'objectless beliefs', to be retained for their power in organizing and maintaining valuable attitudes.[1] It seems tolerably clear that the Anglican Church commended itself to Hobbes, as to Swift later, because, as an 'Erastian' establishment, its deepest intention seemed to coincide with this view. For any religion which makes wider claims, which includes more, in fact, than submission to secular authority, Hobbes has nothing but abhorrence. It was, of course, one of the advantages enjoyed by seventeenth century 'Protestant' writers, that under cover of the usual attack on 'Popery' they could, with every appearance of religious zeal, demolish the very foundations of religion itself. Hobbes's real hostility to religion, in spite of surface protestations, comes out pretty clearly in his tone, and in the direction of his emphasis. In his chapter 'Of Religion', for example, most of the stress is laid upon everything which can render religion suspect: its questionable origin, its employment by unscrupulous tyrants as an instrument of policy, and its constant tendency to degenerate into superstition; and his final word is a thrust at the 'unpleasing priests' to whom he attributes all the misfortunes of history, and who are to be found 'not only among the Catholics, but even in that Church that hath presumed most of reformation'.

SCRIPTURE. It was impracticable for Hobbes, as indeed it had proved for most people until the time of his modern disciples the Soviet rulers, to 'boot the Bible into the dustbin'.[2] And yet it would have saved him a great deal of trouble and hypocrisy if he could have done so. For the Bible, or rather the contemporary attitude towards it, was perhaps the greatest of all the obstacles to the 'exantlation of Truth'. As the 'Word of God' it could neither be denied nor ignored, and there was therefore no alternative but to 're-interpret' it and to confute the current 'misinterpretations'. In his biblical criticism Hobbes employs his usual indirect tactics, so that it is not immediately manifest how little he is really leaving of the supernatural authority of holy writ.

1. Cf. I. A. Richards, *Science and Poetry*, p. 61, and *Principles of Literary Criticism*, p. 280.
2. See Shaw's *Adventures of the Black Girl*.

To begin with, he analyses the phrases 'Laws of God' and 'Word of God'. The Laws of God he identifies with the Laws of Nature, that is to say, the principles of morality which are admitted everywhere and by all men. These are part of the 'natural word of God', for the Scriptures by which God makes himself known to us are threefold: they are, 'Reason', 'Revelation', and the voice of inspired prophets or other trustworthy intermediaries. Of these three scriptures there is little doubt which Hobbes prefers: it is Reason which as the *undoubted word of God* we are never, he says, to renounce.[1] What, then, are we to do when the Scriptures, which we acknowledge as supernaturally inspired, appear to conflict with Reason? Hobbes's reply is characteristic. In the first place there can be nothing in Scripture contrary to reason, but there may be things in it *above* reason. Are we then, as Bacon and Browne taught, to welcome each of these rebuffs as spiritual gymnastics, and perhaps deplore that 'there be not impossibilities enough in religion for an active faith'? Not precisely; there is, I think, a significant difference of tone between Browne's cheerful '*credo quia impossibile*', and even perhaps Bacon's 'Render unto faith the things that are faith's' – and Hobbes's recommendation, in such cases, to 'captivate our understanding to the words'. For what is the real meaning of this 'captivity'? Not submission of the intellect, but of the *will*; so that the reverence we owe to Scripture turns out, rather unexpectedly, to be yet another aspect of our general obligation to obey constituted authority.

We then captivate our understanding and reason when we forbear contradiction; when we so speak, as by lawful authority we are commanded, and when we live accordingly. . . .

A man in love with mystery would not, one feels, have used the image[2] which Hobbes employs in this connexion:

For it is with the mysteries of our religion as with wholesome pills for the sick, which, swallowed whole, have the virtue to cure; but chewed, are for the most part cast up again without effect.[3]

1. *Leviathan*, Ch. 32 (my italics).   2. Quoted above, pp. 90-1.
3. *Leviathan*, Ch. 32.

The tone of this passage differs only by a few degrees of irony from that of the celebrated concluding paragraphs of Hume's essay on miracles:

> Our most holy religion is founded on faith, not on reason; and it is a sure method of exposing it to put it to such a trial as it is by no means fitted to endure. So that upon the whole, we may conclude that the Christian Religion not only was at first attended by miracles, but even at this day cannot be believed by any reasonable person without one.

Just as the attributes of God, then, have been settled by competent authority, so has the question of the scriptural canon, and it is for us to show ourselves well-affected to the sovereign by submitting, here again, to the official ruling.

CHAPTER 7

Rational Theology : Lord Herbert of Cherbury

WE are now to examine the ideas of a group of thinkers who, while fully sharing the desire of their century to separate Truth from Fiction, yet differed profoundly from Hobbes in their conviction that it was through the religious world-view, not the mechanical, that Truth must be sought. It is convenient to consider the 'rational theologians' of the seventeenth century immediately after Hobbes, since it was largely in conscious opposition to Hobbism that they defined their position.

We have seen in Hobbes's work some of the effects of an attempt to turn the contemporary mechanical principles into a philosophy, and to give, in terms of the 'new' philosophy, an exhaustive account of reality. What, we may now ask, would be the position, in the seventeenth century, of those who, though conscious of living in days of 'enlightenment' and eager for whatever illumination might come, yet clung to the central religious affirmations, and sought to justify their validity against the menace of the new teachings? The situation was, of course, highly complicated. Broadly, the problem confronting such men as the Cambridge Platonists, and religious modernists in general, was (as it still is) how to combine 'philosophy' with religion, how to reconstruct old beliefs in the light of new knowledge. As we have seen, the fundamental impulse of the century was towards the 'explanation' of what had hitherto been mysterious; towards the statement in conceptual language of what had hitherto been expressed, or imagined, in pictures and symbols. A vast and august body of beliefs – the Christian religion – had survived with scarcely impaired authority into this philosophic century, together with all its associated imagery, its world-picture, its scale of values, its way of life. It was not likely that the Baconian separation of religion from philosophy would long continue to satisfy. It was inevitable, in this explanatory age, that an effort should be made to 'explain' Christianity, to restate its doctrines in terms which would be felt to be 'reasonable', that is, in accordance with the modern standards of reality. The wheel of history had come full circle, and the seventeenth century reproduced some of the features of the second century A.D. The Cambridge Platonists are the modern analogues of the Alexandrian Fathers, Clement and Origen, with this significant difference – that the Fathers came between a declining philosophy and a rising Christianity, while the seventeenth-century theologians came between a declining Christianity and a rising philosophy. The resemblance between the two schools lies in their effort to maintain religion and philosophy as allies, not as strangers or enemies. Of the modern philosophers, it was Descartes whose system implied the closest union between faith and reason, and it is thus not surprising that the Cambridge movement derived much stimulus from him. But in the negative sense Hobbes counted for as much, for it was Hobbes whose materialism, determinism, and virtual atheism stung the Cambridge men into a philosophic re-examination of the foundations of their beliefs.

Not only the main currents of intellectual development, but also the particular circumstances of political and ecclesiastical history in the seventeenth century, may be said to have given rise to this philosophic type of Christianity. The Reformation, which had originally involved the application of the spirit of inquiry to the system of medieval Christianity, had in fact ushered in a period not of 'enlightenment', but of embittered controversy. The Reformed Churches, appealing to Scripture against Rome, found themselves, in self-defence, compelled to define their positions in creeds and articles; and in the ensuing conflicts the original rationalizing implications of the Reformation were lost sight of. Dogmatic protestantism, indeed, showed itself more hostile to 'rational' religion than the Church had been. Hooker, who at the height of the period of controversy had anticipated the appeal of the Platonists to 'right reason' and the 'light of nature', found Geneva a more formidable foe than Rome. By the middle of the seventeenth century the Confessions had so multiplied that the force of the customary appeal to an external authority – whether of Pope, Council, or Scripture – was inevitably weakened, and religion, like philosophy, was constrained to look within for its certainties. The very same chaos which sent Hobbes flying for safety to his Leviathan, inspired those who cared for the theologico-metaphysical world-view to attempt the task of lifting religion right out of the sphere of controversy, and placing it on a firm, because 'philosophical', foundation. The contests of Puritan and Prelatist wore down the prestige of the authoritarian beliefs, and opened the way for the explanatory spirit of the age to begin its attack on the traditional material.

Before considering the methods and temper of the Cambridge group, it may not be amiss to remind ourselves of the work of an earlier seventeenth-century writer who was alive to the situation, and whose proposals for solving contemporary problems illustrate very clearly the direction in which thought was moving. Lord Herbert of Cherbury is familiarly cited as the 'father of Deism', but as his work *De veritate* has never appeared in English he is less known than he should be by many students of the century. For this reason I have thought fit to present his views by means of extracts rather lengthier than would otherwise have been necessary.[1] In his general aim Lord Herbert shows himself thoroughly representative of the seventeenth-century movement, for he sets himself to discover an infallible touchstone by which Truth may be distinguished from Error. At this point I am only concerned with the application of his general principles to the explanation and restatement of traditional religious beliefs, and it is this which I propose now briefly to examine.

As long as the religious consciousness is being expressed through a single unquestioned system of dogma and imagery, no need is felt to explore its foundations; but when the multiplicity of religions has itself become the most pressing of problems, comparisons are inevitably suggested and attempts will be made to discover what

1. I have translated these from the French version, 3rd ed. 1639. (The work was first published in its original Latin, Paris 1625.)

principles, if any, may be common to them all. The need for principles of comprehension could indeed hardly fail to be felt by many men of very various shades of opinion in this disturbed period. Lord Herbert differs from such men as Baxter, Cromwell, or Jeremy Taylor mainly in that, not content with reducing the creed to the minimum possible number of fundamentals, he goes behind Christianity itself, and tries to formulate a belief which shall command the universal assent of all men as men. It must be remembered that the old simple situation, in which Christendom pictured itself as the world, with only the foul paynim outside and the semi-tolerated Jews within the gates, had passed away for ever. Exploration and commerce had widened the horizon, and in many writers of the century one can see that the religions of the East, however imperfectly known, were beginning to press upon the European consciousness. It was a pioneer-interest in these religions, together with the customary preoccupation of Renaissance scholars with the mythologies of classical antiquity, which led Lord Herbert to seek a common denominator for all religions, and thus to provide, as he hoped, the much-needed eirenicon for seventeenth-century disputes. Herbert's method is strictly in accord with the general tendency of the age which, as we have seen, was towards referring all outstanding problems to an inner tribunal presided over by 'Reason', 'Nature', or 'Truths of first inscription'. Amidst the whirlwinds and the earthquakes of contending doctrine, how shall mankind ever learn the Truth? By attending to the still small voice within. Proceeding in a manner akin to that soon after followed by Descartes, Herbert discovers the principle of certainty in the *natural instinct*, the *common notions* of mankind. Whatsoever is vouched for by the notions commonly inscribed upon the minds of men as such, whatsoever is received by universal consent, that, and that only, is Truth.

Thus universal consent will be the sovereign test of truth, and there is nothing of so great importance as to seek out these common notions, and to put them each in their place as indubitable truths. This is more necessary now than ever, for since it is not only by arguments that we are confused ..., but terrors also are employed, to infuse into the head and into the soul (though conscience and the inner sense cry out against it) the belief that all who are outside the Church of these preachers, whether by ignorance or by error, are so criminal that they must without delay incur eternal damnation: poor mortals, astonished by these fulminations, have no refuge unless we establish certain unshakable foundations of truth supported by universal consent, to which they can have recourse in the doubts of Theology or of Philosophy.[1]

This 'consent' (for which Herbert pleads, it must be admitted, with more enthusiasm than literary charm) must be *universal*, since many errors have been believed in particular times and places. But God has placed within us a certain 'faculty' which 'witnesses' to Truth, and what this faculty certifies is the genuine article.

I add that vulgar doctrines are not altogether false, nor true, for there was never any Religion or Philosophy so barbarous that it had not its portion of truth; yet nevertheless if it has been corrupted by error (as generally happens) there is no other way of restoring it to its splendour than by the separation which depends upon our method. For if the things which are true have the witness of a certain faculty, those which are false will have no such witness. Universal consent, then, should be regarded, in my view, as the first and sovereign Theology and Philosophy, and to this end divine providence greatly assists, for it has, in these last centuries, so largely revealed what was unknown to the earlier ones, that it seems there remains nothing worthy to be known which has not been declared to us.

But our knowledge of Truth is not merely reached by boiling down all that our enlarged culture has taught us; we prove all things by the inner faculty:

Now we derive this universal consent not only from laws, religions, philosophies, and the written remains of all kinds of authors, but we claim further that there are certain faculties innate in us by means of which these truths are vouched for (*conformées*). Nevertheless we leave the mad and the foolish to follow any Church, school, or opinion they like; ... we say merely that it is easy to establish the general truths which are necessary, and that universal consent (which can only be arrived at by divine providence) is the sole criterion of the truth in these necessary things. I undertake this

1. *De la vérité*, p. 51 ff.

labour the more willingly, for in so doing I am espousing the cause of God, who has given these common notions in all times and in all places and to all men, as the means of his universal divine providence.

All that is required is that we should attend to the deliverances of the inner faculty, and give it free play; we fall into error only by neglecting to use the touchstone with which nature has supplied us.

For I boldly say that there have been, and are now, men, Churches, and schools, stuffed with *bagatelles*, which have introduced into succeeding centuries impostures and fables ... having no other foundation than true-seeming stories, or some rude and impertinent reasoning; a thing which would never have happened if my method had been followed.

The common notions are the principles against which it is not permissible to dispute, or indeed they are that part of science which nature has given us, according to her first intention. It is in these notions, as I have many times said, that we see shining a gleam of the divine wisdom, when we separate them from the impurity of opinions.

We, who at this distance of time and for our particular present purpose read these older writers, not in order to agree or disagree with them, but in order to watch their mental behaviour, do not need to ask Lord Herbert by what criterion he can infallibly distinguish a 'common notion' from an 'impure opinion'. A common notion was a notion of the kind which, to a man of his type of culture and at his particular stage of civilization, seemed indisputably 'true' because it satisfied his deepest needs. An 'impure' opinion was one which disappointed or thwarted those particular needs.

What, we next proceed to ask, are the common notions which will serve us in the sphere of religion, and by whose means we may rise above the brawling creed and sect? Herbert is particularly precise in his answer to this question. We must seek the required religious formulation in the two familiar ways – first, by the study of comparative religion:

Religion is a common notion, for there has never been a century nor any nation without religion. We must therefore see what universal consent has brought to light in religion, and compare all that we find on this subject, so as to receive as common notions all the things which are recognizably present and constant in the true religion.[1]

And secondly, there is the oracle within, whose deliverances really render superfluous all this laborious study:

Nay, if you desire a more expeditious method, I will give it to you: Retire into yourself and enter into your own faculties; you will find there God, virtue, and the other universal and eternal truths.

The discovery of the fundamental religious notions common to mankind is indispensably necessary, he continues (in the concluding section of the *De veritate*), since only thus can we defend ourselves against priestcraft – of which Herbert is evidently a sworn foe:

For what is vulgarly spoken about implicit Faith, both among us and in the remotest provinces of foreign lands, is of no service to us in this discussion. As for instance when we are told that human reason is blind, that we ought to yield to Faith, that the Church (which cannot err) has the right to prescribe divine worship, and that, in consequence, we must follow her in all things; that no man should trust so far to the resources of his intelligence as to dare to examine the power and authority of Prelates, and of those who declare the word of God; that there are good reasons for all that is preached (although it surpasses the reach of the human mind) which are so true that one should rather adore than examine them; that God can do all this, and greater things. For all these arguments, and many others like them, which are used according to the diversity of times and places, are as proper for establishing a false religion as the true one, since there is no impostor who cannot use similar language to persuade men to believe his reveries, and to establish his imaginary laws. So that if we do not make plain the path to Truth by means of the common notions ... I see not that one could not establish any opinion one liked. Indeed whatever may be said by those who employ ambiguous and Lesbian rules in matters of faith in order to establish their doctrine, they are nevertheless just like those who, in order to succour the poor wayfarers to whom they have given black eyes, immediately promise, with singular courtesy, to lead them into the right path. But the truth is far otherwise, for the sovereign Judge will not call us to account for what we have done on someone else's authority: each will answer for himself. That

1. This Lord Herbert attempted to carry out in his book *De religione Gentilium*.

is why we must establish preambles and foundations of religion by the light of the universal wisdom, to the end that whatever is added afterwards at the veritable dictation of faith may resemble the roofs of houses, which rest upon and follow the foundations.

We come then, at length, to the list of common notions which Herbert feels, after studying all the accessible religions and consulting his own heart, to be the quintessence of all religious belief. He formulates them in five headings:

I. 'THAT THERE IS A SUPREME POWER'

We call then God, him who has received so many names amongst all sorts of nations.

He is Eternal, Blessed, Sovereignly Good, the Author and Finisher of all things (at least of all things that are good), and he is the 'milieu' in which all things subsist. Besides this universal Divine Providence there is also 'particular' providence, as is proved by the

sentiment of divine aid which commonly assists us, when we seek it in the greatest extremities.

How completely valid this sense of inner assurance was to Herbert himself is vividly seen in the incident he relates at the close of his *Autobiography*, in which the vanity and egoism which are so pleasantly conspicuous all through that book almost reach the sublime. Throughout his career Herbert had, according to his own account, been favoured in exceptional degree by the great and the fair. One supreme favour had as yet, however, been withheld from him: he had not hitherto received any direct testimony of appreciation from the Deity, on whose behalf he had written the *De veritate*. This favour was now to be vouchsafed to him. The book had been read in manuscript and commended by no less a man than Grotius, yet Herbert was uncertain whether to publish it. He felt that his work was revolutionary in its methods and aims, and he feared general censure. One day, while he was in this state of hesitancy:

One fair day in summer, my casement being opened towards the South, the sun shining clear and no wind stirring, I took my book *De veritate* in my hand, and kneeling on my knees, devoutly said these words: O thou Eternal

God, Author of the light which now shines upon me, and giver of all inward illuminations, I do beseech thee of thy infinite goodness to pardon a greater request than a sinner ought to make; I am not satisfied enough whether I shall publish this book *De veritate*; if it be for thy glory, I beseech thee give me some sign from heaven; if not I shall suppress it. I had no sooner spoken these words, but a loud though gentle noise came from the heavens (for it was like nothing on earth) which did so comfort and cheer me, that I took my petition as granted, and that I had the sign I demanded, whereupon also I resolved to print my book: this (how strange soever it may seem) I protest before the Eternal God is true, neither am I any way superstitiously deceived herein, since I did not only clearly hear the noise, but in the serenest sky that I ever saw, being without all cloud, did to my thinking see the place from whence it came.[1]

God is also Just, and Wise; He is just, for not only the common notions, but also history and experience prove that 'all things are administered with piety and justice, although we do not know the causes and the reasons'. He is wise, 'for he not only makes to appear the gleams of his wisdom in the attributes mentioned, but also in his works, in which it shines wondrously'. The attributes of Omnipotence and of Liberty are questioned by some, but that of Infinity, Herbert thinks, is proved 'by the infinity of space, which God surpasses as comprising all things, for the common notion teaches us that God is above and beyond all things'. The notion of the infinity of space, first celebrated in the previous century by Bruno, was of course an essential part of the new world-picture which, in our period, was replacing the Ptolemaic:

As for the attributes which are rejected by our inquiry, they are those which ascribe to God some novelty, or which attribute to him corporality, multitude, and particularity, or which assert that he damns men for his sole pleasure; for such a God is nothing but a pure idol of the imagination, in which alone it subsists.

2. 'THAT THIS SOVEREIGN POWER MUST BE WORSHIPPED'

Common consent ordains this, although men differ as to the means.

1. Lord Herbert's *Autobiography*, concluding pages.

Some religious cult of one kind or another is found everywhere. Herbert postulates this as a fundamental principle, and concludes from it that religion is the distinguishing characteristic of mankind. Those who appear to be atheists are generally those who, disgusted at the horrible things attributed to God by deluded men, prefer believing in no God to believing in this one. Whereas, were the divine attributes rightly conceived, such people would rather be in the mood to believe at all costs; so that even if there were no God they would wish there were one.

3. 'THAT THE GOOD ORDERING OR DISPOSITION OF THE FACULTIES OF MAN CONSTITUTES THE PRINCIPAL OR BEST PART OF DIVINE WORSHIP, AND THAT THIS HAS ALWAYS BEEN BELIEVED'

About ceremonies men have disputed, but about the necessity for good conduct there has been a universal consensus. Piety and holiness of life are forms of worship, for they naturally produce love towards God and faith in him. We have, it is true, our bodily nature; but nature has implanted in us a taste for virtue, so that our souls may be gradually detached from earthly delights, and dwell in the constant enjoyment of inner tranquillity.

4. 'THAT ALL VICES AND CRIMES SHOULD BE EXPIATED AND EFFACED BY REPENTANCE'

Predestinarian doctrines which imply the futility of repentance are inconsistent with divine goodness and justice.

5. 'THAT THERE ARE REWARDS AND PUNISHMENTS AFTER THIS LIFE'

Every religion, all sorts of laws and of philosophy, *and, what is more, Conscience* [my italics], teach openly or implicitly that we shall be punished or rewarded after this life.

Thus it appears, [he concludes], that the common notions which recognize a sovereign Author of all things, which bid us honour him, lead holy lives, repent of our crimes, and expect reward or punishment after death, come from God, and are imprinted in the whole human race, and that those which presume plurality of Gods, which allow sin to remain unrepented of, and which waver as to the eternal state of the soul, are not common notions, nor truths. All religion is not good, . . . and we are not claiming that a man can be saved in all sorts of religions – for how can it be that he who believes more than he need, and does less than he ought, can be saved? But we gladly believe that in every religion, and even in each conscience, whether by grace or by nature, a man has means sufficient to render himself acceptable to God.

Herbert has, in effect, defined some of the principal tenets of what came later to be commonly known as 'natural religion'. This is the archetypal religion imprinted in all men in all times and places, of which all particular religious cults are derivatives. Ceremonies and usages superimposed on these primary common notions may have their use in religion, but they are not essential. The simple articles of natural religion, which underlie all particular rites and sacraments, contain all that is 'necessary for salvation', and so may be used as the basis for religious 'comprehension'.

These then are the common notions on which the universal Church is founded; for it is not the Church which is built of stone and lime, or even of marble, which is infallible, nor that which men establish by words or writing, mingling therewith somewhat of their own opinions and giving their support thereto; neither is it that which fights under some particular flag, or which comprises a certain number of persons in some corner of the earth or in a certain century; but it is simply the doctrine of the common notions, which embraces all sorts of places and times, and all men, which ought to be called *Catholic*, since it is this alone which explains the universal divine providence and wisdom, and which shows the reason why we address God as the common Father of the universe; it is *this* Church outside which there is no salvation – nay, all the praises attributed to 'the Church' belong to *it*, and each of the other Churches is by so much the less true, and the more subject to error, as it is further separated from this.

Lord Herbert is not primarily concerned in this work with 'Revelation', but his few concluding remarks on the subject are of interest as illustrating one of the methods by which the rationalizing seventeenth century dealt with so venerable a concept. That any truth could be 'given' by sheer force of supernatural authority, so that it must be believed without being understood, was a proposition which became less and less acceptable to most minds as the century proceeded. The notion of Revelation, however, was too strongly embedded in traditional ways of thought to be dismissed; it required to be elaborately explained away. It could, for instance, be identified with the process by which the common notions themselves (the starting-point of all reasoning) are imprinted in our minds, 'Reason' thus becoming, in the phrase of Locke, 'natural revelation'. Herbert, though he approaches this point of view, seems to understand by revelation some process or experience (akin to the above-mentioned communication of the divine *imprimatur* for *De veritate*) by which we become more than ordinarily certain of anything. His retaining of the word cannot conceal his entire alteration of its usual meaning. The revelation, to be genuine, must be made *to oneself*; what is 'revealed' on someone else's authority is only story or tradition. We must, moreover, have prepared ourselves for its reception by prayers and vows; and the revelation, when it comes, must bear the hall-mark of authenticity – that is, it must persuade us to something which we know (on *other grounds*) to be 'good'. The recipient of a revelation, too, should be able to attest (as unfalteringly as Herbert did of his celestial noise) that he had experienced a 'particular movement of God' towards him. 'To state the whole in a few words,' he concludes, virtually, though not quite, breaking through from the theological thicket into congenial naturalism:

every divine and happy sentiment that we feel within our conscience is a revelation [my italics], although properly speaking there are no other revelations than those which the inner sense knows to be above the ordinary providence of things.

CHAPTER 8

Rational Theology: The Cambridge Platonists

The Candle of the Lord

THE characteristic task of a century which was gravitating steadily towards 'enlightenment' was to give the true, the 'philosophical' account of matters which had hitherto been misconceived by both the learned and the vulgar. In the field of theology, then, we must expect to find the rationalizers largely concerned with putting an *idea*, and *abstraction*, where formerly there had been a *picture*. For only the abstract, only what could be conceptually stated, could claim to be *real*: all else was shadow, image, or at least 'type' or symbol. As we have seen, the urge towards such restatements came both from the main intellectual movement of the time, and – in the case of religion – from the need to transcend controversy. It is significant that in the seventeenth century most of the religious rationalizing is carried on conservatively; there is no appearance, and usually no intention, of destructive criticism. The assumption always is that the core of religious truth is sound, if only it can be freed from the traditional accretions. The Cambridge Platonists were, in their varying degree, deeply religious and indeed saintly men; and their treatment of older conceptions was ruled throughout by their desire to deepen, while clarifying, the religious consciousness of their time. In so far as they spoke a new or at least an unfamiliar language, it was because they felt that the life of the spirit was perishing in the spent air of polemic. Their aim was not to destroy, but to conserve and reinforce from within what they felt to be vital in the religious tradition. Accordingly their technique is, not to confront the cloud of credal warfare, but to 'put it by'; to dwell always upon the real, the saving truths, and by simply not using the weapons of controversy to let them silently rust away.

For this purpose it was convenient to change the linguistic currency: to speak of religious matters in terms other than those in constant use, and (what is presupposed by this) to *think* of them in modes whose very possibility, as it were, showed up much contemporary thought as inadequate and crude. No finer storehouse of such terms and such ways of thought existed, or none was so available or so powerful in the seventeenth century, as the Platonic and neo-Platonic philosophy. Here was a system, essentially religious in spirit, which taught the sole reality of the spiritual world and the immortality of the soul, which pictured life as the soul's striving for heaven and prescribed a regimen for its upward ascent: a system too which was not only venerated on its own account by the cultured, but which in its long and intimate association with Christianity had flowed into its stream and become part of it. The language of Platonism at that time commanded assent with an authority second only to that of Scripture, and to use it in religious exhortation, therefore, was the happiest available method of implying, without aggressively proclaiming, that there were other ways of faith besides those laid down in the current formulae. Salter, the eighteenth century editor of Whichcote, tells us that it was Whichcote's aim, in his Cambridge preaching, 'to preserve a spirit of sober piety and rational religion in the University and Town of Cambridge, in opposition to the fanatic enthusiasm and senseless canting then in vogue'. There was, I think, less of 'opposition' in Whichcote than Salter's eighteenth-century mind sees in him. Burnet expresses his temper more nearly:

He was much for liberty of conscience, and being disgusted with the dry systematical way of those times, he studied to raise those who conversed with him to a nobler set of thoughts, and to consider religion as a seed of deiform nature (to use one of his own phrases). In order to this, he set young students much on reading the ancient philosophers: chiefly Plato, Tully, and Plotin; and on considering the Christian religion as a doctrine sent from God both to elevate and sweeten human nature; in which he was a great example, as well as a wise and kind instructor.[1]

1. Burnet, *History of His Own Times*, Vol. 1, pp. 186-7 (1724 ed.).

The Cambridge Platonists were mainly Puritan in affinity, as indeed the connexion of several of them with Emmanuel College (then regarded as a 'seminary of Puritans') shows clearly enough. They may therefore be said to illustrate, together with such figures as Milton and George Fox, the tendency of advanced Protestant thought, after passing through its dogmatic post-Reformation phase, to reveal once again its original rationalizing temper, and to fall thus into line with the general movement of the century. The Platonists are celebrated for their appeals to 'Reason'; Reason, which in the text that Whichcote especially never tires of quoting, is 'the candle of the Lord', and to follow which, John Smith declares, is to follow God. But we must be careful not to misconstrue the significance of 'Reason' as the Platonists commonly use the term. 'Follow Reason' was an injunction having, from their standpoint, a twofold application to the special needs of the age. It meant, on the one hand, 'think philosophically' – regard as real only such things as were real to Plato. But it was no mere intellectual emancipation which they advocated. They would have less faithfully interpreted their master had they not gone on to insist, as they did, that the pursuit of 'Truth' involved the purification of the heart and the disciplining of the will; only the pure in heart could see God. 'Nothing is the true improvement of our rational faculties', said Whichcote, 'but the exercise of the several virtues of sobriety, modesty, gentleness, humility, obedience to God, and charity to men.'[1] Thus as philosophers the Platonists found in the metaphysics of Plato a defence against Hobbesian materialism, while as moralists and preachers they found in him authority for their characteristic message, that conduct mattered more than creed.

It is on this latter side of their work that I want primarily to dwell. The metaphysical work of Cudworth and More is interesting, and will be referred to briefly later. But for the purposes of this essay the Platonists are significant mainly because they employ seventeenth-century criteria of the Real towards the restatement of religious belief. We find them here (and the Sermons of Whichcote and John Smith are especially relevant to our inquiry) playing their

1. Quoted by Powicke, *The Cambridge Platonists*, p. 47.

part in the movement towards 'enlightenment' by constantly sub-stituting an *entelechy*, an idea, or a state of mind for one or other of the dramatic or pictorial representations of the traditional scheme. Take, for instance, the doctrine of Salvation. The popular concep-tion of salvation was of course inseparably bound up with all the imagery, biblical and theological, associated with the Fall and the Atonement. The Platonists were opposed to many of the implica-tions of the Fall doctrine, in particular to the customary depreciation of human nature and human Reason by orthodox divines. With their sense of the normality, the 'naturalness' of the spiritual pro-cesses, they could not accept the view, expressed in the traditional insistence upon *supernatural* grace, that there was no 'natural light' left to the sons of Adam since the Fall. The God who was Reason deified would not have cast man off so utterly. Neither had 'reve-lation' ceased after the Apostolic age, and consequently it was not confined to the pages of Holy Writ. God is the perpetual source of illumination to all who can live the life of Reason, and the function of Scripture is to confirm the truths which are discoverable by the light of Nature. 'The written word of God', says Whichcote, 'is not the first or only discovery of the duty of man. It doth gather and repeat and reinforce and charge upon us the scattered and neglected principles of God's creation.'[1] In particular, as might be expected, they abhorred the doctrines of predestination, especially what Henry More called 'the Black Doctrine of absolute Reprobation'. Their whole emphasis was upon the power of the individual to raise him-self unceasingly towards perfection by living after the Spirit. Tradi-tional teaching about Salvation evoked images of Heaven and the hereafter, of redemption and justification in its various forms; the Platonists (like the Quakers in this as in other ways) speak rather of 'here' and 'now'. 'Give me religion that doth attain real effects.'[2] The righteous are to become, in this life, partakers of the divine nature. Salvation is indeed the purpose of the Gospel, but salvation is to be conceived less as an ultimate destination of the soul beyond the horizons of this life than as a present approximation towards

1. Tulloch, *Rational Theology and Christian Philosophy*, etc., Vol. II, p. 100.
2. Whichcote, quoted by Powicke, op. cit., p. 80.

moral purification. To be 'saved' is to be 'good'. This teaching may be said to represent the application within the spiritual sphere of Bacon's scientific method. The purpose of science is to know the real world and master it, but for centuries men have wasted their powers in vain speculations. The purpose of religion is to produce men of godlike temper and lives ('*real* effects'), but for centuries they have been wrangling over creeds and forms, and never so hotly as since the so-called Reformation. The aim of Whichcote and Smith in their preaching was to 'call men off from dogmas and barren speculation', and to urge them to fix upon the 'Real'; that is, to devote themselves, in a spirit of chastened 'reasonableness', to the pursuit of sweetness and light. They reject no article of the Faith, but they shift the emphasis of exhortation, affirming values where orthodoxy affirmed facts.

John Smith's *Discourses*

I can think of no better means of illustrating the methods of the Platonists than by giving some account of the *Discourses* of John Smith. This volume is likely, I think, to outlive many of the more formal treatises by these authors. It contains the sermon of which Matthew Arnold (himself an apostle of Hellenism, though in altered circumstances) wrote: 'I have often thought that if candidates for Holy Orders were simply, in preparing for their examination, to read and digest Smith's great Discourse on The Excellency and Nobleness of True Religion ... and nothing further except the Bible, we might have, perhaps, a hope of at last getting, as our national guides in religion, a clergy which could tell its bearings and steer its way', etc. These same *Discourses* have been called, by a living Cambridge Platonist, 'the best University Sermons that I know'.[1] I shall not scruple to quote Smith freely, since his prose is frequently of rare excellence, and moreover, his exact tone and quality can only be conveyed in his own words.

1. Dean Inge, *The Platonic Tradition*, p. 58.

(1) The Platonist, the anti-scholastic, and the moralist in Smith all appear in his first Discourse, *Concerning the True Way or Method of attaining to Divine Knowledge*. Knowledge of God is knowledge of what is most Real. But though this knowledge is of the spirit and not of the senses, it is not abstract theoretical knowledge; it can, in fact, only be described by metaphors derived from sensation. We must rise above the life of the senses to know God, but in so doing we must reach, not a barren notional idea of him, but a higher and spiritual kind of 'sensation', a *noesis* which is superior to discourse. Divine 'knowledge' then, in effect, is the mystical experience, wherein we become one with the real. It is expressly distinguished as a form of *experience*, from the 'theology' of the schools:

It is but a thin, aiery knowledge that is got by meer Speculation, which is usher'd in by Syllogisms and Demonstrations; but that which springs forth from true Goodness . . . brings such a Divine light into the Soul, as is more clear and convincing than any Demonstration. The reason why, notwithstanding all our acute reasons and subtile disputes, Truth prevails no more in the world, is, we so often disjoyn *Truth* and true Goodness, which in themselves can never be disunited.[1]

Were I indeed to define Divinity, I should rather call it a *Divine life*, than a *Divine Science*; it being something rather to be understood by a *Spiritual sensation*, than by any *Verbal description*.[2]

Learned as these preachers are, 'close up those barren leaves' is one of their constant refrains.

To seek our Divinity meerly in Books and Writings, is *to seek the living among the dead*: we doe but in vain seek God many times in these, where his Truth too often is not so much *enshrin'd* as *entomb'd*: no; *intra te quaere Deum*, seek for God within thine own soul; he is best discern'd νοερᾷ ἐπαφῇ, as *Plotinus* phraseth it, by an intellectual touch of him: we must see with our eyes, and hear with our ears, and our hands must handle the word of life. . . . David, when he would teach us how to know what the divine Goodness is, calls not for *Speculation* but *Sensation*, *Taste and see how good the Lord is*.[3]

1. *Discourse* I, p. 4 (1673 edition).   2. ibid., p. 1.   3. ibid., p. 3.

Henry More, testifying to the same purpose, relates how at the end of a period of intense study he experienced a sudden slackening of his thirst for intellectual knowledge, followed by a 'conversion' which brought with it the real illumination of soul-knowledge:

Whether the Knowledge of Things [with this question the realization had come to him] was really that supreme Felicity of Man, or something Greater and more Divine was: Or, supposing it to be so, whether it was to be acquir'd by such an Eagerness and Intentness in the reading of Authors, and Contemplating of Things; or by the purging of the Mind from all sorts of Vices whatsoever.[1]

In all this do we not recognize the Cartesian self-sufficiency, the Cartesian rejection of authority and reliance upon inward certitude? It was the corollary to this century's rejection of the errors of the past, that it should find within the soul the Candle of the Lord, whose beams, if only they were free to shine abroad, would show up a divine universe in a divine light. In thus identifying religious knowledge with religious experience, the Platonists found a means, congenial to the temper of the age, of superseding both scholasticism on the one hand, and popular picture-thinking on the other. The concept 'God', like any other, must be *realized*; each man must make God real by becoming godlike himself. For John Smith there was no doubt as to what it meant to be godlike, or wherein consisted this holy life which is the 'best and most compendious way to a right belief'. In the seventeenth century no prophets of 'integration' spoke 'in defence of sensuality'. The Platonic, the Catholic, and the Puritan traditions all united in representing the good life as the endeavour 'more and more to withdraw ourselves from these Bodily things to set our soul as free as may be from its miserable slavery to this base Flesh'.[2] One aspired towards the state in which (to quote from a poet of kindred temper) –

1. See *The Philosophical Poems of H. More*, ed. Bullough, Intro d. xvii, xxxi, xxxv, etc.
2. Smith, op. cit., p. 16.

> the light of sense
> Goes out, but with a flash that has revealed
> The invisible world.[1]

'We must shut the Eyes of Sense, and open that brighter Eye of our Understandings.' Smith declares, it is true, that 'when *Reason* once is raised by the mighty force of the Divine Spirit into a converse with God, it is turn'd into *Sense*'; but 'Reason in its most exalted mood' is not, for him, as it was for Wordsworth, a definition of Imagination which could be used in defence of poetry. It was a defence of the mystical experience, and this can, of course, furnish subject-matter for the highest poetry. But Smith's 'Sense' is a very different thing from that contact with 'nature's living images' which for Wordsworth, and probably for most poets, is a necessary condition of poetical creativeness. What he and his like call the 'Imagination' is the image-making faculty – a thing of earthly rather than heavenly affinity – which continually throws up a stream of phantoms which come between the mind and the object of contemplation. Here on earth we see but in a glass darkly, not *in speculo lucido*: 'Our own *Imaginative Powers*, which are perpetually attending the highest acts of our Souls, will be breathing a gross dew upon the pure Glass of our Understandings, and so sully and besmear it, that we cannot see the Image of the Divinity sincerely in it.'[2] Imagination, according to this view, is a weakness incident to the flesh; it must be transcended as far as may be, or used, if at all, only to body forth what eye hath not seen, nor ear heard.

So certain, so indubitable did the nature of virtue appear to these thinkers that they were able, in the manner of their time, to regard the notion of it as one of those *communes notitiae* inscribed upon our souls. Enlightenment had not yet proceeded too far; and it was the good fortune of the age that it could rationalize away the vain imaginations of the past, and yet, on looking into its own heart, find written there, as by the hand of 'nature', all the old certainties.

We want not so much *Means* of knowing what we ought to doe, as *Wills* to doe that which we may know.

1. Wordsworth's *Prelude*, VI, 600.   2. Smith, op. cit., p. 21.

(2) Some further points of theology are treated in the usual explanatory and 'realizing' manner in the Discourse *Concerning the Nature and Existence of God*. God's existence is demonstrated, according to the method of 'natural theology', from the order of nature on the one hand, and the moral sense of man on the other. Although the Heavens declare the glory of God, the most clear and distinct imprint of him is to be found in the rational soul of man. Smith offers us here, indeed, a version of the 'ontological' proof, deducing God from the consideration of certain characteristics of the human mind. We are conscious of our own rationality, but we know also that our souls only participate in it, and are not identical with it. Our minds, too, 'are so framed, as not to admit of any other than *One Infinite* source of all that *Reason* and *Understanding* which themselves partake of, in which they live, move and have their Being'.[1] Similarly our yearning for a *summum bonum* presupposes a real Supreme Good as its object, a good outside and above ourselves. This, as might be supposed, is the aspect of the divine nature which Smith is most concerned to emphasize. Our understandings may realize God as Power and Reason, our wills and affections realize him as Goodness and Beauty.

He is not onely the *Eternal Reason*, that Almighty *Mind* and *Wisdom* which our Understandings converse with; but he is also that unstained Beauty and Supreme Good which our Wills are perpetually catching after: and wheresoever we find *true Beauty*, *Love*, and *Goodness*, we may say, Here or there is God.[2]

Consonant with this account of God is Smith's further teaching that 'Heaven' is to be understood as Happiness, which again means approximation to God; Hell is Misery, or estrangement from him. Again, anxious always to substitute rational conceptions for anthropomorphic imaginings, Smith insists that we shall not think of God as the omnipotent Lawgiver, constituting right and wrong by the mere fiat of his will. 'The Primitive rules of God's Oeconomy in the World', he says, are 'not the sole Results of an Absolute Will, but the sacred Decrees of Reason and Goodness'.[3] We should hold,

1. Smith, op. cit., pp. 118 ff.
2. ibid., p. 132.   3. ibid., heading of Ch. 4.

not that what God decrees is right, but that God decrees what *is* right. The general significance of this teaching, and its relevance for our present study, are, I think, very great. For we here see Smith, in the effort to make 'real' the substance of theology, finding the associations of the word 'God' itself an obstacle to his purpose. God ordains *what is right*; then, if it was already right 'in the nature of things', antecedently to God's decree, what need for the divine decree? The concept 'right' has in effect been deified, made antecedent to 'God'. Deeply ingrained in the minds of the Platonists, and of the greater number of their contemporaries as well, was the assumption that concepts alone are real, and that whatever is concretely imagined is phantasmal. To think of God without allowing the busy imagination to stain his white radiance with its phantasms – this was to be the effort of the enlightened believer. If one must use images – and it was hard to avoid them – one might think of God as Light, or the source of Light (a favourite figure with John Smith). But, as we have seen (and it was this teaching which saved the Platonists from barren intellectualism), better than all *thinking about* God was to feel him, to 'know', and as it were to *be* him; thus restoring upon a higher plane that 'sense' which could only delude upon the lower. Written theology or written poetry must needs be made up of imaginings; one could, however, *live* one's poetry and one's divinity.

If matters stood thus with the central idea of all religion, the idea of God, it is no wonder that much else in so composite a thing as traditional Christianity needed the elucidating touch. In a Discourse entitled *A Christian's Conflicts and Conquests, or a Discourse concerning The Devil's active Enmity and continual Hostility against Man* (one of a series of sermons against witchcraft preached annually at Huntingdon by a Fellow of Queens' College), Smith turns his attention to the Kingdom of Darkness, and deals with it in his accustomed fashion. Rejecting no jot or tittle of the popular mythology, he unobtrusively substitutes, at every turn, the more 'adequate' notion. The devils, he declares,

fell from God not so much by a local descent as by a Mental apostasie and dissimilitude to God. ... Wheresoever there are any in a disposition to sin against God, wheresoever there are any capable of a Temptation or Diabolical impression, here and there are they.[1]

When we say, The Devil is continually busie with us, I mean not only some Apostate spirit as one particular Being, but that spirit of Apostasie which is lodged in all men's natures; ... as the Scripture speaks of Christ not onely as a Particular person, but as a Divine Principle in holy Souls.[2]

Wickedness is the Form and Entelech of all the wicked spirits: it is the difference of a name rather than any proper difference of natures that is between the Devil and Wicked men.

As conversing with God implies not change of place but participation with his nature, so converse with the Devil is 'not so much by a mutual local presence' as by imitation of a wicked 'nature'.

God is but One, and his Name One ... and where we find Wisdom, Justice, Loveliness, Goodness, Love, and Glory in their highest elevations and most unbounded dimensions, That is He: and where we find any true participations of these, there is a true Communication of God; and a defection from these is the Essence of Sin and the Foundation of Hell.[3]

The trouble with the popular picture-thinking about these matters is that it enables men to love 'God' or hate 'The Devil' merely as names or phantoms, without having any 'clear or distinct apprehensions' (observe the Cartesian phrase) of what it is that they should be loving or hating. Thus they often quarrel with the Devil in notion, while their hearts comply with 'all that which the Devil is'. It should be clearly understood that Smith had apparently no thought of *denying* that the Devil was a particular Apostate spirit, any more than that Christ was a particular historical person. The situation in his time (it was also Milton's time) was that 'enlightenment' had proceeded as it were half-way only, so that it was possible for the religious to relegate the traditional mythology to a limbo of the mind, according to it a kind of poetic belief, while dwelling with the daylight part of their minds upon the rational interpretations.

1. Smith, op. cit., p. 448. 2. ibid., p. 451. 3. ibid., p. 454.

(3) Having given his discourses upon the principles of natural theology, Smith died, so his editor informs us, before completing his projected series upon Revealed Religion. It is hard to imagine, however, that if we had possessed these unwritten sermons they would have disclosed any unsuspected aspects of Smith's mind. We have, moreover, his short treatise *Of Prophecy* to indicate how he would have approached the topics of Revelation. In perusing this we again experience the familiar sense that a new ideology is being quietly substituted for an old without any avowed departure from orthodoxy. The technique of this process can in this case be partly described. It includes the following devices: (*a*) Passing over without mention those aspects of a question which are usually most discussed. Here, for instance, there is little or nothing said about the 'scheme' of prophecy, culminating in the Messiah. (*b*) Obliterating, almost casually, the very distinction in question (between 'natural' and 'revealed') by showing that 'natural' knowledge is itself a species of revelation. Smith argues that what the prophetic inspiration often does is simply to arouse a livelier realization of the 'Truths of Natural Inscription'. (*c*) Demonstrating that Scripture is so written as to be adapted to 'vulgar apprehensions'. It has already been pointed out how vital an issue Scriptural interpretation necessarily became in this century which was both Protestant and philosophical. A book like the Bible, containing so much poetry, history, legend, and allegory, and so little that could be called 'philosophy', clearly needed a great deal of firm 'explanation', since it was also indisputably the word of God. I have indicated above[1] how this was attempted; the Scriptures were written in the 'language of accommodation':

> Truth is content, when it comes into the world, to wear our mantles, to learn our language, to conform itself as it were to our dress and fashions: ... it speaks with the most Idiotical sort of men in the most Idiotical way, and becomes all things to all men, as every sonne of Truth should doe, for their good.[2]

In other words, Scripture speaks to us in type, symbol, and parable;

1. See Chapter 4.　　　　　　　2. Smith, op. cit., p. 165.

in it 'the Philosophical or Physical nature and literal veritie of things cannot so reasonably be supposed to be set forth to us, as the Moral and Theological'. It was a queer stroke of historical irony which compelled these philosophers to accept, as the repository of necessary Truth, a book which needed so much 'interpreting' before it would yield up its precious burden. Even if the Bible had not become a danger-zone on account of sectarian disputes, it would still have been a natural impulse, on the part of the Platonists, to 'set young students much on reading the ancient philosophers: chiefly Plato, Tully, and Plotin'. (d) Establishing a series of distinctions separating true from false prophecy, or prophecy from dreams and 'enthusiastick impostures'. In doing this Smith sketches out, with the aid of Plato, the neo-Platonists, and the Rabbinical commentators, a psychology of prophetic inspiration, which I will briefly summarize.

Smith's general notion of prophecy is that it is a process whereby God 'flows in upon the minds of men'. But he distinguishes (following the Rabbinical tradition) several 'degrees of prophecy'. (a) In its highest form – the *gradus mosaicus* – divine knowledge is conveyed by the direct illumination of the highest, or rational, faculty of the soul. Moses was a 'superior' prophet, because he was privileged to converse with God thus 'face to face'. Next below this comes (b) the degree at which the reason is illuminated indirectly, through the medium of the 'imagination' – the imagination being the 'stage' on which appear the 'images' which are to be allegorically and 'anagogically' interpreted. At this level the prophet is dealing, not with naked Truth, but with phantasms and simulacra depicted in his 'fancy' or 'imagination' (equivalent terms), and he will accordingly also speak in figurative language; but if he is a 'true' prophet he will *understand* the truths so represented, and be able to interpret them. In (c) the lowest kind of prophesying ('divination') the prophets, like Plato's soothsayers and poets, know not what they say: they are unable, as it were, to decode their own phantasms. This last group, then, includes all the pseudo-prophets who do actually, it seems, have their 'Phansies' excited, but do not reach 'a true understanding of things in their coherence and contexture'.[1] The inferiority of the mere 'imagination' to 'Reason' could not be more emphatically stated: 'The Pseudo-Prophetical Spirit is seated onely in the Imaginative Powers and Faculties inferior to Reason'; whereas in the *gradus mosaicus* 'all imagination ceaseth, and the Representation of Truth descends not so low as the Imaginative part, but is made in the highest stage of Reason and Understanding'. Smith is the more concerned to show up the true nature of group (*c*), because in it are included all the 'Enthusiastical Impostors of our Age'. The grand distinction between the true prophecy and the false, or mere dream, is that the true never 'alienates the mind', but co-exists with clearness of reason and solidity of judgement; it informs and enlightens, whereas the false merely 'ravishes'. The genuine prophet is convinced by the force and clearness of the influx; he knows he is not merely dreaming dreams because he intuitively apprehends the communication as 'true'. Nevertheless the normal mode of communication was through 'dream' and 'vision'. Smith will accept from tradition that 'angels' (rather than God himself directly) are probably the 'furnishers of the prophetical scene'. The acts and doings of the prophets themselves, as recorded in Scripture, are to be understood, except where there is unmistakable evidence to the contrary, as 'imaginary' and not historical. This Smith justifies by arguing that

The Prophetical scene or Stage upon which all apparitions were made to the Prophet, was his Imagination; and that there all those things which God would have revealed to him were acted over Symbolically, as in a Masque, in which divers persons are brought in, amongst which the prophet himself bears a part. And therefore he, according to the exigency of this Dramatical apparatus, must, as the other Actors, perform his part. . . .[2]

He quotes approvingly a comment of Maimonides on one of the *res gestae* of the prophets – the shaving of Ezekiel's hair and beard. 'Far be it from God', says the Rabbi, 'to render his Prophets like to fools and drunken men', *therefore*, he infers, this and all suchlike actions are imaginary, i.e. 'done' only in a prophetic vision.

1. Smith, op. cit., p. 186.   2. ibid., p. 215.

Maimonides and several other medieval Rabbinical commentators are great favourites with Smith, who evidently found in them a mental constitution akin to his own.

In much of this treatise Smith gives the impression that he is dealing with comparatively uncongenial material. There is, however, another 'degree of Prophecy' of which he can speak with more of his characteristic warmth, because it is more closely allied to the 'natural' illumination he knew and trusted. This is 'that degree of Prophecy called Ruach Hakkodesh, i.e. the Holy Spirit'. It was this which inspired such books as the Psalms, the Proverbs, the Book of Job, and Ecclesiastes. Smith thinks the Jews ascribed this to the 'Spiritus Sanctus', 'not because it flows from the third Person of the Trinity (which I doubt they thought not of in this business), but because of the near afinitie and alliance it hath with that Spirit of Holiness and true Goodness that alwaies lodgeth in the breasts of Good men'. In this way of Revelation there is no 'labour of the Imagination'; its recipients experienced the influx not with frenzy or vision, 'but while they were waking, and their senses were in their full vigour'.

This kind therefore of Divine Inspiration was alwaies more pacate and serene than the other of Prophesie, neither did it so much fatigate or act upon the Imagination. For though these Hagiographi or Holy writers ordinarily expressed themselves in Parables and Similitudes, which is the proper work of Phansie, *yet they seem onely to have made use of such a dress of language to set off their own sense of Divine things, which in itself was more naked and simple, the more advantagiously*, as we see commonly in all other kind of Writings.[1]

All that really distinguished this spirit of inspiration from the 'spirit of goodness' which habitually dwells within the good man's heart was the relative abruptness and 'transport' of its advent; it was 'a kind of vital Form to that Light of divine Reason which they were perpetually possess'd of'. The conditions necessary for the free flowing of the prophetic vein are 'alacrity', 'chearfulness', probity and piety, purity of heart, a 'serene and pacate' temper; for as the Zohar says, 'the divine presence does not reside with Sadness'.[2] Coleridge

1. Smith, op. cit., p. 224 (my italics).   2. ibid., p. 239.

said that an 'unhappy man could not write poetry', and there are obvious analogies between the theories of poetic and prophetic inspiration.

Reflection upon the drift of all that Smith has said seems to show that he has in effect written a 'natural history' of a supposedly supernatural process. True, the notion of divine inspiration clearly implies for him something freely bestowed from outside us, but he feels no essential discontinuity between this and the process, universally felt to be 'natural', whereby the mind is illumined by truth. The truest prophet is really the *philosopher*, who has 'a true understanding of things in their coherence and contexture'. It was this grasp of first principles which constituted the pre-eminence of Moses, and made him a veritable Platonic philosopher-king. For what was the true meaning of the face-to-face converse of Moses with God? It consisted, not merely in the absence of the usual 'angelic mediation', but in the 'clearness and evidence of the Intellectual light wherein God appeared to Moses'. God 'spoke' to him (i.e. truth flowed in upon him)

without any impressions or Images of things in his Imagination in an Hieroglyphical way, as was wont to be in all Dreams and Visions; but *by characterizing all immediately upon his Understanding*: though otherwise much of the Law was indeed almost little more for the main scope and aim of it but an Emblem or Allegory.[1]

Next below the philosopher-prophet who apprehends naked truth without the aid of hieroglyphics comes the allegorist (whether we call him 'prophet' or 'poet' matters little), he who sees and speaks in phantasms, but knows the abstract truths of which they are the images. Lastly, and least worthy, comes the poet-soothsayer, he who lives continually amongst the shadows in the den, and knows nothing of the realities which cast them. Taking the treatise as a whole, one can hardly doubt that it illustrates once again the seventeenth-century effort to apply a 'philosophic' test to traditional material, and to reject, as far as might be, whatever was thereby revealed to be 'fictitious'. I do not think (for a reason mentioned

1. Smith, op. cit., p. 255 (my italics). Smith is here quoting Philo.

below)[1] that the work of the Platonists can be said to have under-
mined religion; but their standards of reality did imply, at least in
theory, a depreciation of the status of poetry. The reappearance in
the later seventeenth century of the Platonic attitude towards
'phantasms' must be counted among the many forces, scientific,
philosophic, and other, which at that time were making poetic
belief, as well as religious belief, increasingly difficult. In the Cambridge Platonists the spirit of Plato aids the spirit of Descartes in
the task of reducing the imagery of religion to 'clear and distinct
ideas'.

(4) I cannot leave this part of the subject without attempting in a
few words to answer an important question still outstanding: How
did this reduction of religious imagery affect the interpretation of
the specific points which distinguish the Christian from other
religions? What account would rational religion give of the 'Gospel' of the person and mission of Christ, of his Incarnation, Atonement, Resurrection, and redemptive grace? It was, of course,
around this body of theological matter, and the issues arising from
it, that the disputes of the Reformation and the earlier seventeenth
century had chiefly raged, and the temper of the Platonists, as we
have seen, was to purge religion of controversy by changing its
vocabulary and setting it in an altered framework. It was to be
expected, therefore, that they would leave unstressed the 'evan-
gelical' parts of Christianity: and this is what we find. They tend,
without ostensible change of creed, to substitute, for the second
Person of the Trinity or the Crucified Redeemer, the divine teacher
whose life and words show God and man in that state of union at
which all religion aims. Christ instituted no new technique of salvation; he rather 'promulgated' and gave supreme confirmation to
the great original laws of the spiritual life, as that purity shall bring
peace of soul, and vice misery.[2] The Gospel, like the prophetic
afflatus, is an 'Influx from God upon the minds of good men'; its
aim and design is to unfold 'the Way and Method of uniting
humane nature to Divinity'.[3] The 'Law' of the ancient Jews aimed

1. See p. 252.
2. Smith's *Discourses*, p. 145.   3. ibid., pp. 278–9.

at the same result, but only in a 'Typical or Emblematical way'. In instituting the Old Covenant God himself was allegorizing or 'shadowing forth' the truths later to be fully revealed. Christians may be, and, alas, constantly are, as 'legal' as the Jews when they rely upon their 'Atonement', or their 'Justification', as an *external* principle needing no translation into the terms of spiritual psychology. The gospel is not a body of doctrines, but a saving influx moulding the heart towards the divine likeness and quickening a godlike life within. We must not count upon being 'Elect', while neglecting the 'Real and Vital Emanations' of God upon us.

It is not all our strong Dreams of being in favour with Heaven that fills our hungry souls ere the more with it: It is not a pertinacious Imagination of our Names being enrolled in the Book of life, or of the Debt-books of Heaven being crossed, *or of Christ being ours, while we find him not living within us, or of the washing away of our sins in his bloud, while the foul and filthy stains thereof are deeply sunk in our own Souls.* . . . And a meer Conceit or Opinion as it makes us never the *better in reality within our selves*, so it cannot render us ere the more acceptable to *God who judges of all things as they are.*[1]

It must not be supposed that Smith tries to substitute the 'Jesus of history' for the Christ of theology. It is rather that the person of Christ represents to him a 'type' of the union of the divine and human natures, and an earnest of what God would further do for believers. Sometimes, indeed, he uses language which betrays, less in words than in tone, how far he has moved away from the formulae of orthodox Christology. He concludes his Discourse *Of Legal Righteousness and the Righteousness of Faith*, for instance, by showing how '*the whole business and Undertaking of Christ is eminently available* both to give relief and ease to our Minds and Hearts, and also to encourage us to Godliness or a Godlike righteousness';[2] and stating that it is 'very advantageous', 'highly accommodate', and 'very agreeable every way and upon all accounts' that there should be such a Mediator. The whole tendency and scope of Smith's teaching, and his own conception of its relation to the needs and problems of his own age, may be summed up in this passage which he himself quotes from Plutarch:

1. Smith, op. cit., p. 320 (my italics). 2. ibid., p. 335.

God hath now taken away from his Oracles Poetrie, and the variety of dialect, and circumlocution, and obscuritie; and hath so ordered them to speak to those that consult them, as the Laws doe to the Cities under their subjection, and Kings to their people, and Masters to their Scholars, *in the most intelligible and persuasive language.*[1]

The Metaphysical Teaching of the Platonists

RALPH CUDWORTH

No account of what was considered 'real' in the seventeenth century would be complete without some mention of the metaphysical teaching of the Platonists, which is to be found mainly in the works of Ralph Cudworth and Henry More. We have already given some hint of what in John Smith's world counted as most real, and the general agreement between these thinkers on first principles was such that quite a brief summary will perhaps serve our purpose sufficiently here. It will be recalled that the starting-point of the Cambridge philosophers was opposition to Hobbes. To Hobbes, as we have seen, the only view consistent with modern enlightenment was one which allowed reality to 'body' alone. The Cambridge school, on the other hand, inspired by the wish to save the religious world-view from what they justifiably felt to be hostile doctrine, made it their concern to criticize the assumptions of Hobbes's materialism, and to show that it failed to give a complete account of reality. To this end they fused the testimony of Plato and Descartes with their own spiritual intuitions and those of spiritually minded men of all times into an impressive affirmation of the reality of God and of the soul. Disputes of this kind about ultimate reality, in spite of the elaborate ratiocination and learning displayed on both sides, seem to be reducible after all to a straight contest between one affirmation and its opposite. Hobbes affirmed the reality of 'body', Cudworth and More of 'spirit'. Each disputant proclaims the primacy of what seems most real to himself.

1. Smith, op. cit., p. 257 (my italics).

In his quest for reality Cudworth feels that he will not have discovered what he seeks until he has found that which is 'self-existent', not dependent for its reality upon anything else. This principle, for him, is God; and conversely the root of all atheism consists in 'making senseless matter the only self-existent thing, and the original of all things'.[1] 'The true and genuine idea of God in general is this, A perfect conscious understanding being (or mind) existing of itself from eternity, and the cause of all other things.' The point at issue, as Cudworth sees it, is whether Mind is secondary and derivative, 'the youngest and most creaturely thing in the world', or whether it is not rather 'senior to the world, and the architect thereof'.[2] For the atheist-materialist, Mind is

but a mere whiffling, evanid, and fantastic thing; so that the most absolutely perfect of all things in the universe is grave, solid, and substantial senseless matter.

– a view which to Cudworth is simply inconceivable. This recognition of Mind as senior to the world involves also the recognition of thought or soul in man as a real substance not dependent upon body. This standpoint enables Cudworth to detect what was incomplete in Hobbes's theory of knowledge. His point is that even if the processes of perception can be analysed into motions in matter, our *awareness* of those motions has still to be accounted for. Every 'seeming' may have behind it a certain configuration of material particles, but that does not alter the fact that only in a certain setting – namely, in a conscious being – do these configurations generate 'seemings'. Some new element must then be present here, 'to' which there can be such a thing as a 'seeming'. What is this element? It will not do to dismiss the 'seemings' as 'mere apparitions', phantasms, while conceding 'reality' only to the configurations. The seemings (i.e. phenomena of consciousness) are amongst the events in *rerum natura*; what possible ground, then, can there be for denying to them, or at any rate to that which is aware of them, reality save an atheistic unwillingness to admit the existence of soul?

1. *True Intellectual System*, Vol. I, p. 321 (Tegg, 1845).
2. ibid., Vol. III, pp. 60 and 420.

A modern atheistic pretender to wit hath publicly owned this same conclusion, that 'mind is nothing but local motion in the organic parts of man's
body'. These men have been sometimes indeed a little troubled with the
fancy, apparition or seeming of cogitation – that is, the consciousness of it,
as knowing not well what to make thereof; but then they put it off again,
and satisfy themselves worshipfully with this, that fancy is but fancy, but
the reality of cogitation nothing but local motion; *as if there were not as much
reality in fancy and consciousness as there is in local motion.* That which inclined
these men so much to this opinion was only because they were sensible and
aware of this, that *if there were any other action besides local motion admitted,
there must needs be some substance acknowledged besides body.*[1]

Cudworth develops his theory into a denial of the passivity of the
mind in the act of perception and an assertion of our freedom in
Volition. Human Knowledge is 'a thing independent upon singular
bodies, or proleptical to them, and in the order of nature before
them'; it is 'not a mere passion from sensible things'.[2] If Knowledge
were merely the inevitable response of one group of particles to
a stimulus from another group,

then would everything that suffered and reacted motion, especially polite
bodies, as looking-glasses, have something both of sense and understanding
in them. It is plain, that there comes nothing to us from bodies without us,
but only local motion and pressure. Neither is sense itself the mere passion of
these motions, but the perception of their passions in a way of fancy. But
sensible things themselves (as for example light and colours) are not known
or understood either by the passion or fancy of sense, nor by anything
merely foreign or adventitious, but by intelligible ideas exerted from the
mind itself, that is, by something native and domestic to it: nothing being
more true than this of Boetius, that *omne, quod scitur, non ex sua sed ex com-
prehendentium natura, vi, et facultate cognoscitur.*[3]

And if sensation, although having its origin in material motions, yet
cannot be *defined* as the mere passive reception of those motions, but
involves 'a perception of that passion' and therefore a percipient
entity, still less can 'mental conception' be attributed to the motion

1. *True Intellectual System*, Vol. III, p. 418 (my italics).
2. ibid., Vol. III, pp. 64–5.
3. ibid., Vol. III, p. 62.

of external bodies (Cudworth means, I take it, what he calls our 'universal and abstract ideas of the intelligible natures or essences of things'). And least of all can our volitions be so determined, 'there being plainly here something ἐφ'ἡμῖν "in our own power" (by means whereof we become a principle of actions, and accordingly deserving commendation, or blame), that is, something of self-activity'.

The affirmations here imperfectly summarized may be said to be the corner-stones upon which that vast and unwieldy fabric, the *True Intellectual System of the Universe*, was built; it was by their means that he felt he could refute atheism, materialism, and determinism. Into the merits of his refutation it is not our purpose to go; indeed metaphysical beliefs, having their roots in the emotions, are probably incapable of proof or disproof. All we can say is that Cudworth showed with considerable acumen what metaphysical formulae were the necessary intellectual counterpart of a set of feelings opposed to Hobbes's. The Cambridge Platonists were contemplative, mystically-minded men to whom the realm of essence was more real than the material world. Their philosophy was a rationalization of this way of life. One further aspect of Cudworth's teaching, however, deserves to be dwelt upon for a moment because of its bearing upon the theory of poetry. It will doubtless have occurred to readers of Cudworth that in his account of knowledge we have some of the materials for a theory of the 'imagination' akin to Coleridge's. The view that there is 'as much reality in fancy and consciousness as in local motion' involves the greater part of what Coleridge, in the philosophical chapters of the *Biographia Literaria* and elsewhere, was labouring to demonstrate. What was chiefly needed before a theory of the imagination satisfactory to poets could be evolved, and what was lacking for the most part until Coleridge and Wordsworth, was precisely such a confidence as Cudworth's in the *reality* of the mind's images. As we have suggested, intellectual conditions in the seventeenth and eighteenth centuries on the whole discounted as fictional all mental shapings other than the 'clear and distinct ideas' of mathematics and of 'philosophy'. But if, not only every process of abstract thought, but every *perception* contained some element contributed by the mind, if the mind was constitutive in some degree of reality, then the way was clear for a theory which could give the highest possible truth-value to the products of the shaping power. Cudworth, of course, makes no such application of his theory. There was no compelling reason, in his time, why any lofty theory of the creative imagination should be produced; on the contrary, as we have seen, there were the strongest philosophic grounds for regarding the works of the imagination as 'gross dew upon the pure Glass of our Understandings'.[1] At best the imagination could be made to serve the understanding by deliberately using it, after the manner of the prophets, to produce what Coleridge, defining 'allegory', called 'the translation of abstract notions into a picture-language'. The philosophical poems of Henry More were the outcome of a conscious attempt to produce poetry on these principles, and may be taken as a comment on the usefulness, for poetry, of such a theory. The fact is, that Cudworth and More, although they were probably better equipped theoretically to vindicate the imagination than any of the moderns before the Italian critics of the eighteenth century, were simply not poets or critics, but moralists and religious philosophers. What they therefore wanted was a theory to support their belief in the self-existence and autonomy of the soul. Thus no real succour for the dwindling forces of poetry was forthcoming from this, the most likely quarter in the seventeenth century; rather, on the whole, the reverse. Many far-reaching changes had to take place in the intellectual climate before there would come a theoretic justification of the power which could cast 'modifying colours' over the 'inanimate cold world', the 'universe of death', which science had substituted for

> That which moves with light and life informed,
> Actual, divine, and true.[2]

We know, of course, that Coleridge studied and found much to admire in the Cambridge Platonists;[3] and I may be permitted,

1. See above, pp. 130 and 138-9.   2. Wordsworth, *Prelude*, XIV, 160.
3. Cf. his remarks on Cudworth, *Omniana*, No. 123.

perhaps, to illustrate and conclude these remarks by placing side by side a passage from Cudworth and one from Wordsworth:

Knowledge and understanding is not a mere passion from the thing known, existing without the knower, because to know and understand, as Anaxagoras of old determined, is κρατειν, to 'master' and 'conquer' the thing known, and consequently not merely to suffer from it, or passively to lie under it, this being κραταισθαι, to be 'mastered' or 'conquered' by it.[1]

> Not prostrate, overborne, as if the mind
> Herself were nothing, a mere pensioner
> On outward forms – did we in presence stand
> Of that magnificent region. On the front
> Of this whole Song is written that my heart
> Must, in such Temple, needs have offer'd up
> A different worship.[2]

HENRY MORE

With Henry More, as with Cudworth, the existence of the spiritual world was the first of certainties, and most of his works are designed to prove its reality. More was the most mystical of the Cambridge Platonists; with him the reality of 'spirit' was more than an intellectual conviction, it was an experience. As with Coleridge, a sense of the divine presence interpenetrating all things seems to have been inborn in him, and he was conscious of it very early in his life. He speaks of 'that exceeding hail and entire sense of God which nature herself had planted deeply in me', and declares that his mind 'was enlightened with a sense of the noblest theories in the morning of his days'.[3] So little of earth was there in his make-up that his very body (if we are to believe him) gave forth a flower-like fragrance. One can fancy him like one of the angelic beings described by himself, whose bodies are ethereal vehicles for the spirit that

---

1. op. cit., Vol. III, p. 432.   2. *Prelude*, VI, 736.
3. Quoted by Tulloch, *Rational Theology and Christian Philosophy, etc.*, Vol. II, p. 308.

informs them. He can discourse with the familiarity of Milton's affable archangel, only at much greater length, on the affairs of the supramundane world. As a youth he was possessed, like Donne and Milton, with a 'mighty and almost immoderate thirst after Knowledge'. But after ransacking the philosophies he found himself unsatisfied and uncertain of his bearings, and remained in this condition, apparently, for three or four years. Upon this 'dark night of the soul' there broke, then, the light of the new spiritual realization to which I have already referred.[1] It came to him that the road to divine knowledge lay not through 'such an eagerness and intentness in the reading of authors and contemplating of things', but through the purgation of the mind from all sorts of vices whatsoever. This realization allayed his 'insatiable desire and thirst after the knowledge of things' and awoke in him an impulse towards the inward discipline which is the condition of spiritual vision. More's 'dying into life' was also accompanied by the sense that the will of the ordinary self must be extinguished, so that the divine will might be all in all. He had been guided to this wisdom by the reading of the Platonists, especially Plotinus, who insists always that vision springs from ethical purification: 'if you have been this, you have seen this'. 'I was fully convinced', says More, 'that true holiness was the only safe entrance into divine knowledge'.[2] Furthermore,

When this inordinate Desire after the Knowledge of things was thus allay'd in me, and I aspir'd after nothing but this sole Purity and Simplicity of Mind, there shone in upon me daily a greater Assurance than ever I could have expected, even of those things which before I had the greatest Desire to Know.[3]

From this one impulse, which taught him more than all the sages could, all the work of his life took its origin and its specific direction. It is important, in trying to follow him through his many elaborate arguments in defence of 'spirit', to remember that beneath all his reasonings, and supporting them, lay a certainty born of mystical experience. The experience was the determinant, the

1. See above, p. 129.   2. Tulloch, op. cit., p. 312.
3. Ward's *Life of More*, quoted Bullough, op. cit., p. 35.

philosophy was its rationalization; and in saying this one is virtually absolving posterity from the onus of reading the philosophy. Experience is always interesting and more or less communicable, as the permanence of great poetry shows; but the rationalizations of one age generally mean little to later centuries. Nevertheless, since our present concern is with the workings of the seventeenth-century mind in its efforts to define the most 'real', I will give a short account of some of More's methods of procedure.

Beginning life, then, with his interpretation of existence unalterably fixed by his emotional experience, More was at once confronted with the two main philosophical systems of his own time, those of Hobbes and Descartes. His repugnance for Hobbism may be guessed, and indeed he clearly regarded himself as the champion of all vital truth against Hobbes's materialism and its dire consequences. Nothing, he felt, was of more urgent importance than 'to root out this sullen conceit' of Hobbes, 'that the very Notion of a Spirit or Substance Immaterial is a perfect Incompossibility and pure Nonsense'. For the implications of this view, as he clearly saw, were

That it is impossible that there should be any God, or Soul, or Angel, Good or Bad; or any Immortality or Life to come. That there is no religion, no Piety nor Impiety, no Vertue nor Vice, Justice nor Injustice, but what it pleases him that has the longest Sword to call so. That there is no Freedome of Will, nor consequently any Rational remorse of Conscience in any Being whatsoever, but that all that is, is nothing but *Matter* and *Corporeal Motion*; and that therefore every trace of man's life is as *necessary* as the tracts of Lightning and the fallings of Thunder; the blind *impetus* of the *Matter* breaking through or being stopt every where, with as certain and determinate *necessity* as the course of a Torrent after mighty storms and showers of Rain.[1]

In his *Immortality of the Soul* he places Hobbes, 'that confident exploder of *Immaterial Substances* out of the world', as it were in the witness-box by quoting eight of his clearest statements for the sole reality of body, and then proceeds to refute him point by point. We shall understand his position best, perhaps, by considering what he

1. *Immortality of the Soul*, Ch. 9 (in F. I. Mackinnon, *The Philosophical Writings of Henry More*, pp. 86–7).

took to be the *True Notion of a Spirit*.[1] In this treatise, which belongs to his last period, we find him in opposition to Descartes as well as to Hobbes. More had formerly been one of the earliest transmitters of Cartesian ideas to England, and had corresponded with Descartes himself (in 1648) in a vein of flamboyant compliment conceivable only in the seventeenth century, when eminent men in the various European countries could salute each other like kings across sea and frontier, and over the heads of the uninstructed. What had especially attracted him in Descartes, apart from the precision and charm of all his work, was his clear affirmation of the existence of the soul and of God as the fundamental certainties. Here, he felt, was the great, the incomparable philosopher of the modern age, who could not only explain the hidden workings of nature but who could do it without falling, like Hobbes, into materialism. A theory of the world which accepted the last results of science, but which yet confirmed the metaphysics of Platonism and Christianity: what more could be desired? Gradually, however, More's youthful enthusiasm for Descartes, like Coleridge's for Hartley, gave way to a misgiving that there was a fundamental cleavage between them; and Descartes, to whom he had written in 1648 that 'All the great leaders of philosophy who have ever existed, or who may exist, are pygmies in comparison with your transcendent genius',[2] at length became for him 'that pleasant Wit *Renatus des Cartes*, who by his jocular *Metaphysical Meditations* has so luxated and distorted the rational faculties of some otherwise sober and quick-witted persons'.[3] This remarkable change was brought about by the realization that Descartes did not teach the 'True Notion of a Spirit'; that his conception of 'soul', that is, was not 'true' to More's own experience. More's technique for expressing his divergence from Descartes was strictly confined by the contemporary modes of thought, but he seems nevertheless to be feeling after and endeavouring to expose

1. The treatise so headed, which was a translation of part of More's *Enchiridion Metaphysicum* (1671), was appended to Pt 1 of Glanvill's *Sadducismus Triumphatus* (1681). The references here are to the 1700 edition of the *Sadducismus*.

2. Tulloch, op. cit., Vol. II, p. 369.   3. *True Notion of a Spirit*, p. 2.

that very quality in Cartesianism which, as I have suggested above,[1] made it ultimately a force hostile to poetry and to religion. He singles out for attack Descartes' definition of the soul as a *res cogitans*, a thinking substance, having no extension in space. For one who, though affirming the reality of spirit, yet denies it 'extension' or location in space, More coins the term 'Nullibist'. To say that a thing is, and yet is nowhere, seems to him dangerous nonsense. He agrees with the Nullibists that 'whatever real Being there is that is somewhere, is also extended', but differs in believing that the soul, which his adversaries agree to be real, not only is, but is *somewhere*, that is, occupies space. To strip spirit of all attributes save that of thought is, he fears, to reduce it to a mere abstraction. The Cartesians have wrongly assumed that because we can conceive the soul merely as cogitation, therefore it has no other conceivable attributes, such as location. He points out that the mind can conceive many things in abstraction from many of their attributes, and urges that

from the precision of our thoughts to infer the real precision or separation of the things themselves is a very putid and puerile sophism.[2]

The view that the Mind is not 'in space' seems to More to imply that 'the Mind, in so far as it is conceived to be an *Incorporeal Substance*, is to be exterminated out of the Universe, as a useless figment and Chimaera.'

Such authority had the notion of 'Extension', in the seventeenth century, as the essential attribute of the admittedly 'real' (matter), that unless one could attribute extension to a substance, that substance was in danger of evaporating into nothingness. This was More's fear for 'spirit'; Descartes by affirming spirit as a mere abstraction was really, in spite of all appearances to the contrary, beginning upon the slippery slope towards materialism and atheism. It was safer, in More's opinion, to admit frankly that extension is a necessary attribute of all that exists, and to demonstrate, further, that spirit, as a real being, must be extended also. He was anxious to claim extension for spirit

1. pp. 82 ff.   2. *True Notion of a Spirit*, op. cit., p. 11.

that it may be conceived to be some real Being and true Substance, and not a vain Figment, such as is everything that has no Amplitude and is in no sort extended.[1]

It is a queer situation: More, the champion of 'spirit', appears, at least at first sight, to be paying unconscious tribute to the sovereignty of 'matter', for he can only defend the reality of spirit by endowing it with extension, which was supposed to be the peculiar and essential attribute of matter. He attempts to avoid the implications of this in two ways. First he denies that extension is the formal principle of matter, and substitutes for it 'impenetrability'; spirit, on the other hand, is penetrable. Secondly, the property of 'divisibility', which was agreed to be inseparable from extended matter, does not belong to extended spirit. The extension of spirit is true extension, and yet it is different from material extension; it is what he calls 'metaphysical extension', a notion which becomes little clearer when he describes it as a 'fourth dimension'[2] or 'essential spissitude'. Spirit, it seems, is to have extension so that it may be deemed as real as matter, but it must have it without any of the awkward conditions which attend upon material extension; it must be penetrable and 'indiscerpible'. More retorts the charge of 'corpority' upon his opponents; they cannot conceive of extension apart from matter because they wrongly hold that whatever is extended is the object of imagination, not of intellect. The fact is, he continues, in a characteristic manner of philosophic invective, that they are suffering from that very 'materious disease' of which I was accusing More himself a moment ago:

their Imagination is not sufficiently defecated and depurated from the filth and unclean tinctures of corpority; their mind is so illaqueated and lime-twigged, as it were, with the Ideas and Properties of corporeal things,[3]

that they mix up metaphysical with physical extension. Metaphysical extension, then, is the idea of extension contemplated by the intellect in abstraction from 'corporeal affections'. In trying to substantiate this conception More frequently appeals for proof to the

1. *True Notion of a Spirit*, op. cit., p. 41.
2. op. cit., p. 32. 3. op. cit., p. 30.

idea of 'infinite extension' which, he says, is imprinted on our intellects (not our *imaginations*) so that we cannot think it away. He asks his readers to refer to the 'internal sense' of their minds, and see whether they can fail to conceive of a certain infinite, immovable extension, having necessary, actual existence – the equivalent, I take it, of infinite space – and of themselves as in this. The conception of infinite space seems to him to be an example of extension conceived without the attributes of matter, and hence to be a proof of his proposition. As is well known, this infinite extension or space became with More, by a very natural analogy, an attribute of God, the Infinite Spirit. In thus making space the divine ground of the universe he was followed by Locke and Newton.[1]

More's arguments can perhaps best be viewed, from our present point of view, as an endeavour to reunite matter and spirit, which the rigid logic of Descartes had left in unbridgeable opposition, and to give greater 'body', or actuality, to both conceptions, which in Cartesianism were too nakedly abstract. More wants his 'spirit' to be more than abstract 'cogitation'; he will have it to be activity, and the activity must be *there where* it is at work, penetrating and moving matter.

More had thus demonstrated to his own satisfaction that the notion of a spirit contained no inherent contradiction of absurdity. His further proofs, from reason, of the actual existence of spirit, as a substance distinct from matter – proofs from the necessary existence of God, from the incapacity of matter to think, move, or organize itself, and so forth – follow the usual lines, and need not be recapitulated here. But there was a further class of proofs on which he placed increasing reliance in his later years, the 'proofs' from testimonies of apparitions and witchcraft. In his treatise on the *Immortality of the Soul* he had spoken of the 'pre-eminence of the arguments drawn from reason above those from story'. But later he appears to have felt that the increase of infidelity made well-attested stories of witches and apparitions especially requisite, since the sceptics and worldlings who denied 'spirit' were still afraid of 'ghosts', and their 'dull souls', unable to rise to rational conviction,

1. Cf. Mackinnon, op. cit., pp. 293–4.

might thereby be 'rubbed and awakened with a suspicion, at least, if not assurance, that there are other intelligent beings besides these that are clad in heavy earth and clay'.[1] More includes evidence of this kind in several of his works, devoting to it, for instance, the whole of Book III even of his early *Antidote against Atheism* (1652). For More

> Millions of spiritual creatures walk the earth,[2]

and ascend upwards, in unbroken hierarchical degrees, through the air to heaven. It was typical of the seventeenth-century situation that this pilgrim of the skies should welcome blasts from Hell as 'evidence' for the reality of the heavenly spirit-world in which he was so entirely at his ease; that this Cambridge rationalist, after proving his faith in the language of loftiest metaphysics, should proceed to buttress it by stories of 'Coskinomancy', of 'Margaret Warine discharged upon an Oake at a Thunder-clap', or of the 'vomiting of Cloth stuck with Pins, Nails, and Needles, as also Glass, Iron, and Haire, by Wierus his Patients'. The fact is that in appealing to demonology More, like Browne and Glanvill, was tapping a reservoir of traditional supernatural belief which lay deeper in the national consciousness than Christianity itself, and deeper, certainly, than the new ice-crust of rationalism which now covered it. Christianity, as is well known, had not abolished the older divinities, it had merely deposed and demonized them; and Protestantism, aiming at the purification of Christianity from the 'pagan' accretions of the Middle Ages, had produced at first not a diminished but a greatly heightened Satan-consciousness, so that the later sixteenth and earlier seventeenth centuries, when witch-burnings reached their maximum, were Satan's palmiest time in England. By the time of More, it is true, this Puritan horror of the powers of darkness, which had persecuted without pity much that had been tolerated in the less self-conscious pre-Reformation days, had greatly weakened, under 'philosophic' influences. But primitive picture-thinking is not destroyed at a blow, and the persistent if furtive acknowledgement of things undreamed of in the 'new

1. Tulloch, op. cit., Vol. II, p. 390. 2. *Paradise Lost*, IV, 677.

philosophy' was now unexpectedly available as a reinforcement to the philosophic defence of the faith. It may be, one may now conjecture, that in making the most of this crude material the defenders of religion were guided by a sound instinct. They may have obscurely felt, though they could not have realized or admitted it, that the ancient springs of popular demonology were also those of religion itself, and that in the emotion of the supernatural, however evoked, they had a surer foundation for faith than all the 'proofs' of philosophic theism.[1]

In this side of his work More is closely associated with his friend Joseph Glanvill, and as Glanvill is in more ways than one a significant figure for our present purposes, I shall include what remains to be said on this topic in the next chapter, which is devoted to him.

1. Cf. above, pp. 55–6.

CHAPTER 9

Joseph Glanvill

GLANVILL is, of course, best known as the source of Matthew
Arnold's Scholar Gypsy, but anyone who assumed from the extract
printed at the head of that poem that Glanvill's works were a mere
storehouse of 'quaint' lore would be greatly mistaken. He is better
represented by his admirable phrase 'climates of opinions',[1] which
has been put into currency of late by Professor Whitehead. Glanvill
was, in fact, a typical 'modern churchman' of the Restoration
period, a Fellow of the Royal Society, interested in every up-to-
date theory and discovery, an ardent upholder of 'modern' versus
'ancient', and especially concerned, as befitted his profession, to
demonstrate 'the agreement of reason and faith', and to explain
how religious the 'science' of the Royal Society really was. Though
not a member of the Cambridge group, he was a great admirer of
the Platonists, especially of Henry More; and Wood tells us that he
regretted having been at Oxford instead of at Cambridge where, at
any rate in his undergraduate days (he entered Exeter College in
1652), the 'new philosophy' was held in greater esteem. But Glanvill's work is not all of one piece; he is definitely a 'transitional',
and serves admirably to link the ages of Browne and Boyle. He
might be termed 'Browne with a difference', and the difference is
chiefly due to the fact that although he predeceased Browne he was
born a generation later, and was consequently much affected by the
Post-Restoration climate. He was not an original thinker, but he
could state with admirable clearness, and with real charm of style,
the views with which he most sympathized; and it is perhaps for
this very reason that his development reflects in miniature the transi-
tion from the earlier to the later phases of the century. In his first
work, *The Vanity of Dogmatizing* (1661), he shows something of

1. Cf. below, p. 175.

Browne's peculiar mental poise, and in occasional coruscations echoes the very quality of the Brownese wit more closely than any other writer I know. In his later work, on the other hand, in such an essay as *The Agreement of Reason and Religion*,[1] for example, he has strained out all 'metaphysical' qualities (doubtless remembering what was expected of Fellows of the Royal Society),[2] and writes the sober, transparent prose of Sprat, Boyle, or Tillotson. A few examples will not be out of place here, for they illustrate one aspect of the process which it is the main purpose of this book to study.

From *The Vanity of Dogmatizing*:

(*a*) Nature, that was veil'd to *Aristotle*, hath not yet uncover'd, in almost two thousand years. What he sought on the other side of *Euripus*, we must not look for on this side *Immortality*. In easie disquisitions we are often left to the uncertainty of a guess: yea after we have triumph'd in a supposed Ευρηκα; a new-sprung difficulty marrs our Ovations; and exposeth us to the Torments of a disappointment: so that even the great *Master of Dogmatists* himself concludes the scene with an *Anxius vixi, Dubius morior*.[3]

(*b*) For our initial age is like the melted wax to the prepared seal, capable of any impression from the documents of our Teachers. The *half-moon* or *Cross*, are indifferent to its reception; and we may with equal facility write on this *rasa Tabula*, Turk, or Christian. We came into the world like the unformed *Cub*, 'tis *education* is our *Plastick*: we are baptized into our opinions by our Juvenile nurture, and our growing years confirm those unexamined Principles.[4]

I have kept the best, though shortest, example for the last:

(*c*) The Sages of old live again in us; and in opinions there is a Metempsychosis. We are our reanimated Ancestours, and antedate their *Resurrection*.[5]

The derivative quality of this writing would be clear enough without the reference to the 'ingenious Dr Browne' which Glanvill makes in this treatise,[6] and without the use of the Brownese word

---

1. Essay 5 in *Essays on Several Important Subjects*, 1676.
2. See below, pp. 190 ff. 3. p. 66 (1661 edition).
4. p. 128. 5. p. 138.
6. p. 204.

'digladiations',[1] which is also to be found here. Glanvill has caught something of Browne's attitude to his subjects, his play of fancy steadied by wistfulness and pity, and has reproduced some of his devices of style, the progression by allusion, image, and antithesis, the varied repetition, the intellectual somersault, the flash of paradox. But Glanvill's is a thinner medium, and if you surrender to it for a while, allowing yourself to pretend that it is Browne's, you will soon sink. His sallies are less native to his way of thought, they are the conscious flourishes of a mind less molten, more set in the 'philosophic' mould. Ten years later he was writing like this (one example should suffice):

[Reason, he is saying, supports Religion by showing] that the Divine Nature is infinite, and our Conceptions very shallow and finite; that 'tis therefore very unreasonable in us to indeavour to pry into the Secrets of his Being, and Actions; and to think that we can measure and comprehend them: That we know not the Essence and Ways of acting of the most ordinary and obvious Things of Nature, and therefore must not expect thoroughly to understand the deeper Things of God; That God hath *revealed* those Holy Mysteries to us; and that 'tis the highest *reason* in the world to believe, that *what he saith is true, though we do not know how these things are.*[2]

There, one feels, speaks the Fellow of the Royal Society, the Chaplain-in-Ordinary to Charles II, and Rector of Bath Abbey.

In order to explain how it was that this rational divine and ardent modernist held the views that he did about witchcraft, I propose now to consider two of his most characteristic works, *The Vanity of Dogmatizing* and *Sadducismus Triumphatus*. The first of these, his earliest work, is also the most interesting, both for the richness of its prose style and the completeness with which it conveys Glanvill's outlook. It is also valuable as a summary of the main topics which were being discussed, in 'philosophic' circles, in the middle of the century, and as revealing the processes by which, it was hoped, 'true' views of nature could be substituted for vain ones. It is a strangely double-faced book, for in spite of its sedulously maintained tone of scepticism it is, in essence, a paean of triumph

1. The word is also to be found in Bacon (*Advancement of Learning*, IV, 6).
2. *Essays on Several Important Subjects*, V, p. II.

in celebration of the new philosophy. Purporting to humble us with the extent of our ignorance, it really congratulates us on our wonderful progress in knowledge. To the humility of Bacon and the scepticism of Descartes he adds the jubilation of a later age over the new world which the scientific meekness had inherited. Of course we know nothing; our faculties are prone to err: but consider what we have achieved by recognizing this fact! The main controversial aim of the book is an attack on the 'dogmatizing' of the scholastics and the ancients; it is against these that he urges the insignificance of our knowledge. Dogmatism is vain when it is a schoolman who dogmatizes; not so when it is Descartes. In spite of his reservations about the provisional nature of the Cartesian explanations, it is they alone that satisfy him. The book belongs, therefore, to the story of the rejection of scholasticism,[1] and in the battle of the books Glanvill is a redoubtable champion of Modern versus Ancient.

The Vanity of Dogmatizing

He opens his argument with the conjecture that Adam, in his primal innocence, must have known all that we now, in our 'decay and ruins', strive vainly to guess at. Prelapsarian Adam 'needed no spectacles'; neither did he need a 'Galileo's tube' to perceive the 'Celestial magnificence and bravery'. The real significance of these fancies lies in the two 'philosophic' principles by which Glanvill justifies them. The first of these is, that 'as far as the operation of nature reacheth, it works by corporeal instruments';[2] or, in other words, a purely physical or 'natural' account can be given of every occurrence in nature. Secondly:

Sense is made by motion, caus'd by bodily impression on the organ and continued to the brain, and centre of perception.

Hence where we fail to perceive the chain of causes behind a natural

1. Cf. Chapter 1 above.
2. Cf. Bacon's 'God worketh nothing in nature but by second causes' (*Advancement of Learning*, 1, 3).

event, this is simply due to failure of our bodily organs. Now Adam, as the 'medal of God', stamped with the divine image, must be supposed to have had perfect 'organs'; what we surmise or deduce, he could perceive by his senses alone. It was much discussed in the seventeenth century, for instance, how the loadstone attracted iron; and a mechanical explanation being necessary, it was imagined that it did this by 'Atomical Effluviums', by emitting, that is, a stream of material particles which enveloped the iron and dragged it towards the magnet. Adam, says Glanvill, could *see* with his own eyes whether or not this was indeed what occurred. 'Adam', in fact, becomes here a form of wish-fulfilment for the mechanico-material-ist; he sees and therefore knows what the philosopher is firmly persuaded of, but cannot demonstrate.

Leaving our Cartesian ancestor in the enjoyment of his philo-sophic Eden, Glanvill now changes these notes to tragic, and begins to catalogue the manifold ignorances of fallen humanity. It ill befits us to be dogmatic when we know nothing of the matters that con-cern us most – of the nature of the soul, to begin with. Whence comes it? Is it newly created for each new individual, or handed down by 'seminall traduction'? Then there are all the difficulties arising out of the Cartesian dualism;[1] the problem of how body and soul – distinct substances – the one extended in space, the other unextended ('no where', as More expressed it) and immaterial – could possibly cohere. The thought of this fundamental riddle moves Glanvill to one of his best-known utterances:

How the purer Spirit is united to this Clod, is a knot too hard for fallen Humanity to unty. . . . How should a thought be united to a marble-statue, or a sun-beam to a lump of clay! The freezing of the words in the air in the northern climes, is as conceivable, as this strange union. . . . And to hang weights on the wings of the winde seems far more intelligible.[2]

Nor do we know by what hidden mechanism the soul is able to move the body. We can construct imaginary material analogies to illustrate this: but, says Glanvill (the paradox warming his imagina-tion to the point of a Brownese scintillation), if we consider the soul

1. Cf. above, pp. 80 ff.   2. *Vanity of Dogmatizing*, p. 20.

under the notion of the ingenious Sir K. Digby as a pure *Mind and Knowledge*, or as the admir'd *Des-Cartes* expresses it, *une chose qui pense*, as a *thinking substance*; it will be as hard to apprehend as that an empty wish should remove Mountains: a supposition, which, if realized, would relieve *Sisyphus*.[1]

Nor are we helped by the theory of 'the most excellent *Cantabrigian* Philosopher' (Henry More), that the soul is an extended penetrable substance;[2] for if it penetrates all bodies 'without the least jog', how can it impart to them any motion? Similarly we are at a loss for a scientific theory of sensation (perception). We think we know that it is the soul that perceives, and that the body is only the transmitter of 'corporeal impressions'; at least we have for this view the authority of Aristotle, Plato, and above all 'that wonder of men, the Great *Des-Cartes*'. But

how the soule, by mutation made in matter, a substance of another kind, should be excited to action; and how bodily alterations and motions should concern it which is subject to neither; is a difficulty which confidence may triumph over sooner, then conquer.[3]

We are ignorant, too, of the inner mechanics of Memory. Glanvill passes in review the theories of Descartes, Sir Kenelm Digby, Aristotle, and Hobbes on this subject, and finds them all inconclusive. The theories of memory propounded by the seventeenth-century philosophers, and Glanvill's reasons for dissatisfaction with them, are indeed worthy of some notice in passing; for they illustrate the contemporary effort to explain all natural processes – even as in this instance, those of mind – by constructing an illustrative mental picture of the process on mechanical principles. Descartes, for instance, to whom Glanvill as usual gives a respectful hearing, conjectured that impressions left, as it were, tracks or channels behind them in the porous matter of the brain, and that when we perform an act of memory, the pineal gland radiates the animal spirits around

1. *Vanity of Dogmatizing*, p. 22. Compare this passage, in which the philosopher has the air of deliberately ornamenting his point with a fancy, with the more *organic* allusiveness of Browne's: 'Some graves will be opened before they be quite closed, and Lazarus be no wonder' (*Urn Burial*, Ch. 5).

2. See above, pp. 150 ff.   3. *Vanity of Dogmatizing*, p. 29.

until they find the track representing the relevant impression. The spirits at once flow into this track, which admits them more readily than any of the non-relevant tracks, and the pineal gland registers its satisfaction in a motion which the soul translates into the object sought for. Glanvill credits this theory (and that of Digby, which need not be retailed) with ingenuity, and admits that conjecture could hardly further go; he finds the explanation, however, less 'false' than 'unconceivable'. That is to say, you have only to try to elaborate this imaginary mechanical model of the mind still further to find it unworkable. How is it, for instance, that we have distinct and separate remembrance of objects whose images must, in fact, have originally passed through the *same* aperture in the brain? Moreover, how do the spirits infallibly find the right track? Amongst the myriads that there must be, would there not inevitably be others which would admit the spirits as readily as the appropriate ones? And surely these 'tracks' made in such soft matter as the brain would tend to be filled up by the pressure around them; or else 'the opening of other *vicine passages* might quickly obliterate any tracks of these: as the making of one hole in the yielding *mud*, defaces the print of another near it'.[1] In a word, by the time you have reduced the brain to a lump of jelly riddled with impossible millions of wormholes, your imaginary picture has ceased to seem credible or explanatory. Similarly with Hobbes's theory, to the effect that memory is 'decaying sense', that is, awareness of motions which were formerly impressed by objects upon the brain, and which continue there still, though less vigorously than when the object was present. To this Glanvill replies that the brain is not composed of the kind of matter that can retain vibratory motions for any length of time; it is, on the contrary, 'of such a clammy consistence, that it can no more retain it than a *Quagmire*'. Moreover, if each thing remembered were represented by a conserved motion in the brain, our memories would be stored 'with infinite variety of divers, yea contrary motions, which must needs interfere, thwart and obstruct one another: and there would be nothing within us, but *Ataxy* and disorder'.

1. *Vanity of Dogmatizing*, p. 35.

Passing from mind to body, Glanvill next observes that the organization and persistence of generic and specific forms in vegetables and animals are great mysteries. The suggestion that they are accidental is preposterous, neither has any satisfactory mechanical solution been found. But even what might be supposed the simpler problem of the composition and cohesion of inorganic bodies is unsolved. By what principle do the 'parts' of a body hold together? Here again we observe the effort to explain the problem by conceiving the inner structure of matter pictorially. Descartes has said that 'rest' is the cohesive principle; but if this be so, why are some things firm and others brittle? The thought of the absurd consequences of this theory provokes Glanvill to a passage of Brownese paradox:

if the *Union* of the *Parts* consist only in Rest; it would seem that a bagg of *dust* would be of as firm a consistence as that of *Marble* or *Adamant*: a Bar of *Iron* will be as easily broken as a Tobacco-pipe; and *Bajazet's* Cage had been but a sorry *Prison*.[1]

What of the suggestion that the material particles are to be imagined as grappling each other in an intricate tangle by 'hooks' or 'angulous involutions'? Well, but the 'hooks' themselves are further divisible into lesser hooks, and either we must picture a series of dwindling hooklets extending to infinity, or we must come at last to 'indivisibles' which are holding together by nothing but juxtaposition. As usual, however, after showing the weakness of all proposed mechanical solutions, Glanvill praises the illustrious Descartes, 'that miracle of men', for having given an account which, though imperfect, is yet 'the most ingenious and rational that *hath* or (it may be) *can* be given'. It is evident that although mechanical explanations have hitherto proved inadequate, it is along such lines that Glanvill looks for our nearest possible approach to truth. He freely admits, however, that it is a 'disease of our Intellectuals', one of the frailties incident to fallen humanity, that we can conceive nothing but by sense-analogies, or what he calls, in a phrase worth remembering, a 'return to material phantasms'.[2] It is only Nature's grosser

1. *Vanity of Dogmatizing*, p. 49.   2. ibid., p. 67.

ways of working which are sensible; her hidden machinery is for ever hidden, and all we can do is to 'imagine' it on the analogy of the perceptible. But even our senses themselves impose deceits upon us. Glanvill enumerates several examples in which motion is imperceptible, the grand instance being, of course, the apparent quiescence of the earth. Glanvill writes, it may be observed, as if few were yet convinced of the earth's motion; 'its assertion', he says, 'would be entertained with the hoot of the Rabble'. He is anxious to suspend his own judgement on the matter, though he is clearly swayed by the authority of the great wits such as 'Pythagoras, Des-Cartes, Copernicus, Galileo, More, Kepler, etc.', and thinks it 'no heresy' to believe in the earth's motion. Furthermore, we are prone to the error of 'translating the Idea of our Passions to things without us'. We make the familiar mistake of attributing secondary qualities to objects themselves, and imagine that the heat is 'in' the fire, the colour 'in' the flower, and so on.

The next class of errors which Glanvill deals with is the deceits and fallacies of our 'Imaginations', and it is important for our purpose to attend with some care to his observations on this vital topic. We have learnt to expect little mercy for the imagination from seventeenth-century writers, and it certainly gets no quarter from Glanvill. The age was too intent on separating 'truth' from 'error', and too convinced that truth resided in abstraction, to have much respect for the source of all fiction – the faculty that dealt in 'material phantasms'. As we have repeatedly seen, it was held to be precisely the mark of the philosophically and spiritually minded to be able to transcend the level at which phantasms seem to be real. Glanvill begins the attack at once by speaking of the 'evil conduct of our *Imaginations*, whose irregular strength and importunity doth almost perpetually abuse us', and proceeds to give a brief analysis of the soul's intellectual actions, so as to be able the better to expose the deceptiveness of that 'mysterious faculty'. (1) First, then, there is 'simple apprehension'. Simple apprehension of a present corporal object is called 'Sense'; of an absent object, Imagination. But if we would reach an apprehension of 'spirituals', we must 'denudate them of all material Phantasmes' so that they may become the object of our 'Intellects'. (2) Next comes the framing of propositions from 'simple intellections', whence springs our knowledge of distinctions and identities. When such a judgement of identity or distinction relates to material objects, it is made by the imagination; if otherwise, by the understanding. (3) Lastly, we have the connecting of propositions and deducing conclusions from them: this process is called Discourse, or Reason. Correct deductions are made when the essential principles of all discourse are employed (he mentions a few of the familiar axioms, e.g. *Impossibile est idem esse et non esse; Quodlibet est, vel non est*, etc.). But when the conclusion is deduced from 'mis-apprehended or ill-compounded phantasmes' we ascribe it to the Imagination. Imagination does not deceive us at the first stage since our senses always correctly inform us of the only truth within their scope, namely, that they are affected in such-and-such a manner. Our sight, which reports the 'crookedness' of a stick half under water, is correctly informing us of the true behaviour of light when passing through media of differing densities. It is at the second stage that imagination deceives, when we begin to judge that the phantasms are copies of realities, and hence to draw wrong inferences from them. We begin at this stage to mistake 'motions within the cranium' for 'exterior realities' – hence the 'Visions, Voyces, Revelations of the Enthusiast', or the delusions of 'hypochondriacal imaginants'. But it is in our reflections about spiritual matters that imagination so easily besets us. In his ensuing remarks about the soul and angels, Glanvill, in his anxiety to preserve their spirituality, declares boldly for what Henry More called 'nullibism':

That the *Soul* and *Angels* are devoid of *quantitative dimensions*, hath the suffrage of the most; and that they have nothing to do with grosser *locality*, is commonly opinion'd. But who is it, that retains not a great part of the imposture, by allowing them a *definitive Ubi*, which is still but *Imagination*? He that said, a *thousand* might dance on the *point of a Needle*, spake but grossly; and we may as well suppose them to have *wings*, as a proper *Ubi*.[1]

To be 'in a place' is incompatible with 'so depurate a Nature'. We

1. *Vanity of Dogmatizing*, p. 100.

do not ask 'where' a thought is, or 'where' Virtue is. Yet so strong is imagination, that we can only with great effort avoid mixing something of corporeity with our most abstracted contemplations. It is, of course, with reference to our conceptions of the Deity that this weakness becomes most serious. We ascribe 'Intellections, Volitions, Decrees, Purposes' and the like to 'that nature, which hath nothing in common with us, as being infinitely above us'. We may allowably use these and similar terms as figurative expressions, 'as himself in his Word is pleased to *low* himself to our capacities'; but to conceive of human faculties or affections as being really and formally in the Divine Essence is the 'Imposture of our *Phancies*'. Thus our very Reason itself, provided as it is with so much spurious material wherewith to discourse, is bound to be liable to error, indeed the 'Reason of the far greatest part of mankind, is but an aggregate of mistaken phantasms'. Even the 'highest and most improved parts of Rationality, are frequently caught in the entanglements of a tenacious Imagination'. Glanvill infers from this that we should not talk of Reason being opposed to Faith; the disharmony, if any, is only in the 'Phancy'; true Reason, which is the image of the divine wisdom, corrects the impious suggestions of imagination.

It is unnecessary to attend Glanvill so closely all through his catalogue of our errors, especially as we have already considered the kindred works of Bacon and Browne, whom Glanvill often follows. It will suffice merely to mention the 'praecipitancy of our Understandings'; the difficulty we find in all close application to the quest for truth; our propensity to judge 'feasibles' impossible, or to ascribe effects to wrong causes – particularly natural events to supernatural causes.[1] We are misled, too, by our affections: '*facile credimus quod volumus*'. That opinions and beliefs are often merely rationalizations of our instinctive preferences or aversions is a truth which Glanvill perceived with exceptional clearness for his time:

Congruity of Opinions, whether true or false, to our *natural constitution*, is one great incentive to their belief and reception: and in a sense too the *complexion* of the *mind*, as well as *manners*, follows the Temperament of the Body.[2]

1. That this should proceed from the author of *Sadducismus Triumphatus* is characteristic of the period.   2. *Vanity of Dogmatizing*, p. 121.

Moreover, 'opinions have their Climes and National diversities', and we can account in this way for the 'sensual expectations of the Mussel-men', the 'fopperies of the deluded Romanists', and other human aberrations, otherwise inexplicable. Custom and education fill us with prejudices and presuppositions, as we see from the tenacity with which men of other races and religions cling to their ridiculous delusions; and "tis to be feared, that Christianity itself by most, that have espoused it, is not held by any better tenure'. Interest, too, often fixes the colour of our belief, witness that Pope[1] whose saying it was, 'Quantum nobis lucri peperit illa fabula de Christo!'

We come now to that portion of the book in which Glanvill's controversial purpose declares itself, and to which all these sceptical arguments have been leading up, namely, the attack on 'peripateticism', and the corresponding eulogy of the Moderns. Amongst the irrational prejudices which generate false opinions, slavish reverence for ancient authority is one of the most pernicious. In our superstitious dread of going beyond the ancients, we 'come short of genuine Antiquity, Truth'. Like Montaigne, Glanvill urges that

'tis better to own a Judgement, tho' but with a curta supellex[2] of coherent notions; then a memory, like a Sepulchre, furnished with a load of broken and discarnate bones.[3]

Let us away with the pedantry of continual citations from 'authorities'; 'Authorities alone with me make no number, unless Evidence of Reason stand before them'. The peripatetic philosophy has acquired and retained an authority above all others; it has indeed so much absorbed our veneration that we have overlooked other and more fruitful schools of thought amongst the ancients themselves:

Thus the Aristotelian Philosophy hath prevailed; while the more excellent Hypotheses of Democritus and Epicurus have long lain buried under neglect and obloquy: and for ought I know might have slept for ever, had not the ingenuity of this age recall'd them from their Urne.[4]

1. I have not ascertained which Pope this was.
2. Scant equipment.   3. Vanity of Dogmatizing, p. 143.
4. ibid., p. 146 (cf. above, p. 14).

I have tried to explain (in Chapter 1) why the hypotheses of Democritus and Epicurus inevitably seemed 'more excellent' in the seventeenth century. The whole direction of interests and demands was then favourable to their revival, and we see Glanvill here unconsciously illustrating his own statement, just quoted, that 'Congruity of opinions, whether true or false, to our natural constitution, is one great incentive to their belief, and reception'. And as long as the 'Congruity' lasts, we may add, the hypothesis or opinion will be so persuasive as to be mistaken for fact. Beneath all his show of scepticism, Glanvill believed, I think, almost as firmly in the assumptions of the new philosophy as any scholastic dogmatist did in his own.

In attacking the Aristotelian tradition, Glanvill evidently writes as one who is expressing sentiments which he knows will find an echo in every heart, at any rate in his own circle and country. As we have seen, the repudiation of scholasticism is a constant refrain in the philosophical and scientific writers of the age. I need not recapitulate what has been suggested above (Chapter 1) as to why this was so generally felt to be necessary; it will be enough to indicate the quality of Glanvill's contribution to the cause. The philosophy of the schools, then, according to him, is 'insignificant' and 'dry', because it deals with words, 'creatures of the brain', not with 'things'. The concepts of modern science, on the other hand, such as 'matter', 'particle', 'space', 'location', 'extension', 'motion', are, it is to be noted, felt by Glanvill, as by his contemporaries, to be *things*, not 'creatures of the brain' – and this in spite of his special preoccupation with the weaknesses and limitations of knowledge. In their wordy 'digladiations' the schoolmen neglected 'the more profitable doctrines of the *Heavens, Meteors, Minerals, Animals*', as well as 'the indisputable Mathematicks, the only Science Heaven hath yet vouchsaf't Humanity'.[1] The complaint against Aristotle, as usual, is that he 'explains' nothing, but merely restates every problem in terms of 'qualities', 'sympathies', 'antipathies', 'gravity', and the like. Aristotle's explanations seem to veto further inquiry by saying

1. Cf. Hobbes: 'Geometry, which is the only science that it hath pleased God hitherto to bestow on mankind' (*Leviathan*, Ch. 4).

in a roundabout way, 'this is so because it is so': fire burns because it has the quality 'heat', the loadstone attracts by 'occult sympathy', a stone is seen because it emits a 'visible species', and so on. In this portion of his argument Glanvill echoes Hobbes, even at times striking out a phrase in which Hobbes and Browne jostle oddly together:

A Schoolman is the Ghost of the Stagirite, in a body of condensed Air: and *Thomas* but *Aristotle sainted*.[1]

He is with Bacon in his insistence that the Aristotelian philosophy is 'inept for New discoveries', and therefore serves for no 'use of life'. All arts and professions are capable of improvement, and

that there is an *America* of secrets, and unknown Peru of Nature, whose discovery would richly advance them, is more then conjecture.

As long as we stick to Aristotle,

we are not likely to reach the Treasures on the other side of the *Atlantick*: the directing of the World the way to which, is the noble end of true Philosophy.

The mere sense of the existence of 'the America and untravelled parts of Truth',[2] aptly symbolized for that age by the New World, filled the intellectual explorers of the seventeenth century with a matchless zest which appears in the animation and optimism of their writings.

Amongst all these complaints against scholasticism, which are common to so many of the Moderns of the century, Glanvill brings forward another which proves that he had grasped with unusual clearness what must now be demanded of a theory which should be felt to be really explanatory. Scholasticism, he says, left the world *'intellectually invisible'*,[3] whereas, as we have seen, the effort of Glanvill's time was precisely to *visualize* the hidden processes of Nature on the lines of a mechanical model. The schools speak of 'Celestial

1. *Vanity of Dogmatizing*, p. 152. Cf. Hobbes, 'the Papacy is no other than the "ghost" of the deceased "Roman Empire" sitting crowned upon the grave thereof'.
2. Browne's *Pseudodoxia epidemica*, Preface 'To the Reader'.
3. op. cit., p. 172.

influences, elemental combinations, active and passive principles',
and suchlike dry generalities, but leave us as ignorant as before of
just what we want to know, namely, the inner mechanism of
phenomena. The old phrases signified ignorance of all but the very
effects which called for explanation; the new theory, to be explanatory, must furnish intellectual diagrams which will make 'visible'
what the schools were content to leave hidden, or 'occult'. The
revival of the 'more excellent hypotheses of Democritus and
Epicurus', and the work of Galileo, had made it possible to picture
a great many phenomena as the result of the mechanical inter-
relations of atoms; and those that still resisted mechanical solution
would probably, it was hoped, some day succumb to it.

Yea, the most common *Phaenomena* can be neither known, nor improved,
without INSIGHT[1] into the more *hidden* frame. For *Nature* works by an *Invisible Hand* in all things.

In Fontenelle's *Pluralité des Mondes* (1686), a popular exposition of
Cartesianism, the same topic is treated of, but this time with the
refined insouciance and good breeding of the *honnête homme*. Here
the philosopher, who is represented as instilling the principles of
true philosophy into the willing ear of a fair Countess, makes use of
the following illustration:

[It has just been remarked that 'we see things quite otherwise than as
they are'.]
Upon this I fancy to myself, that Nature very much resembleth an Opera;
where you stand you do not see the Stage as really it is; but it is plac'd with
advantage and all the Wheels and Movements are hid, to make the Representation the more agreeable. ... An Engineer in the Pit is affected with
what doth not touch you. ... This Engineer then is like a Philosopher,
though the difficulty is greater on the Philosopher's part, the Machines of
the Theatre being nothing so curious as those of Nature, which disposeth her
Wheels and Springs so out of sight, that we have been long a guessing at the
movement of the Universe.

Let us suppose, says Fontenelle, that the opera is *Phaeton*, and that
several philosophers of various schools are sitting in the audience

1. *Vanity of Dogmatizing*, p. 180 (my capitals).

watching the protagonist ascending through the air in his chariot. The scholastically-inclined doctors would without doubt explain Phaeton's extraordinary movements as due to 'magnetic virtue', or the 'love' or 'affinity' of the chariot for the top of the theatre.

But now comes M. Descartes, with some of the Moderns, and they tell you Phaeton ascends because a greater weight than he descends; so that now we do not believe a body can move without it is push'd and forc'd by another body, and as it were drawn by Cords, so that nothing can rise or fall but by means of a Counterpoise. . . . I perceive, *said the Countess*, Philosophy is now become very Mechanical. So mechanical, *said I*, that I fear we shall quickly be asham'd of it; they will have the World to be in great, what a watch is in little; which is very regular, and depends only upon the just disposing of the several parts of the movement.[1]

Shaking the dust of the Schools off his feet, Glanvill now launches out in rapturous praise of the 'glorious Undertakers' of his own day, and allows his imagination to riot in prophetic visions of the wonders to come, many of which have since been realized, to an extent probably beyond his anticipation. He foretells not only aviation –

To them, that come after us, it may be as ordinary to buy a *pair of wings* to fly into remotest *Regions*; as now a pair of *Boots* to ride a *Journey*.

– but even 'wireless':

And to conferr at the distance of the *Indies* by *Sympathetick* conveyances, may be as usual, to future times, as to us in a *litterary* correspondence.[2]

We may see, too, deserts turned into paradise by irrigation: the 'restauration of gray hairs to Juvenility', and voyages to the 'Southern unknown Tracts', or even possibly to the moon. Could Glanvill have seen the whole future in his vision, one might guess that his naïve exultation at the opening of the scientific Pandora-

1. Translated by John Glanvill (apparently unrelated to Joseph Glanvill), 1688. The translation was republished by the Nonesuch Press in 1929. (Cf. motto to Chapter 1 above.)
2. *Vanity of Dogmatizing*, p. 182.

box would have been exceeded by the horrified astonishment with which he would have contemplated the world which actually possessed these and other 'marvels'. The existence of this strain of tense expectancy in the seventeenth-century consciousness must be taken count of if we would understand their notions of 'Truth'. A 'true' theory, at that time, was one which would add all this and more glory to the Kingdom of Man.

Glanvill concludes this section, much in the manner of Browne, by an obeisance to 'Divinity'. Though in Philosophy he is a 'seeker', and sceptical of authority, in Divinity he hopes to entertain no opinion less than sixteen hundred years old.

From this point onwards Glanvill's argument widens into a general condemnation of all philosophical arrogance or 'opinionative confidence', and we begin to see still more clearly that his scepticism is a double-edged weapon, as serviceable against the presumptuous modern as against the jejune scholastic. Or, we might say, he begins to reveal by what channels his scientific enlightenment is linked with 'credulity', and we are provided with one more illustration of the truth of Browne's remark that 'by acquainting our Reason how unable it is to display the visible and obvious effects of nature, it becomes more humble and submissive unto the subtleties of faith'.[1] Glanvill does not in this book work out all the implications of his argument, but he reveals the foundations on which his belief in witchcraft and apparitions rested. It makes one a little giddy to watch this convinced 'Modernist' mining away at the foundations of all certainty. He even anticipates Hume's critique on our ideas of 'causation',[2] urging that we cannot be certain that any one thing is the *cause* of another, since we are aware only of 'concomitances' – as the cock was who thought his crow produced the dawn. We must not judge Nature by the analogy of the mind, or judge that what seems impossible to us must necessarily be so in Nature. Nevertheless, it is to be observed that Glanvill here keeps the argument strictly within the region of the 'natural', and suggests explanations

1. *Religio medici*, I, sect. 10.
2. A point duly noted by Leslie Stephen, in his article on Glanvill in the *Dictionary of National Biography*.

on scientific lines for the rarities he mentions. It is at this point,[1] for instance, that the story of the Scholar Gypsy is introduced, its purpose being to demonstrate the telepathic power of the 'imagination'. The Scholar, on being rediscovered by some of his Oxford friends, undertakes to prove to them that the 'mystery' of the gypsies is not all imposture, and that he has mastered some part of their ancient wisdom. Placing them in a room of the inn where they have met, he retires to another part of the house, declaring that he will repeat their conversation to them correctly when he returns. He duly performs this, explaining to his astonished companions that he had done it by sheer exertion of his own mental energy, himself having 'dictated' the whole conversation to them by what we should now call telepathy. It would be 'vain dogmatism' to reject such a 'well-authenticated' story as this because of its seeming 'impossibility'. Glanvill is anxious to show that his own acceptance of the marvel is not due to vulgar credulity, but is based on the conviction that a 'philosophic' explanation for such things probably exists, if we are not too prejudiced to look for it. He accordingly propounds two hypotheses to remove what appears to be the element of 'impossibility' in the Scholar Gypsy's performance, namely the apparent action at a distance. One is 'that of a *Mundane* Soul, lately reviv'd by that incomparable *Platonist* and *Cartesian, Dr H. More*', which supposes a 'spirit of Nature' of *anima mundi* as the medium of transmission; the other – 'if any would rather have a *Mechanical* account' – is that 'the Aether', that is, a 'liquid medium' of 'subtil matter' which is supposed to fill all space, receives the motions from the brain of the Scholar and transmits them to those of his friends. ''Tis only an hint of the *possibility* of mechanically solving the *Phaenomenon*,' he modestly concludes; but he has said enough to show how the scientific attitude may be preserved even towards the 'marvellous'. His polemic is beginning to be diverted away from the schoolmen, and towards the unbelieving worldlings of Restoration England. Glanvill's readiness to accept the 'spirit of Nature' as explanatory while scornfully rejecting the 'active principles', 'celestial influences', and other phrases of the schools, illus-

1. *Vanity of Dogmatizing*, pp. 196 ff.

trates admirably how 'explanation' often consists merely in a change of nomenclature. To us, all alike are sounds signifying the philosopher's inability, after a certain point, to render causation 'intellectually visible'.

Fired by his theme – that what seems impossible to us may not be so in Nature – and stimulated, too, by the thought of triumphs to be achieved 'when *Magical* History shall be enlarged by riper inspections', Glanvill adduces a few more 'probable impossibilities' of a similar type, which may be mentioned in passing to illustrate the quality of his scientific faith. There is, for instance, communication by 'sympathized dials', that is, by means of needles touched by the same magnets. If two persons, each possessing one such needle set in a lettered dial, will agree upon a time, one of them may send a message at 'very distant removes' by moving his needle to the various letters required, when its 'fellow' will move in correspondence. Even though this particular experiment might fail, Glanvill maintains (with some show of right instinct, as we now see) that on similar lines, at least, communication at a distance will one day be possible, 'without unwarrantable assistance from *Daemoniack* correspondence'. He has heard, too, of communication by 'sympathized hands', where a piece of one person's flesh is grafted on to that of his friend and vice versa, so that pin-pricks may be 'sympathetically' felt and messages sent thereby. This is attested by the true story of a 'Gentleman' who requested his 'Chirurgeon' to amputate one of his arms, which was apparently quite healthy, explaining that the hand was sympathized with that of a friend, and that the friend having died the hand would now rot away. Glanvill, covering his credulity with an unusually impressive display of Brownese latinity (it is in this chapter that he refers to the *Pseudodoxia*), argues that the Gentleman was justified in his surmise, for 'that which was so sensibly affected with so inconsiderable a touch, in all likelyhood would be more immuted, by those greater alterations which are in *Cadaverous Solutions*'. Lastly, there is the 'sympathetick medicine' for wounds invented by Sir Kenelm Digby, the principle of which consisted in anointing not the wound itself, but the weapon which had caused it, or the 'cruentate cloth'. Of the truth of this marvel Sir Kenelm Digby has given unexceptionable proof, and he has also 'explained' it 'by Mechanism', assuming that there are

atomical aporrheas, which passing from the Cruentate cloth or weapon to the wound, and being incorporated with the particles of the salve carry them in their embraces to the affected part: where the medicinal atomes entering together with the effluviums of the bloud, do by their subtle insinuation better effect the cure, then can be done by any grosser Application.[1]

Whether the anima mundi be the true explanation, though it be the more 'desperate', or the mechanical, which has 'more of ingenuity than solid satisfaction', the 'facts' still remain to prove Glanvill's case against ignorant unbelief. The moral of all this, once more, is that the deeper springs of causation remain hidden from us, and we can only guess at them by analogy with 'palpable causalities, conceiving them like those within the sensible Horizon'. 'To say that the principles of Nature must needs be such as our Philosophy makes them, is to set bounds to Omnipotence'. Even the 'Grand Secretary of Nature, the miraculous Des-Cartes', who has so infinitely outdone all his predecessors, intends his theories to be considered only as provisional working hypotheses, and never pretends that things must necessarily be as he has supposed them to be. In reading this book one has to pause continually to take one's bearings. The argument is directed against undue certainty, but it often has more the air of a plea for the universal applicability of the mechanical explanations. Glanvill seems almost to admit this when, after using the flower-in-the-crannied-wall argument, and our ignorance whether our neighbour does not see 'blue' when we see 'white', in further confutation of the dogmatists, he admits that he has not meant all this quite seriously: he has merely 'play'd with the Dogmatist in a personated Scepticism'. 'Opinionative confidence', we may agree with him, is 'the effect of ignorance'. But when he declares that

Opinions are the Rattles of immature intellects, but the advanced Reasons have out-grown them,

1. Vanity of Dogmatizing, pp. 207–8.

we may suspect that the 'opinions' are the 'Reason' of other ages, and 'Reason' the 'opinions' of his own. Nevertheless his intellectual disinterestedness is remarkable for his century, and it is this quality which gives him the wisdom to write that while

they that never peep'd beyond the common belief in which their easie under-standings were at first indoctrinated, are indubitably assur'd of the Truth, and comparative excellency of their receptions ... the larger Souls, that have travail'd the divers *Climates* of *Opinions*, are more cautious in their *resolves*, and more sparing to determine.[1]

The book concludes with an eloquent defence of Philosophy as the noblest and most heavenly of all pursuits. The ignorant think it atheistic because it refuses to acknowledge a miracle in every extra-ordinary effect, whereas it is in reality the best friend of religion. It accustoms the soul to withdraw itself from the level of ordinary experience, and expatiate in the ampler air of reason. In spite of all that has been said of its limitations, it is folly to neglect what know-ledge we can attain here below, just because full knowledge is post-poned to a future state. All this defence, Glanvill concludes, is supremely applicable to the Cartesian philosophy, of which he prophesies, in his peroration, that its virtues

will bear it down to Posterity with a *Glory*, that shall know no *term*, but the *Universal ruines*.

Sadducismus Triumphatus[2]

We have seen enough of Glanvill's sceptical principles to under-stand by how natural a development they could be used in defence

1. *Vanity of Dogmatizing*, p. 227.
2. First published as *Philosophical Considerations Touching Witches and Witch-craft*, 1666. The fourth edition (1668) was called *A Blow at Modern Sadducism*; and in 1681, a year after Glanvill's death, this was republished as *Sadducismus Triumphatus*, with the addition of More's *True Notion of a Spirit*, translated from his *Enchiridion metaphysicum*.

of the Faith. If it be further asked, What has the defence of the Faith to do with witches and witchcraft? the reply is, as already suggested,[1] that in the seventeenth century disbelief in a spirit-world was supposed to be associated with the materialistic temper which disbelieved in a *spiritual* world, and consequently denied the immortality of the soul and all the truths of religion. It may seem a roundabout way of defending religion to demonstrate the reality of Satan; but in Glanvill's time believers were just awakening to the danger that science might abolish the category of the supernatural altogether, and it seemed the shortest way of preventing this to insist upon that class of supernatural phenomena which most of the scoffers themselves acknowledged, if not in their daylight theories, then subconsciously, when alone in the dark.[2] Moreover, it must be remembered that since the period of divine miracles was assumed by Protestantism to have closed with the Apostolic Age, and since the relations between God and man had been still further rationalized by the most recent theologians, the field of supernatural interventions had become almost exclusively the province of the Devil. Witchcraft thus furnished the only available contemporary evidence of a tangible kind for the existence of supernatural activity. Glanvill knew that there were more direct methods of defending the attitude of faith: was there not the ontological proof of the incomparable Descartes, besides the evidence of Nature, and of the human heart? But he saw that in the age of the Royal Society the climate of opinion was becoming more and more unfavourable to belief in witchcraft, and he roused himself to secure what seemed to him 'the outworks of Religion, and to regain a parcel of Ground which bold Infidelity hath invaded'. So completely did he see the existence of witches and the immortality of the soul as the same issue, that he describes his purpose simply as being to defend the belief in a future life against 'those who will stupidly believe that they shall die like Beasts, that they may live like them'.[3] Thus we get the queer spectacle of a Fellow of the Royal Society lashing his age for a type

1. See above, p. 153.
2. Cf. Hobbes, who is said to have been afraid of the dark.
3. *Sadducismus* (1700 edition), prefatory Letter to the Duke of Richmond.

of 'unbelief' which Lecky and others celebrate as one of the finest triumphs of the scientific movement. He carries his campaign against *dogmatizing* so far as to attack the latent dogmas of 'scepticism' itself. 'That there are no witches or apparitions' seems to him a piece of unwarrantable cocksureness, and to accept such a current assumption merely because the climate of opinion has encouraged it, is the mark of an unphilosophic mind.

Atheism is begun in *Sadducism*: And those that dare not bluntly say, There is no GOD, content themselves (for a fair step and Introduction) to deny that there are Spirits and Witches.[1]

Such infidels are not common amongst the 'meer vulgar', but abound amongst their 'superiors'.

And those that know anything of the World, know that most of the looser *Gentry*, and the small Pretenders to *Philosophy* and *Wit*, are generally deriders of the belief of *Witches* and *Apparitions*.

And this is no mere indifferent matter which may be left to opinion (like the question of the earth's motion): it 'hath a core in it that is worse than Heresie'. Glanvill knows that the obstacle he has to contend with is

a *mighty confidence* grounded upon *nothing*, which *swaggers* and *huffs*, and swears there are no Witches.

After these prefatory remarks Glanvill offers his considerations about witchcraft, arranged in a series of answers to objections, as his contribution to the worsting of Sadducism and the defeat of the Devil's last stratagem, his pretence that 'there is no such thing as himself, but that Fear and Fancy make Devils now, as they did Gods of old'.[2]

(1) The first objection he answers is that the notion of 'spirit' is itself an absurdity. If so, then the notions of God, of the soul as distinct from matter, and thus of immortality as well are also

1. *Sadducismus*, Preface.
2. ibid., p. 2. Cf. Browne's similar view, referred to above, p. 56.

absurdities. It would follow that the world was 'jumbled into this elegant and orderly Fabrick by Chance'; it would also follow that our ideas are merely material motions. But even granting that 'immaterial substance' is a contradiction, is it not reasonable to suppose that the air and all the regions above us – 'the Upper Stories of the Universe' – are peopled with intelligences? The microscope has shown us that the infinitely little is aswarm with life; why suppose otherwise of the infinitely great?

(2) That the actions attributed to witches are absurd or impossible. The more absurd, the likelier not to be faked As for impossibility, how can we 'measure the World of Spirits by the narrow rules of our own impotent Beings'? 'We are ignorant of the most *obvious* things about us,' and so on, in the vein of *The Vanity of Dogmatizing*. Glanvill then tries to show (for he never forgets the Royal Society, even at his most credulous) not how these marvels *do* take place, but how they may reasonably be *conceived* to happen, without contravening 'the rules of Reason and Philosophy'. And what even we can conceive as being done by the laws of physics, could *a fortiori* be affected by the superior power and knowledge of spirits. Glanvill assumes that the devils always operate by setting in motion the existing mechanisms of nature, and that their technique can therefore be conjecturally pictured as well as that of the Scholar Gypsy, or the action of Digby's sympathetick medicine. In this way he preserves his scientific integrity. Indeed he is never unscientific, for to believe in a spirit-world actively mingling in our affairs was then the most obvious commonplace; one could assume it, as one could assume the world-soul, or the animal spirits, as a scientific postulate, where mechanism failed to suffice. Thus he argues that if, as philosophers nearly unanimously agree, the soul is separable from the body without death, we can easily understand that a spirit could convey a witch's soul through the atmosphere clothed in air or 'some more subtile Matter', to the place of rendezvous. And that marks or injuries sustained by this aerial body should be transferred to the grosser body is no more incomprehensible than the 'signatures' stamped upon the foetus by the mother's imagination.

(3) That 'tis very improbable that the Devil, who is a wise and mighty Spirit, should be at the beck of a poor Hag, and have so little to do, as to attend the Errands and impotent Lusts of a silly Old Woman.[1]

The reply to this objection (it will be noticed that Glanvill lets his objector speak with force and point) is brief: the 'sagess and grandure' of the Prince of Darkness need not be brought into question, there are plenty of minor devils for these low tasks.

(4) That as it is commonly children who are the victims of the supposed evil practices, to believe in these stories is virtually to accuse Providence of neglecting the innocent, whom it should surely have under its especial care.

Glanvill's reply to this plea is significant: it is to the effect that there are, for that matter, plenty of *other* things for which we could also 'accuse Providence' – in a word, the miseries and injustices of human life; and yet 'we believe there is a *beauty* and *harmony* and goodness in that *Providence*, though we cannot unriddle it in *particular instances*'.[2] Providence has not secured children against other disasters – 'we accuse *It* not when a whole Town full of *Innocents* falls a *Victim* to the *rage* and *ferity* of *barbarous Executioners* in *Wars* and *Massacres*.' And what of the doctrine, cheerfully swallowed by many of the devout, that children are heirs of hell at birth? Glanvill also seems to think – and here he is in distinguished company – that he can assert eternal providence, and justify the ways of God to children, by laying all the blame on the witch instead of on the devil. He thence launches forth on a characteristic attempt to show that 'fascination' can be mechanically explained, on the analogy of contagion in disease, as produced by the passage of 'particles' from the witch to the victim,

which way of acting is ordinary and familiar in all natural *Efficiencies*. And 'tis now past question, that *Nature* for the most part acts by subtile *Streams* and *Apporreaea's* of *minute Particles*, which pass from one Body to another.[3]

If devils can hurt us at the instigation of a witch, why should they not do so with no such intermediary, and thus annoy us continually? To this and other such objections Glanvill's stock reply is a

1. *Sadducismus*, p. 11.   2. ibid., p. 13.   3. ibid.

characteristic appeal to our ignorance; how can we expect to fathom 'the projects of the Dark Kingdom', 'the Policy of Hell'? And yet he is always ready to 'suggest' how these matters may be 'conceived'; it is perhaps the lower orders of the infernal society who do most of the chaffering for souls, and these degenerate natures may be eager to satisfy their lust for dominion by catching whomsoever they most easily can (e.g. 'poor and miserable old women'), and making them their vassals. It is vain to argue too, that the effects of witchcraft are produced by 'imagination' in the witch or in the observer; whoever believes that 'imagination' can convey, for instance, pins and nails into the human body, believes something more incredible than sorcery itself. At the same time we should expect to find the discontented, the melancholy, and the imaginative the readiest victims of devils, since spirits probably act upon us not directly, with their 'naked essence', but by appropriate instruments, and the 'imagination', especially of those in whom that faculty predominated over reason, would be the aptest of instruments. If, unaided, the imagination of the Scholar Gypsy could work such wonders, what might we not expect of imaginations fanned by breathings from Hell?

(5) In answering the question why spirits work upon so few, and appear so seldom, Glanvill states his belief, which is comparable with that of More and of Milton, that spirits may be 'embodied'. The

Analogy of *Nature*, which useth not to make *precipitous leaps* from one thing to another, but usually proceeds by orderly *steps* and *gradations*,[1]

suggests that there must be an order of beings between us, 'who are so deeply plung'd in the grossest Matter', and the pure unbodied intelligences, which are the highest order of created Beings. If this be so, no spirit would be happy out of its own medium, but would be pained by the need to compress its tenuous body into a 'visible consistence'; and this would naturally apply more to good spirits (whose visits are notoriously brief) than to evil ones, who are more 'foeculent and gross', and hence more easily reducible to visibility. These conjectures about spirits are interesting because they show a

1. *Sadducismus*, p. 23.

disposition both to believe in a supernatural world, and at the same time to visualize or 'imagine' it, with the result that the Spirits inevitably become phantasms invested with ethereal 'bodies'. Further, Glanvill's ensuing comparisons between the heavenly and the infernal forces in their relations with man illumine for us the contemporary state of belief about the different grades of the supernatural. These comparisons arise when he is trying to answer the objection that if fiends traffic with the wicked, then why do not angels commune with the good? First he says that they do, but he has no universal and contemporary testimony to confirm this; instead, he appeals somewhat desperately to Deuteronomy, Origen on Jeremiah, and the Book of Daniel. But he relies mainly upon the Baconian principle – the foundation-stone of all science – that *God works in nature by second causes alone, whatever the Devil may do.* It is as if he felt that a more dignified procedure befitted the governing-classes of the universe, whereas the lower and criminal orders of the spirit-hierarchy might quite well employ cruder methods. To support them in their faith and conduct of life, the righteous have all the consolations of religion and the means of grace, the mediation of the Saviour and the ministration of the Spirit – *'any of which are more than the apparition of an angel'*.[1] He goes further, and declares that such an apparition

would indeed be a great *gratification* of the *Animal Life*, but it would render our *Faith* less Noble and less Generous, were it frequently so assisted.[2]

The fact seems to be that in approaching the region of *religious* experience Glanvill insensibly falls into modes of thought and of language very different from those he uses in dealing with sorcery. Centuries of theological insight had purged the Christian supernatural of cruder elements, and by the seventeenth-century 'angels', in spite of More and Milton, were really a superfluity of the faith.

1. *Sadducismus*, p. 26 (my italics).
2. ibid., p. 26. Cf. Coleridge: 'It [the existence of God] could not be intellectually more evident without becoming morally less effective; without counteracting its own end by sacrificing the *life* of faith to the cold mechanism of a worthless because compulsory assent' (*Biographia Literaria*, Ch. 10).

The official 'supernatural' of religion occupied the place of honour in the universe and in the minds of the faithful; within this region, spiritual and 'rational' conceptions were predominant. It was the blessedness of faith to believe in this, but not to 'see'. But side by side with or concealed beneath this Christian consciousness, there still persisted mental habits more deep-rooted and more ancient, which expressed themselves in the pictorial beliefs Glanvill is defending. The religious tradition had itself brought this about by rationalizing its own field and deliberately handing over the 'pagan', the sub-rational, to the Devil. It is, of course, easier to think pictorially than abstractedly, hence the vitality of the popular demonology. Thus it comes about that whereas faith can dispense with the luxury of angels (and Glanvill writes a beautiful Cambridge-Platonic chapter[1] on the possibility, and the conditions, of direct communication between purified souls and God, rendering angelic intermediaries unnecessary), wickedness still keeps its demons. And the righteous keep them too, as we see, though for opposite reasons. It is odd to find that because Glanvill does not himself *want* angels, he allows himself, in *this* direction, to share the 'enlightenment' of his age, and to use the same sort of language about stories of angelic intervention as he condemns where witchcraft is concerned:

for my part I scorn the *ordinary Tales of Prodigies*, which proceed from *superstitious* Fears, and *unacquaintance* with *Nature*.[2]

However, in this case he deems it prudent to cover his retreat by a screen of soft phrases: 'I know not why it may not be conjectured', 'it seems to me not unreasonable to believe', and so forth.

(6) I shall only refer to his treatment of one further objection, the 'last and shrewdest', which is that if the Devil can work miracles, how can we distinguish them from true miracles, the great inducement to faith? Glanvill first gives it as his opinion – hardly consistent, perhaps, with his oft-repeated denial that we can pronounce with any certainty about the ways of God or of the Devil – that in matters of such concernment Providence does not allow us to be deceived. If the events of the whole gospel narrative were the out-

1. *Sadducismus*, sect. XIII.   2. ibid., p. 27.

come of devilry, then indeed we are deceived in all things, and are of all men the most miserable. But Glanvill has a stronger argument in reserve; he is prepared to subordinate miracles to the truth or morality they illustrate. This is the true mark or 'signature', showing whether a miracle be divine or diabolical. A definition of 'miracle' being needed, Glanvill lays down that it is not simply an 'unaccountable' event, for so are the 'magnalia' of nature; neither is it an act or event 'beyond mere Nature', for we do not know the limits of 'Nature'; miracles are, then, wonderful or unaccountable acts performed by holy persons to confirm some divine doctrine. Strictly, then, it is the divine doctrine (already known) which proves the miracle to be genuine, rather than the miracle which proves the doctrine to be true.

Glanvill's proofs from Scripture do not concern us, though it is important to realize that the authority of Scripture was then supposed to be on the side of belief in witchcraft. Neither need we speak of the 'choice collection of modern relations', which fills the greater portion of his Second Part. In concluding these remarks on Glanvill, I would point out that in order to obtain a balanced idea of his outlook one should pass immediately from his stories about the Demon of Tedworth, the disturbances at Mr Mompesson's House, or the villainous Feats of that rampant Hag Margaret Agar (of Brewham in the County of Somerset), to his tranquil utterances about the reasonableness of Christianity in an essay like *The Agreement of Reason and Religion*.[1] It is here that we get the Glanvill of the Royal Society, exhibiting what might be called the official foundations of his belief. What he says in this capacity shows him in full accord with the 'rational' tone which became universal in the religious writings of the later seventeenth century. He reveals his mastery of the technique of proving religion by pure reason, certainly 'without unwarrantable assistance from Daemoniack correspondence', and almost – in the deistical manner – without unwarrantable assistance from Revelation. The fundamentals of natural religion, he says, in a passage which recalls Lord Herbert of Cherbury, are all proved by Reason, and by Reason alone. The first article of belief, the existence

1. Essay 5 in *Essays on Several Important Subjects*, 1676 (cited above, pp. 156–7).

of God, is proved by Reason, not by Revelation, for the very notion of Revelation presupposes a God who reveals. Similarly it is Reason which proves the authority of Scripture by showing good cause for believing it to be from God, by demonstrating the truth of its testimony, and the harmony of its teachings with those of nature. If we abandon Reason, we abandon the firmest support of religion, and shall find ourselves defenceless against Rome and against the Enthusiasts. Reason he defines as the principles of thought implanted in us, or, more fully, the

Fundamental Notices, that God hath implanted in our Souls; such as arise not from external Objects, nor particular Humours or Imaginations, but are immediately lodged in our Minds; independent upon other Principles or Deductions; commanding a sudden assent, and acknowledged by all sober Mankind.

Amongst the principles of Reason are the familiar propositions: That God is a being of all perfection, That a thing cannot be and not be, That a whole is greater than any of its parts, and so forth. 'Conclusions' are

those other Notices that are inferred *rightly from* these; and *by their* help, from the Observations of *Sense*; And the *remotest* of them that can be conceived, if it be *duly inferred* from the *Principles* of *Reason*, or rightly circumstantiated *Sense*, is as well to be reckoned a Part or Branch of Reason, as the more *immediate* Conclusions, that are Principles in respect of those distant Truths.[1]

The only comment I will make at this point is that in phrases like 'commanding a sudden assent', 'acknowledged by all sober Mankind' and 'implanted in our souls', we get a hint of how 'Reason', like its yoke-fellow 'Nature', could become equivalent, in less guarded moments, to 'the usual assumptions of contemporary good sense' – or more simply (to conclude with Glanvill's own most famous phrase) the 'Climate of Opinion'.

1. *Sadducismus*, pp. 5–6.

CHAPTER 10

The Heroic Poem in a Scientific Age

The Climate of Opinion

IT happens that the development of English poetry since the Renaissance has coincided with one of the most determined and prolonged efforts ever made by man to arrive at a 'true' world-view along scientific lines. In the seventeenth century, as we have abundantly seen, the boundaries between 'truth' and 'fiction' were being laid down with unexampled energy, rapidity, and precision. I have already suggested that during the period of such a systematic effort to displace older world-pictures by 'philosophical' conceptions the position of poetry was likely to be precarious. For in poetry thought is not pure; it is working in alliance with the feelings and the will. In Bacon's phrase, it 'subjects the shows of things to the desires of the mind' – which is the exact reverse of the process called science. It can thus appear, and often has appeared to certain kinds of philosophers, as the enemy of 'truth'. Something has been said in foregoing chapters to indicate that in the seventeenth century these developments did actually lead to a lowering of the prestige of poetry. The degree of assurance with which serious poetry can be written at any period depends upon the prevailing state of certainty or scepticism about ultimate issues. The tone, the rhythm, and the imagery of poetry vary according to the stage reached in the development of belief and unbelief. A poet, that is, who feels that his constructions are 'true' as well as agreeable or expressive will write a different sort of poetry from that of one who feels that they are 'fictions' – misrepresentations of actuality, even though they be symbols of it; and different again from that of one for whom the boundaries of 'truth' and 'fiction' have either never yet become clear, or else have become less clear than they once seemed. I have presented some evidence to show that in our century 'truth' was being handed over more and more to 'philosophy', and to prose as its proper medium, while poetry was being reduced to the role of catering for delight by means of agreeable images from which we derived pleasure without being 'cozened by the fiction'.[1] Some further corroboration may not be amiss at this stage in order to make the situation clearer.

THOMAS SPRAT's *History of the Royal Society*

I know of no work which more fully illustrates the climate of opinion in post-Restoration days than Sprat's *History of the Royal Society*. This work, which has something in common with Glanvill's celebrations of the triumphs of modern learning – though it is clearly the product of a much blunter sensibility – is full of jubilation over the 'exantlation of truth', and of panegyrics upon those who 'remov'd the rubbish' of ages, and 'freed our understandings from the charms of vain apparitions'.

And we may well guess that the absolute perfection of the True Philosophy is not now far off, seeing this first great and necessary preparation for its coming is already taken off our hands.[2]

In several passages which clearly reveal the temper of his time and of his circle, Sprat justifies the ways of prose in a 'learned and inquisitive age', and sets aside with a confident and heavy hand the vain fancies of the poets. Learning originated, he tells us, in the East and in Greece; and the primitive philosophers, in order to render their views comprehensible and acceptable to their hearers, 'set them off with the mixture of Fables, and the ornaments of Fancy'. Hence it came about that

the first masters of knowledge among them were as well Poets, as Philosophers; for Orpheus, Linus, Musaeus, and Homer, first softened men's

1. Cf. above, p. 83.
2. Sprat's *History of the Royal Society*, p. 29. (The first ed. appeared in 1667. My references are to the second ed., 1702.)

natural rudeness, and by the charms of their Numbers, allur'd them to be instructed by the severer doctrines of Solon, Thales, and Pythagoras. This was a course that was useful at first, when men were to be delightfully deceiv'd to their own good. But perhaps it left some ill influence, on the whole Philosophy of their Successors; and gave the Grecians occasion ever after of exercising their wit, and their imagination, about the works of Nature, more than was consistent with a sincere Inquiry into them.[1]

The notion of the early poet as 'vates' was of course a commonplace of the Renaissance, but it is interesting to find the seventeenth century emphasizing the *scientific* in addition to the moral, theological, or political meanings which were supposed to be wrapped up in the fables of antiquity. Bacon, who regarded poetry as 'fained history', whether Narrative, Dramatic, or Allegorical (satire, elegy, epigram, ode, etc., he relegates to the 'arts of speech'), sets down 'the philosophy of ancient fables' as the only deficiency of learning in the province of poetry.[2] He specifies the functions of 'parabolical' or 'allusive' poetry as being either to render something explicit to the unlearned, or the opposite – namely, to envelop mysteries and keep them from the profane.[3] Yet, after giving a few 'explanations' of well-known fables, he adds:

> Nevertheless, in many the like encounters, I do rather think that the fable was first, and the exposition devised, than that the moral was first, and thereupon the fable framed.[4]

Homer, he thinks, 'had no such inwardness in his own meaning'. But Bacon had a further interesting suggestion; the fables themselves, he concludes, may have embodied the Wisdom of the Ancients even if Homer or Hesiod did not know or intend to convey it. The fables are much older than the poets who versified them, and many of them are to be regarded

not as the product of the age, or invention of the poets, but as sacred relics, gentle whispers, and the breath of better times, that from the traditions of more ancient nations came, at length, into the flutes and trumpets of the Greeks.[5]

1. *History of the Royal Society*, p. 6.   2. *De augmentis*, Bk 11, Ch. 13.
3. Cf. *Advancement of Learning*, Bk 11, Ch. 4.   4. ibid.
5. Preface to *The Wisdom of the Ancients*. Cf. *De augmentis*, Bk 11, Ch. 13.

Bacon was so certain of this that he not only devoted a long chapter in the *De augmentis*[1] to decoding the fables of Pan, Perseus, and Bacchus, but also composed his *Wisdom of the Ancients*, in which thirty-one classical fables are rationalized into moral, political, or philosophical lessons. This dream of a primeval golden age and its 'wisdom', like the doctrine of divine inspiration in Scripture, allows its exponents to see depth on depth of meaning in their texts, and Bacon, in expounding his fables, exhibits a great deal of his own wisdom, if not that of the ancients. It is hardly necessary to give examples, but to illustrate the treatment of primitive material by an acute but unhistorical intelligence, it may suffice to mention that Pan, who stands for Nature, or 'the nature of things', had 'horns broad at the roots but narrow and shorn a-top, because the nature of all things seem pyramidal: for individuals are infinite; but being collected into a variety of species, they rise up into kinds; and these again ascend, and are contracted into generals, till at length nature may seem collected to a point'; that he is called the messenger of the gods, next after Mercury, 'as, next after the word of God [= Mercury], the image of the world [Pan] is the herald of the divine power and wisdom'; that Orpheus denotes learning, Eurydice 'things', or the subject of learning; that Cupid is an allegory of the corpuscular philosophy, and so forth.

A curious by-product of the Baconian speculations is to be found in the *Mythomystes* of Henry Reynolds (*c.* 1633),[2] who applies the argument to the depreciation of modern poets. The moderns are ignorant triflers, whereas the ancient poets were all-wise. Reynolds is anxious to prove that the fables are all profound allegories not only of ethical truth, as often asserted, but of natural philosophy. In this scientific age it is our main concern to study God in his works, and here in these fables are to be found the secrets of his inner procedures. His talk is of Orpheus, Musaeus, Homer, Hesiod, and Zoroaster, whom he regards as divinely illumined (comparable, indeed, to Moses in this respect), and cites Plato, Pico della Mirandola, and Allessandro Farra as authorities for the doctrine of 'in-

1. Bk II, Ch. 13.
2. Spingarn, *Criticial Essays of the Seventeenth Century*, Vol. I, p. 141.

spiration'. He quotes Conti,[1] 'one of our late Mythologians', to the effect that philosophy, when it first appeared, was only 'the senses and meanings of fables taken out and separated from their huske and involvements'. He praises the ancients for the care with which they wrapped up their meanings, thus ensuring that only the discerning should understand them.

It is nowhere suggested, either by Bacon or by Reynolds, that poetry should still be used, in the manner of antiquity, for conveying profound intuitions and glimpses of 'truth'. On the contrary, it is everywhere implied that though poetry may have been the 'mental rattle that awakened the attention of intellect in the infancy of civil society',[2] its usefulness is now exhausted, and our present concern is with the serious work trying to behold face to face what was formerly seen in a glass darkly. Bacon concludes his section on Poetry with:

> But it is not good to stay too long in the theatre. Let us now pass on to the judicial place or palace of the mind, which we are to approach with more reverence and attention.[3]

And Reynolds tells us that *nowadays the philosophers are the true poets.* This is certainly the feeling of Thomas Sprat, to whom we now return.

> When the fabulous age was past, says he, Philosophy took a little more courage; and ventured more to rely upon its own strength, without the Assistance of Poetry.

Heroes and giant-killers, it is said, were followed of old by law-givers, and Sprat will presume to give a 'philosophical sense' to this story too ('as many others have done before me'):

> First then, the Phantasms, and Fairies, and venerable Images of Antiquity, did long haunt the World: against these we have had our Champions; and without all question they had the better of the Cause: and now we have good ground to trust, that these Illusions being well over, the last finishing

1. d. 1582.
2. T. L. Peacock, *Four Ages of Poetry.*
3. *Advancement of Learning*, Bk II, Ch. 4, end.

of this great Work is nigh at hand, and is reserv'd for this undertaking [the Royal Society].[1]

The most important passages in Sprat's book, for our purposes, occur where, after narrating the early history of the Royal Society, he proceeds to give 'a model of their whole design'. It is noticeable that in the forefront of this account he places the intention of the Society to purge the present age of the errors of antiquity –

> And to accomplish this, they have endeavour'd, *to separate the knowledge of Nature from the colours of Rhetorick, the devices of Fancy, or the delightful deceit of Fables*.[2]

– in a word, they have determined to declare war upon poetry. As for the scope of their inquiries – God, Men, and Nature comprising the whole possible field – they propose to 'forbear' God and the Soul, as being likely to lead to more talking than working. With God they 'meddle no otherwise than onely as the Power, Wisdom, and Goodness of the Creator, is display'd in the admirable order and workmanship of the Creatures'. When they have made more progress in the exploration of material phenomena they may, perhaps, tackle the Soul; for though man is no mere 'natural Engine' of whose motions we may give a mechanical account, yet a further study of 'spirits', 'bloud', etc., may bring us nearer to accurate guesses about even the more exalted acts of the soul, 'and that, too, without destroying its spiritual and Immortal Being'.

> *These two subjects*, God and the Soul, *being onely forborn*: In all the rest, they wander at their pleasure.[3]

To this, then, the rendering to Faith that which is Faith's has by now brought us, that this eminent Restoration divine can really feel that in omitting God and the Soul from their programme the Royal Society are omitting nothing of serious importance. It is axiomatic that God and the Soul exist, so why worry any further about them? Besides, the study of the Creation is the best study of the Creator, and therefore philosophy is not only the true poetry of the age (as Reynolds has said), but the true religion as well.

1. Sprat, op. cit., pp. 29–30.   2. ibid., p. 62 (my italics).
3. ibid., p. 83 (my italics).

'There is one thing more', Sprat continues, in what has become the best known passage of his book,

about which the Society has been most sollicitous; and that is, the manner of their Discourse: which, unless they had been very watchful to keep in due temper, the whole spirit and vigour of their Design, had been soon eaten out by the luxury and redundancy of speech.[1]

The famous attack on 'poetic' language, which follows, is a blend of Platonic and Baconian ardour for 'truth' with dislike for scholastic and metaphysical wit. It is a manifesto, comparable in a sense to Wordsworth's Preface to *Lyrical Ballads*, proclaiming the Augustan return to 'nature'; but whereas Wordsworth is concerned to distinguish true from false poetry, the 'imaginative' from the 'imaginary', Sprat rejects, on behalf of his age, all forms of poetic utterance as undesirable 'ornaments of speech'. These embellishments 'were at first, no doubt, an admirable Instrument in the hands of Wise Men', who used them to clothe moral and philosophical instruction; but now –

they are generally chang'd to worse uses: They make the fancy disgust the best things, if they come sound, and unadorn'd: *they are in open defiance against Reason: professing not to hold much correspondence with that; but with its Slaves, the Passions;* they give the mind a motion too changeable, and bewitching, to consist with right practice. Who can behold, without Indignation, how many mists and uncertainties, these specious Tropes and Figures have brought on our knowledge? . . . in few words, I dare say, that of all the Studies of men, nothing may be sooner obtain'd than this vicious abundance of Phrase, this trick of Metaphors, this volubility of Tongue, which makes so great a noise in the world.

They have therefore been most rigorous in putting into execution, the only Remedy that can be found for this extravagance: and that has been, a constant Resolution, to reject all the amplifications, digressions, and swellings of style: *to return back to the primitive purity, and shortness,* when men deliver'd so many things, almost in an equal number of words. *They have exacted from all their members, a close, naked, natural way of speaking; positive expressions, clear senses; a native easiness; bringing all things as near the Mathematical*

1. Sprat, op. cit., p. iii ff.

plainness, as they can: and preferring the language of Artizans, Countrymen, and Merchants, before that, of Wits, or Scholars.[1]

Not only Tropes and Figures, but the 'yellow-skirted fays' will now be banished for ever by the light of common day. Sprat complacently announces the passing of the beliefs ('superstitions') which his co-Fellow of the Royal Society, Glanvill, was labouring to defend. In thus dismissing into outer darkness the beliefs which had lived for centuries on the borderland of poetry and religion, Sprat exhibits something of the sense of safety and inner assurance which was characteristic of Addison, and often approaches him closely in the tone of his writing. The poets of old, he says, reverting to his former accusation,

to make all things look more venerable than they were, devised a thousand *false Chimaeras;* on every Field, River, Grove, and Cave, they bestowed a Fantasm of their own making: With these they amaz'd the world. . . . And in the modern Ages these Fantastical Forms were reviv'd and possess'd Christendom, in the very height of the Scholemen's time: An infinit number of Fairies haunted every house; all Churches were fill'd with Apparitions; men began to be frighted from their Cradles. . . . All which abuses if those acute Philosophers did not promote, yet they were never able to overcome; nay, even not so much as King Oberon and his invisible Army.

But from the time in which the *Real Philosophy* has appear'd there is scarce any whisper remaining of such horrors: Every man is unshaken at those Tales at which his Ancestors trembled: *The cours of things goes quietly along, in its own true channel of Natural Causes and Effects.* For this we are beholden to Experiments; which though they have not yet completed the discovery of the *true world, yet they have already vanquish'd those wild inhabitants of the false world*, that us'd to astonish the minds of men.[2]

No clearer proclamation could be desired of the victory of the new world-picture, the fact-world, over the older worlds of traditional feeling. 'Truth' was the exclusive possession of the Real Philosophy; all besides could only, from the point of view of the time, be false and chimerical. For Sprat the entry into the 'true world' was a

1. My italics.
2. Sprat, op. cit., p. 340 (my italics). Cf. Addison, *Spectator*, No. 419.

glorious emancipation; he would have been staggered to know that one hundred and fifty years after him men not out of their senses (though poets) would be lamenting that glory and loveliness had passed away; that later on, the recovery of every fragment of information about primitive beliefs would be the life's work of a distinguished succession of scientists; and that an outstanding mind of the third century after his would be passionately striving to bring back the pre-scientific consciousness, and reanimate the world which science had 'killed'. Sprat himself was of course far from admitting that his science was a danger to 'Religion' as he understood it. He devotes a long and characteristic section to proving the contrary, making use of the arguments common to all the harmonizers of religion and science in his day. Reason and Religion aim at the same objects, and cannot possibly conflict. As for the Gospel miracles, they, like the Tropes of the early poets, were necessary in an ignorant age, but have been discontinued since men became capable of rational conviction. The Church of England at any rate (whatever may be said of others) will not fear the new light, for she has always stood for Reform, the Rights of the Civil Power, and Reason. The Anglican Church stands firm, midway between Superstition and Enthusiasm, and will gain, not lose, by the spread of the scientific temper. 'The universal Disposition of this Age is bent upon a rational Religion,'[1] and this is exactly what the Church exists to provide. He admits, indeed, with a coolness surprising in a bishop, that *the influence which Christianity once obtain'd on men's minds is now prodigiously decay'd*,[2] that its condition, in fact, resembles that of the cults of antiquity just before their destruction – when their ceremonies were observed in public and ignored in private. But for this he blames, not science, but the vices of the time; and the cure for it is not more mystery, but more rationality. The practice of moral virtue, the observance of the Laws of Nature, and the contemplation of God's works – these are the remedies. As for the supernatural doctrines of Christianity, there is nothing better, he says, than 'to believe them in gross'. 'The spiritual and supernatural part of Christianity no philosophy can reach'; the 'experimenter' can

1. Sprat, op. cit., p. 374.   2. ibid., p. 376 (my italics).

193

therefore believe them as easily as a schoolman. At first sight Sprat's language on this subject may seem to resemble that of the modern segregators of religion from science; yet his purpose is really opposite to theirs. While Barth or Otto insist on the transcendence of the supernatural in order to vindicate its autonomy, Sprat is honouring it with a cold salute after banishing it to a safe distance.

Finally, in enumerating the benefits to be expected from science, Sprat gives us a short and not very gracious section on 'this *pleasant but unprofitable sort of men*',[1] the wits and writers, who also, it appears, may profit from the Real Philosophy. Friend and biographer of Cowley though he be, Sprat feels he must apologize for including this topic 'amidst so many matters of greater weight'. What he says of the sources of poetic imagery is, however, of considerable interest and significance for our present purpose. Wit, he tells us, is founded upon images derived from the various spheres of familiar or traditional knowledge. These images have at all times been drawn, he continues, from

the Fables and Religions of the Ancients, the Civil Histories of all Countries, the Customs of Nations, the Bible, the Sciences, the Manners of Men, the several Arts of their hands, and the works of Nature. In all these, where there may be a resemblance of one thing to another, as there may be in all, there is a sufficient Foundation for Wit.

Now some of these sources of imagery are by this time *exhausted*, and Sprat, curiously anticipating at once Johnson and Wordsworth, writes as follows:

The Wit of the Fables and Religions of the Antient World is well-nigh consum'd: They have already serv'd the poets long enough; and it is now high time to dismiss them; especially seeing they have this peculiar imperfection, that they were only Fictions at first: whereas Truth is never so well express'd or amplify'd, as by those Ornaments which are True and Real in themselves.

Classical mythology is thus exploded and obsolete, and can no longer infuse life into modern poetry. The old nature-images of the poets are also too hackneyed to be repeated any more. The ancients

1. Sprat, op. cit., p. 419 (my italics). For this discussion see ibid., pp. 413 ff.

had long ago 'quite devour'd' the sweetness of flowers, fruits, and herbs; and they had 'tir'd out the Sun, and Moon, and Stars with their Similitudes, more than they fancy them to be wearied by their daily journeys round the Hevens'. The moral of all this is, of course, that the new knowledge of nature will supply poets with what they most need, a source of new and true images.

HOBBES AND DRYDEN ON FANCY AND JUDGEMENT

Further testimony to the same effect is to be found in the psychological theories of the time, in which 'judgement' is customarily valued above 'fancy'. In his *Answer to Davenant* (1650) Hobbes gives this account of the 'creative' process:

Time and Education begets Experience; Experience begets memory; Memory begets Judgement and Fancy: Judgement begets the strength and structure, and Fancy begets the ornaments of a Poem. The Ancients therefore fabled not absurdly in making memory the Mother of the Muses. For memory is the World (though not really, yet so as in a looking glass) in which the *Judgement, the severer Sister*, busieth her self in a grave and rigid examination of all the parts of Nature, and in registering by Letters their order, causes, uses, differences, and resemblances; Whereby the Fancy, when any work of Art is to be performed, findes her materials at hand and prepared for use, and needs no more than a swift motion over them, that what she wants, and is there to be hand, may not lie too long unespied.[1]

Fancy is thus a process whereby the contents of the mind, which consist of sense-impressions preserved in the storehouse of the Memory, are rapidly reviewed, and suitable images picked out for ornamental use. It is associated by Hobbes with the act of finding 'unexpected similitude' in 'things otherwise much unlike', from whence proceed 'those grateful similies, metaphors, and other tropes, by which both poets and orators have it in their power to make things please or displease, and show well or ill to others, as they like themselves'. On the other hand, Judgement is the act of

1. Spingarn, *Critical Essays of the Seventeenth Century*, Vol. II, p. 59.

discerning dissimilitude in things that otherwise appear the same. Fancy and Judgement together make up what Hobbes and his contemporaries knew as Wit.[1] Elsewhere[2], speaking of Wit as one of the intellectual virtues, he tells us outright that 'Fancy, without help of judgement, is not commended as a virtue', whereas judgement is commended for its own sake. In a good poem – that is to say, in an epic or dramatic poem, for 'sonnets', etc., are dismissed as 'other pieces' – both are required, and Hobbes even concedes that 'the fancy must be more eminent'; but this is for a reason which itself 'places' poetry – it is because such poems 'please for the extravagancy, but ought not to displease by indiscretion'. We *may* use language, he tells us in a chapter *Of Speech*,[3] 'to please and delight ourselves and others, by playing with our words, for pleasure or ornament, innocently'. But this is not the serious employment of words, which are properly signs for real things and their connexions. He classes metaphor as one of the abuses of language and a source of deceit, misconception, and absurdity.

Dryden, as a professional man of letters and a critic, has wider views on poetic speech, and knows how to put up a sound apology for what he terms 'poetic licence'. But his psychology of poetry is very much like Hobbes's. In one of his earliest prose writings[4] he defends the use of rhyme in plays on the ground that it 'bounds and circumscribes the fancy'.

For imagination in a poet [synonymous with 'fancy'] is a faculty so wild and lawless, that like a high-ranging spaniel, it must have clogs tied to it, lest it outrun the judgement.

The obligation to rhyme forces the poet to curb his magnanimity, and allows time for his judgement to assert its proper sway. Similarly, in the *Essay of Dramatic Poesy* (1668) Dryden calls judgement 'the master-workman in a play', and describes 'verse' as 'a rule and

1. See Hobbes's *Human Nature*, Works (Molesworth ed.), Vol. IV, Ch. 10.
2. *Leviathan*, Ch. 8.
3. ibid., Ch. 4.
4. *Epistle Dedicatory of The Rival Ladies*, 1664. (*Essays of J. Dryden*, ed. W. P. Ker, Vol. I, p. 8.)

line by which he keeps his building compact and even, which otherwise lawless imagination would raise either irregularly or loosely'.[1]
In a later essay[2] he speaks – in language more congenial to the twen-
tieth than to the nineteenth century – of the 'coolness and discretion
which is necessary to a poet'. We are here as far removed as possible
from the *furor poeticus*, the 'afflatus', which in all 'inspirational'
theories of poetry from Plato onwards have been said to accom-
pany poetic utterance. We are equally distant from the plastic
Imagination of Wordsworth and Coleridge, which moulds the
mere *natura naturata* into something 'truer' than itself. It was a stock
reproach against poets during the Renaissance and the neo-classic
period that they were not merely makers of sugared trifles but actually forgers of lies. The poet speaks the thing that *is* not. Two principal kinds of answers were devised by the apologists: either that
the poet speaks 'higher' truths in parable, or that he '*nothing
affirmes, and therefore never lyeth*'[3] – that is, that his work is really
play and must not be taken seriously. On the whole, it was the latter
which in the end came to hold the field. It is implicit, for example,
in Dryden; and although poetry saved its dignity in the next century
by becoming satirical and reflective, it remained essentially an
embellishment upon a prose fabric: complimented and honoured
indeed like women in the 'utopia of gallantry', but like them,
of no serious account.

Milton

With all these forces, scientific and philosophic, working together
for 'Truth', and tending more and more to show up the traditional
imagery of poetry and religion as obsolete, phantasmal, or fictitious,
how was it that the seventeenth century nevertheless produced what
Dryden himself called 'one of the greatest, most noble, and most
sublime poems which either this age or nation has produced'[4] –

1. *Essays of Dryden*, Vol. I, p. 107.
2. *Apology for Heroic Poetry and Poetic Licence*, 1677, ibid., p. 186.
3. Cf. Sidney's *Apologie*.
4. *Apology for Heroic Poetry*, op. cit., Vol. I, p. 179.

Paradise Lost? This is obviously a question which must receive serious attention in a study like the present, which is largely concerned with the relation between what was held for 'truth' and what for 'poetry' in this century. In attempting to account for the appearance of this great religious poem in the middle of the seventeenth century I shall have to discuss, as briefly as may be, its form and subject-matter, and some aspects of Milton's own mind and character.

THE HEROIC POEM

In the first place, then, it must be emphasized that in the seventeenth century there was one poetic genre which enjoyed such peculiar and special prestige that it was proof against the cold climate of 'an age too late' – the Heroic Poem. Only the Bible could claim a greater share of reverence than Homer and Vergil. This was a legacy of the Renaissance, when, as is well known, the desire to emulate the noblest achievements of the ancients had become fused with the patriotic nationalism of the time, and poets in each country had aspired to 'illustrate' their vernaculars by composing in them works worthy to be set beside the *Iliad* and the *Aeneid*. The continued vitality of this tradition is well illustrated in Dryden's describing the Heroic Poem, at the very end of the century and of his own life (1697), as 'undoubtedly the greatest work which the soul of man is capable to perform'.[1] It is outside my purpose to account for this veneration for epic poetry, but a few of its credentials may well be mentioned. The ancients had produced their crowning masterpieces in this kind, Aristotle had canonized it; and Dante, Ariosto, and Tasso had in their several ways raised Italian nearly to a level with the classical languages. Not until a work of equal scope, ordonnance, and elevation had been produced in French, for instance, or in English, could those modern dialects claim to have emerged from medieval barbarism. Moreover, the subject-matter of epic was normally some great act in the drama of national history, and through it, therefore, could be expressed the new-found pride of

1. *Dedication of the Aeneis*, op. cit., Vol. II, p. 154.

nationhood, and the passion for great doing, which distinguished the Renaissance. Above all, the comparative invulnerability of heroic poetry, even in an age of scientific enlightenment, was due to this, that though it might make use of fiction, though its history might be 'fained', its object was something as important as Truth itself, namely moral edification. On this point the critics from the Renaissance onwards were unanimous, and Dryden's remark, which recalls Spenser's, may be taken as typical:

The design of it is to form the mind to heroic virtue by example; 'tis conveyed in verse, that it may delight, while it instructs.[1]

In order to acquit himself worthily in heroic poetry, then, a poet must possess the loftiest genius as an artist and the highest qualities as a man. The very difficulty of the task invested the whole topic with a glamour which can now be more easily understood than felt; and this to some extent explains the extraordinary fact, noted by W. P. Ker,[2] that

The 'Heroic Poem' is not commonly mentioned in histories of Europe as a matter of serious interest: yet from the days of Petrarch and Boccaccio to those of Dr Johnson, and more especially from the sixteenth century onward, it was a subject that engaged some of the strongest intellects in the world (among them Hobbes, Gibbon, and Hume); it was studied and discussed as fully and with as much thought as any of the problems by which the face of the world was changed in those centuries. There might be difference of opinion about the essence of the Heroic Poem or the Tragedy, but there was no doubt about their value. Truth about them was ascertainable, and truth about them was necessary to the intellect of man, for they were the noblest things belonging to him.

English poetry had had its Spenser, who had hoped to overgo Ariosto. But he was not felt to have succeeded; for, as Dryden remarked, in reviewing the achievement in this field,[3] there was no uniformity in his design; he had a new hero for each adventure, and as each one represented a particular moral virtue, they are 'all equal,

1. *Dedication of the Aeneis.* 2. *Essays of Dryden*, Vol. I, Introduction, p. xvi.
3. *Discourse Concerning the Original and Progress of Satire*, op. cit., Vol. II, p. 28.

without subordination or preference'. And apart from these and other faults (the 'ill choice of his stanza', for instance), the work was incomplete. The absolute epic in English was still unwritten. Part at least of Milton's purpose was to write it, and so to realize at last, for England, this cherished ambition of the Renaissance. In a famous passage of the *Reason of Church Government*, Milton relates how the great idea came to him,

that by labour and intense study ... joined with the strong propensity of nature, I might perhaps leave something so written to aftertimes, as they should not willingly let it die.

And it became clear to him, also, that like a true poet of the Renaissance his aim must be the adorning of his native tongue, and the honour and instruction of his country:

That what the greatest and choicest wits of Athens, Rome, or modern Italy, and those Hebrews of old did for their country, I, in my proportion, with this over and above, of being a Christian, might do for mine; not caring to be once named abroad, though perhaps I could attain to that, but content with these British islands as my world. . . .[1]

Dryden will not grant that even Milton had realized the idea of the heroic poem, for reasons which will be best discussed when we come to the question of subject-matter. But he would have agreed that Milton was pre-eminently fitted, both in genius and in character, to succeed where others had failed. Loftily as they conceived of the heroic poem, no poet or critic of the Renaissance could approach Milton in grandeur of purpose and intensity of self-devotion. It is not for me here to do more than remind readers how, 'long choosing and beginning late', Milton dedicated himself to the intellectual and moral discipline which he considered necessary for his purpose; of his realization that

he who would not be frustrate of his hope to write well hereafter in laudable things, ought himself to be a true poem; that is, a composition and pattern of the best and honourablest things; [2]

1. Milton's Prose Works (Bohn), Vol. II, p. 478.
2. *Apology for Smectymnuus* (Bohn), Vol. III, p. 118.

and of his magnificent request, twenty years before the completion of *Paradise Lost*, for yet more time, since his was

a work not to be raised from the heat of youth, or the vapours of wine; like that which flows at waste from the pen of some vulgar amourist, or the trencher fury of a rhyming parasite; nor to be obtained by the invocation of dame memory and her siren daughters, but by devout prayer to that eternal Spirit, who can enrich with all utterance and knowledge, and sends out his seraphim, with the hallowed fire of his altar, to touch and purify the lips of whom he pleases.'[1]

Nor was Milton actuated, it need hardly be said, merely by the literary and patriotic ambition to rival the ancients in English; with him the moral purpose, always a part of the Renaissance theory of epic, was of supreme importance. His work was to be 'doctrinal and exemplary to a nation', for it was the true office of poetic genius, he held,

to imbreed and cherish in a great people the seeds of virtue and public civility, to allay the perturbations of the mind, and set the affections in right tune; to celebrate in glorious and lofty hymns the throne and equipage of God's almightiness, and what he works, and what he suffers to be wrought with high providence in his church; to sing victorious agonies of martyrs and saints, the deeds and triumphs of just and pious nations, doing valiantly through faith against the enemies of Christ. ... Teaching over the whole book of sanctity and virtue, through all the instances of example. ...[2]

The appearance of *Paradise Lost* in the midst of the seventeenth century, then, may be attributed in the first place to the fact that in Milton the Renaissance idea of the heroic poem, alive as ever though hitherto 'laid up in some heaven to which the true scholar might rise',[3] at last found its destined English exponent.

1. *Reason of Church Government* (Bohn), Vol. II, p. 481.   2. ibid., p. 479.
3. Ker, op. cit., Introduction, p. xv.

MILTON'S CHOICE OF SUBJECT

It is not part of my purpose to discuss the stages in Milton's own
development which finally led to his choosing the Fall of Man as
the theme of his heroic poem. It is well known that this was not his
original intention; that he had meant to write an Arthuriad, and that
Paradise Lost had been, at the time of the Trinity Manuscript,[1] his
favourite idea for a Tragedy. Dr Tillyard, in his admirable recent
work on Milton,[2] has also shown, by a careful examination of the
prose works, that at the beginning of the Parliamentary régime
Milton was in a state of high-wrought excitement, expecting an
imminent divine event in England, and that he then hoped, in his
Arthuriad or other epic of kindred theme, to sing the glorious
coming of the Kingdom of God and the victories of his saints. In
one of his most incandescent passages of impassioned prose, composed in that dawn when it was a bliss to be alive, England then
standing on the top of golden hours,[3] Milton wrote:

Then, amidst the hymns and hallelujahs of saints, *some one may perhaps be
heard offering at high strains in new and lofty measure* to sing and celebrate thy
divine mercies and marvellous judgements in this land throughout all ages;
whereby this great and warlike nation, instructed and inured to the fervent
and continual practice of truth and righteousness, and casting far from her
the rags of her whole vices, may press on hard to that high and happy emu-
lation to be found the soberest, wisest, and most Christian people at that
day, when thou, the eternal and *shortly expected King*, shalt open the clouds to
judge the several Kingdoms of the world, and distributing national honours
and rewards to religious and just commonwealths, shalt put an end to all
earthly tyrannies, proclaiming thy universal and mild monarchy through
heaven and earth; where they undoubtedly, that by their labours, counsels,
and prayers, have been earnest for the common good of religion and their
country, shall receive above the inferior orders of the blessed, the regal
addition of principalities, legions, and thrones into their glorious titles, and

1. *c.* 1640–1.
2. E. M. W. Tillyard, *Milton* (Chatto & Windus, 1930).
3. The parallel with Wordsworth's state of mind in 1790 is irresistible.

in supereminence of beatific vision, progressing the dateless and irrevoluble circle of eternity, shall clasp inseparable hands with joy and bliss, in over-measure for ever.[1]

Dr Tillyard has shown convincingly that Milton changed these notes to tragic only after the disappointment of his political hopes, that *Paradise Lost* itself is thus in a sense the work of disillusion, and that the 'embers' of his projected heroic poem, the poem of hope and achievement, must be sought in the prose works, and (eminently, of course) in the verse of the early books of *Paradise Lost* and in the character of Satan.

To this it may be added that in finally choosing his theme, Milton, like Wordsworth when he wrote *The Prelude*, was probably guided by the irresistible bent of his own nature towards the kind of subject with which his genius was best fitted to deal. As Dr Johnson truly remarked, Milton's characteristic port is 'gigantick loftiness', and it is permissible to doubt whether he could have employed his great powers to such effect upon any subject of a more 'human' or 'dramatic' kind. It is true, as Dr Tillyard has pointed out,[2] that had Milton been able to achieve his poem of hope we might still have had his poem of disillusion in a second long work, instead of what we actually have – one single long poem of strangely blended texture. Nevertheless one may surmise that even then the greater of those two possible poems would have been that which approached the more closely in scope and setting to *Paradise Lost*. We must believe, I think, that Milton is not merely rationalizing his own sense of frustrated hopes when he calls his theme

> argument
> Not less, but more heroic than the wrath
> Of stern Achilles on his foe pursu'd
> Thrice fugitive about Troy wall . . .

and describes himself as:

> Not sedulous by nature to indite
> Wars, hitherto the only argument

1. *Of Reformation in England*, 1641 (Bohn), Vol. II, pp. 418–19 (my italics).
2. op cit., p. 112.

> Heroic deem'd, chief mast'ry to dissect
> With long and tedious havoc fabl'd knights
> In battles feign'd . . .

adding:

> Me of these
> Nor skill'd nor studious, higher argument
> Remains, sufficient of itself to raise
> That name, unless an age too late, or cold
> Climate, or years damp my intended wing.[1]

What I am especially concerned here to suggest, however, is that, at any rate after the failure of the Saints, it was not only the bent of his own nature but the intellectual climate of his age which impelled Milton towards a biblical theme for his heroic poem. It is true that Milton's outlook seems never to have been influenced by the post-Restoration and Royal Society atmosphere; he had nothing about him of the 'experimental philosopher'. Indeed, his work is much like an isolated volcano thrusting up through the philosophic plains, and drawing its fire from deeper and older levels of spiritual energy. But Milton was 'protestant' to the core, and this meant that in the moral sphere he *was* an 'experimenter', and had the same disdain for all that was not 'truth' as the natural philosopher had in his. The protestant abhorrence of the tinsel ('carnality') of Laudian religion, well seen in Milton's anti-episcopal tracts, was the moral counterpart of the philosopher's scorn for scholastic verbiage. Intolerance of all except what seemed to him *most real* was, then, a characteristic of Milton which linked him with his age, and vitally affected his choice of poetic subject. In the conditions of the century, and to a man of Milton's temper, what kind of theme would appear worthy to be sung in new and lofty measure? Only one which he could feel to be in the highest sense 'true' as well as 'heroic'. Milton's dismissal of 'fabled Knights' and 'battles feigned' and all the 'tinsel trappings' of romance constitutes a rejection of 'fiction' by the protestant consciousness, which is strictly comparable with the rejec-

---

1. *Paradise Lost*, preamble to Bk ix.

tion of scholasticism by the scientific consciousness, and can be ascribed to the same underlying cause. The traditional sources of poetry were running dry; mythologies were exploded and obsolete; no poet with Milton's passion for reality could pour all the energies of his nature into such moulds any longer. But there still remained one source, and one only, from which the seventeenth-century protestant poet could draw images and fables which were not only 'poetic' but also 'true': the Bible. Thanks to the work of several recent scholars, notably M. Saurat and Dr Tillyard, we now appreciate the range and daring of Milton's speculation, and realize that it is unsafe to ascribe to him the purely naïve beliefs he was formerly thought to hold. Milton could twist Scripture to his purpose, or, as we have seen,[1] override it on occasion.[2] Yet when all is said, Milton's attitude to the Bible was still that of protestantism. The Bible remained a numinous book for Locke, and Toland, and Swift, and Addison, and innumerable polite savants in the eighteenth century; how much more, then, must its authority have been felt as a fact by a man of Milton's stamp? That he deferred instinctively to it, even while 'interpreting' it, is shown by his composing that laborious treatise, the De doctrina christiana,[3] in which he is seen exercising the right, and discharging the duty, of every intelligent protestant to search the scriptures for himself and to construct his faith from its pages alone, without regard to the vain notions of other men, or the glosses of priestly tradition. To be left alone with Scripture might, indeed, mean to be left alone with one's own soul, for 'Scripture' was wide enough to bear almost any construction. This may all along have been the inner logic of the protestant appeal to Scripture. But all this leaves unchanged the central fact that Milton, together with nearly everyone else in his century, felt all proper contact with biblical material to be, in quite a special sense, contact with Truth. When contemporary history, which alone could have given 'reality' to his Arthuriad, ceased to furnish matter for heroic

1. See above, p. 70.
2. Cf. 'No ordinance, human or from heaven, can bind against the good of man.' Quoted from Tetrachordon by Tillyard, op. cit., p. 164.
3. Cf. above, pp. 69 ff.

and sacred song, Milton, too old, too disillusioned, and too noble to spend his stored resources on anything but highest truth, could only turn to the Bible for his 'fable'. Science might dismiss old picture-thinking as phantasmal; Platonists might strive to wipe off the gross dews of the imagination from the clear glass of the understanding; puritans might banish as carnal the poetry of ritual and symbol: all these and other agencies might be at work, as they were, undermining and destroying older forms of religious and poetic experience; nevertheless here, in Scripture, God himself had condescended to be a poet, and his divine revelation could therefore still be sung by a Milton with undamaged assurance. The existence of the Hebrew scriptures, then, in the particular setting of seventeenth-century protestantism, must be accounted, together with the idea of the heroic poem, as the cause which made possible a great serious poem at just the period when poetry was coming to be thought of as elegant and agreeable rather than 'true'. Poetry, like Popery, might be an affront to the common sense of a Locke or a Tillotson; but as Prophecy it was still admissible. Calliope could not defend the Thracian bard from the wild rout in Rhodope; and no mere Muse could protect a modern poet from the barbarous dissonance of Restoration England. But Milton invokes Urania, a higher than Calliope:

> So fail not thou, who thee implores:
> For thou art Heav'nly, she an empty dream[1]

The seventeenth-century feeling about Scriptural subjects for poetry is also expressed by Cowley, who, as a man of his own age rather than of all time, may be taken to reflect contemporary sentiments more closely than Milton. Speaking of his own Scriptural epic, the *Davideis*, he indulges in an outburst, rather of wit than of passion, on the way in which poets have laid waste their powers on frivolous topics while all the time the Bible contained subjects not only far more poetical, but also, of course, true.

When I consider this, and how many other [i.e. besides the story of David]

1. *Paradise Lost*, preamble to Bk VII.

bright and magnificent subjects of the like nature, the *Holy Scripture* affords and *proffers*, as it were, to *Poesie*, in the wise managing and illustrating whereof, the *Glory of God Almighty* might be joyned with the singular utility and noblest delight of *Mankind*; It is not without grief and indignation that I behold that *Divine Science* employing all her inexhaustible riches of *Wit* and *Eloquence* either in the wicked and beggerly *Flattery* of great persons, or the unmanly *Idolizing* of *Foolish Women*, or the wretched affectation of scurril *Laughter*, or at best on the confused, antiquated Dreams of senseless *Fables* and *Metamorphoses*.[1]

Amongst all holy things stolen by the Devil, there is none he has so long usurped as poetry, and it is time we restored it to God, its true Father:

There wants, methinks, but the *Conversion* of *That* and the *Jews*, for the accomplishing of the *Kingdom of Christ*.

Cowley expresses, too, the feeling we have already met with in Sprat,[2] that the Fables of antiquity are now exhausted and obsolete, and, having served the poets long enough, should now be abandoned – more particularly as they were 'only fictions at first'. Even if 'these boasted *Feasts of Love* and *Fables*' were wholesome (which they are not), a continuance of them would be nauseating, for it is

almost impossible to serve up any *new Dish* of that kinde. They are all but the *Cold-meats* of the *Antients*, new-heated, and new set forth.

The 'old Poets' themselves were indeed able to reap a rich harvest in this field, for the ground was then untilled; and besides, 'those mad stories of the *Gods* and *Heroes*', ridiculous as they may now seem, were then 'the *whole Body* (or rather *Chaos*) of the *Theologie* of those times'. But to an enlightened modern Christian poet, who should be impatient with their follies, such subjects

ought to appear no better arguments for verse than those of their worthy *Successors*, the *Knights Errant*.

1. *Poems of A. Cowley*, Cambridge English Classics edition, p. 12ff.
2. Cf. pp. 194–5 above.

The tone of Cowley's exhortation suggests that his zeal is less for the justification of God's ways to man than for vindicating 'modern' versus 'ancient', the Bible counting, paradoxically, as 'modern' because it 'belonged' to Christendom and not to pagan antiquity. The rest of his argument seems to amount virtually to this: Ancient fables and wonders are nonsensical, but as poetry is bound to treat of marvels, why should it not sing of such as, being in the Bible, must needs be true, and which, moreover, have not become poetically hackneyed? Wonder for wonder, the Bible is more than a match for Greek mythology and legend. Is not Noah as suitable a subject for poetic ornament as Deucalion, or Samson as Hercules?

Why is not *Jeptha's Daughter* as *good a woman* as *Iphegenia*, and the friendship of *David* and *Jonathan* more worthy celebration then that of *Theseus* and *Perithous*? Does not the passage of *Moses* and the *Israelites* into the *Holy Land* yield incomparably more Poetical variety then the voyages of *Ulysses* or *Aeneas*? etc.

Such statements, whether critically justifiable or not, would sound pious and incontrovertible to seventeenth-century ears. They are of interest to us as evidence of a realization, at this period, that the Bible was a poetic source of unique value, inasmuch as its contents could not, even by modern philosophy, be dismissed as fabulous.

Both Cowley and Milton speak as if to be a 'Christian poet' gave one an obvious and overwhelming advantage over all others. Yet whatever superiority of insight the Christian poet might owe to his Faith, he was also involved by it, as an artist, in peculiar difficulties. Coleridge has indicated one of the chief of these in a passage of the *Biographia Literaria*.[1] After censuring the use, by eighteenth-century poets, of personifications taken from an exploded mythology, Coleridge continues:

Yet when the torch of ancient learning was re-kindled, so cheering were its beams, that our eldest poets, *cut off by Christianity from all accredited machinery*, and deprived of all acknowledged guardians and symbols of the great objects of nature, were naturally induced to adopt, as a poetic language,

1. Vol. II, p. 58 (ed. Shawcross). (The italics are mine.)

those fabulous personages, those forms of the supernatural in nature, which had given them such dear delight in the poems of their great masters.

Christianity, as an exclusive, complete, and final revelation of the divine meaning of the universe, did indeed reduce to the level of fiction all other efforts of the human spirit to express its dealings with the Ultimate; and however eagerly 'our eldest poets' may have appropriated the imagery of antiquity, they did so in full consciousness that what they were employing was 'machinery' only, beautiful and compelling perhaps, but at best having no truth-value except sometimes as allegory. But the Christian poet, even if 'cut off' in this sense from all pagan machinery, had still at his disposal, it will be said, the machinery of Christianity itself? This was, as we have seen, just what Cowley and Milton (and certain French poets of the time) were insisting; and in the Hebrew antiquities they possessed a store of materials which had been supernaturally preserved from destructive criticism. But the use of the Christian machinery for the purposes of a seventeenth-century heroic poem was no simple matter. (Dante's *Divine Comedy*, being a wholly different kind of work, offered no example.) One might, indeed, celebrate the deeds of a David, a Samson, or other Old Testament heroes, and feel with Cowley that to do so was an act as well of piety as of artistry. But what if the central divine drama from the Creation to the Day of Judgement were itself to furnish matter for the song? Owing to its historical development in union with Greek philosophy, Christianity was in the peculiar position of possessing not only a Hellenic God, who was the Absolute of theology, but also a Hebrew Jehovah whose personality and behaviour were not altogether unlike those of 'the gods'. The discrepancy between the two conceptions would be felt to be due to the progressive quality of the divine revelation, whereby one kind of relationship between God and man would be fitting before Christ's appearance, and another afterwards. In the seventeenth century, however Hebraically many Puritans thought and spoke about God, there is no doubt that for the best mind (Milton of course among them) God was 'omnipotent, immutable, immortal, infinite',[1] and this meant difficulty for any one who

1. *Paradise Lost*, III, 372.

should speak of divine subjects in poetry, which can only proceed by giving to everything it touches 'a local habitation and a name'. Boileau, who may be taken as representative of the critical intelligence of the end of the century, declares frankly for the continued use of pagan machinery in epic, and pronounces the Christian faith unsuitable for poetic treatment. Heroic poetry, he says,

> Se soutient par la fable, et vit de fiction.
> Là, pour nous enchanter, tout est mis en usage;
> Tout prend un corps, une âme, un esprit, un visage.
>
> .   .   .
>
> Ce n'est plus la vapeur qui produit la tonnerre,
> C'est Jupiter armé pour effrayer la terre;[1] etc.

It is the business of the epic poet to leave no common incident unadorned and unelevated; he must set each action in a mythological framework, for

> C'est là ce qui surprend, frappe, saisit, attache.
> Sans tous ces ornemens le vers tombe en langueur:
> La poésie est morte, ou rampe sans vigueur.

Consequently the scriptural school of poets are misguided zealots:

> C'est donc bien vainement que nos auteurs déçus,[2]
> Bannissant de leurs vers ces ornemens reçus,
> Pensent faire agir Dieu, ses saints, et ses prophètes,
> Comme ces dieux éclos du cerveau des poëtes;
> Mettent à chaque pas le lecteur en enfer;
> N'offrent rien qu'Astaroth, Belzébuth, Lucifer.
> De la foi d'un chrétien les mystères terribles
> D'ornemens égayés ne sont pas susceptibles;
> L'Évangile à l'esprit n'offre de tous côtés
> Que pénitence à faire et tourmens mérités;
> Et de vos fictions le mélange coupable
> Même à ses vérités donne l'air de la fable.

1. *L'Art poétique*, III, 160.

2. Ker says that Boileau is thinking here especially of Desmarets de Saint-Sorlin, author of *Clovis* (see *Essays of J. Dryden*, Vol. II, p. 279).

So completely has poetry, even epic, its most serious genre, assumed the role of 'enchanting' us with its fictions, its '*ornemens égayés*', that it cannot touch Truth without infecting it with its own fictitious quality. It had therefore better leave religion alone, lest it run the risk

> Du Dieu de vérité faire un Dieu de mensonges.

This view reappears in Johnson's censure of Milton's *Lycidas* for its mingling with 'trifling fictions', of 'the most sacred and awful truths such as ought never to be polluted with such irreverend combinations'. We see in this forced separation of religion from poetry a characteristic outcome of the intellectual movement of the century. As 'enlightenment' increased poetry could be dismissed (or enjoyed) as fiction; religion could not yet be similarly dismissed, so it was pigeon-holed as 'revelation' and 'mystery'. At all costs the two dangerous elements must be kept from combining, for if religion became poetical, or poetry religious, the ensuing explosion might disturb the peace of the Augustans. Dryden, reviewing in his old age the achievements of the century in heroic poetry, admits with Boileau that

the machines of our Christian religion, in heroic poetry, are much more feeble to support that weight than those of heathenism,[1]

and considers this as a reason for

the failings of many great wits amongst the Moderns, who have attempted to write an epic poem.

Milton, as before mentioned,[2] was not considered by Dryden to have written the long-awaited epic:

His subject is not that of an Heroic Poem, properly so called. His design is the losing of our happiness; his event is not prosperous, like that of all other epic works; his heavenly machines are many, and his human persons are but two.

1. *A Discourse Concerning the Original and Progress of Satire.* (Ker, Vol. II, pp. 31 ff.)
2. Cf. p. 200 above.

Although his censure of Milton is thus mainly the criticism of a man of letters upon a fellow-craftsman, rather than that of a man concerned with the relations between poetry and beliefs, Dryden does proceed, in one of the most unexpected passages of his prose, to consider the possibilities for a genuine Christian epic, and to offer what can only be described as an extraordinary suggestion of his own. Christian poets, he says, have neglected their own resources. In the angelology of the Book of Daniel, judiciously combined with 'the principles of the Platonic philosophy, as it is now Christianized', they may find the desired Christian substitute for the gods of paganism. The necessary supernatural machinery would then be provided by angelic creatures acting as tutelary genii or guardian angels presiding over the destiny of nations. Unlike the pagan gods, these angels would have the immense advantage of being non-fictitious, for their existence is 'a doctrine almost universally received by Christians, as well Protestants as Catholics'; and thus both poet and reader would have the satisfaction of feeling in contact with something truer than mere fable. Moreover, the contests between the guardian angels of rival tribes would be free from the objections attaching to all portrayals of Divine omnipotence in conflict with Satan. To defy the omnipotent to arms is a palpable absurdity, and there can be no epic interest in a battle wherein the 'poor devils' are sure to get worsted in the end. Whereas we should no more foresee the outcome of a conflict between two tutelary angels than of one between Juno and Venus.

It is strange to contemplate the aged Dryden writing thus hopefully of the prospects of heroic poetry so late in the seventeenth century, for as we can now see, the Renaissance impulse to excel in this kind was by then nearly exhausted, and 'the town' which in the next generation became excited over the *Essay on Man* would have scorned Dryden's proposed machinery, unless it had been used, like Pope's sylphs in the *Rape of the Lock*, in a mocking vein. *Paradise Lost* had in fact been, in spite of Dryden, the nearest realization of the epic ideal that England would have. The reasons for the solidity and lasting-power of Milton's epic lay outside the critical purview of Dryden or Boileau. It was based upon the one 'fable', the one piece of machinery, which could still be 'accredited' as real by almost everybody. True, it was bristling with 'inconveniences', but these were only those of the faith itself. God the Father might argue like a school-divine; Satan might be allowed an inexplicable degree of freedom; the whole business of the Fall might seem an arraignment rather than a justification of the ways of God to men; the geography and administration of heaven and hell might be grossly pictorial and incompatible with any rational theology; but all these difficulties were not created by Milton: they were inherent in a religion which grafted an Aristotelian or Platonic theology upon a stock of Hebrew mythology. Milton, like many in his own generation, was in the peculiar position of being able to hold advanced speculative views and yet at the same time to 'believe' in the traditional imagery of Christianity. The exact quality of that 'belief' is difficult to define, but we may perhaps help ourselves to conceive it by remembering the instinctive deference of that age for ancient authority. If a Bacon could guess at an antique wisdom embalmed in the classical myths, how much rather could not a Milton infallibly *know* that divine truth was contained in the sacred narratives? Like a good protestant, Milton held that every passage of Scripture has only one plain sense, and that in all things necessary for salvation the Bible is plain and perspicuous.[1] Yet he agreed so far with Philo and the allegorists[2] as to believe that in the Old Testament, at any rate, the sense is 'sometimes a compound of the historical and typical'.[3] I have already[4] quoted Milton's statement that, in the biblical accounts of God and his procedure, we are to understand that God is

exhibited not as he really is, but in such a manner as may be within the scope of our comprehension.

Thus, with regard to the Creation, Milton, like Philo or Sir Thomas Browne, considered that it must 'in reality' have been instantaneous, for

> Immediate are the acts of God, more swift
> Than time or motion. . . .[5]

1. Cf. *De doctrina christiana*, Ch. 30, Bohn, IV, p. 440–2.
2. Cf. above, p. 62.   3. *De doctrina christiana*, loc. cit.   4. Above, p. 69.
5. *Paradise Lost*, VII, 176

He even, if M. Saurat be right in his conjectures, entertained the remoter supposition, derived from the Zohar, of a Creation by the 'retreat' of God from part of Total Being. Nevertheless, in condescension to our capacity, the process of creation is successively related in Scripture – 'so told as earthly notion can conceive' – and Milton accordingly follows the Scriptural account in *Paradise Lost*. In practising the method he ascribes to Raphael –

> What surmounts the reach
> Of human sense, I shall delineate so,
> By lik'ning spiritual to corporal forms
> As may express them best – [1]

Milton undoubtedly felt that he was employing the technique of Scripture itself. We could not *know* what God 'really is', nor the true manner of his actions, and though we were free to conjecture speculatively it was wisest to accept the Bible narrative. God's own allegories could at least contain no falsehood, even if they concealed the whole truth; our own invented notions, on the contrary, would be sure to err. In trusting to Scriptural (and Miltonic) imagery, moreover, there was this further reassuring thought:

> What if Earth
> Be but the shadow of Heaven, and things therein
> Each to other like, more than on earth is thought?

Milton's strongly protestant cast of mind inclined him to a literal understanding of Scripture wherever possible; there might be an admixture of the 'typical' in a Bible story, yet it remained for him historical as well. I do not think Milton read the first chapters of Genesis, as Browne had suggested they might be read, *simply* as an allegory illustrating the seduction of Reason by the Passions,[2] though of course the story could mean that also. Had the Fall of Man not been for him a real historical fact as well as an allegory or dogma, I do not believe he could have made it the central theme of his greatest work. Similarly, 'Christ' might be for Milton, as for John Smith, a 'type', a 'principle', representing Right Reason, or the executive

1. *Paradise Lost*, v, 571. (Cf. above, p. 70.)   2. Cf. above, p. 67.

power of God, yet one cannot doubt that for him that principle was historically incarnated, in a unique sense, in Jesus of Nazareth. Dr Tillyard has well noted[1] that in a famous passage of *Areopagitica* Milton juxtaposes, without change of tone, the legend of Psyche with the story of Genesis as if these were for him on exactly the same plane of reality. One might add that in the *Nativity Ode* there is nothing to mark the baroque figure of the 'meek-ey'd peace' as more fictional than the shepherds, the Virgin blest, or the Babe. The 'reality' of the false gods of heathendom was, we know, saved for Milton by their identification with the defaulting angels. On the whole, however, I think we must conclude that whereas the pagan myths were to him but husks from which truth could be winnowed (as in the theory of Bacon and Reynolds), the biblical events, if allegorical at all, were the deliberate allegories of God himself; and when God allegorizes he does not merely write or inspire parables, he also *causes to happen the events which can be allegorically interpreted.*[2] At the same time we may agree with Dr Tillyard that Milton's mind was not consciously preoccupied with the demarcation of truth from fiction. He did not belong to the scientific movement of the seventeenth century, which, as I have repeatedly indicated above, was preoccupied with precisely this task. He lived in a moral rather than a physical world, and was ready to imbibe wisdom wherever he could find it. 'Wisdom', for most Renaissance minds – and as we have seen, Milton's was of that, rather than of the 'modern' or 'philosophic' order – was to be sought above all in antiquity. Antiquity for the seventeenth-century scholar meant two great traditions, the classical, in which he had been intellectually trained, and the Christian, in which he had been spiritually moulded. Great reverence was felt for both traditions – hence the apparent equipollence of Greek and Scriptural myths in parts of Milton's writings – but a special degree of belief was, I think, accorded to the Christian. To the end of the century, and beyond it, the events of the Christian revelation were saved as 'real' by the belief that in them God had, for exceptional and non-recurrent reasons, made a deliberate

1. op. cit., p. 223.
2. Cf. Saurat, *Milton, the Man and the Thinker*, p. 212.

infraction of the 'laws of nature'; but that elsewhere and ever since for all time those laws would be found to operate in their ordinary course. It was only later, when science had familiarized a sharper division between 'real' and 'unreal' phenomena, that the miraculous elements of Christian doctrine could be attacked directly as 'mere' fictions.

MILTON AND THE FALL OF MAN

The foregoing considerations have been advanced, first to show how a great epic poem could arise out of this scientific century; and secondly, to explain why, in spite of all attendant difficulties, a Scriptural theme for this poem was almost inevitable. It remains now to indicate a few of the contradictions which, owing to Milton's partial exposure to the seventeenth-century climate, are to be found embedded in his poetry.

There would be less discussion than there has been about the real meaning of *Paradise Lost* were it not for the fact that we know Milton to have had affinities, on one side of his nature, with the rationalizing spirit of his age, so that it is not always quite certain exactly what he is understanding by a given doctrine. He departed from current protestant orthodoxy in certain important respects. Not only in his radical views on divorce, but in some of the capital points of the faith, he showed an intrepid independence of mind, taking his adventurous flight, like his own Satan, straight through the palpable obscure of current opinion. He abandoned the Calvinist doctrine of predestination; he refused the Son equal status with the Father; he asserted that God created the universe, not out of 'nothing', but out of Himself; and that therefore 'matter' was in itself a divine principle. To this materialism he added the belief that God endowed matter with the principle of life and thought, and that body and soul in man are one, not two. The corollary of this belief, which Milton unflinchingly accepted, was 'mortalism', that is the doctrine that at death 'all of me then shall die',[1] to be revived again only at

1. *Paradise Lost*, X, 792.

the Last Judgement.[1] It will be recalled that he also believed that 'the Spirit which is given to us is a more certain guide than Scripture'.[2] But what I wish to emphasize, rather than these more startling heterodoxies, is the humanism of Milton, which links him both ✓ with the Renaissance and with the Cambridge Platonists. By humanism I merely mean, here, a belief in the natural dignity and virtue of man, provided that by due discipline the passions are subjected to Right Reason. Milton stands half-way between those who, like Pascal or Blake, hold the utter depravity of the natural man, and those who, like Rousseau, believe unreservedly in his goodness. Nature, and human nature along with it, being originally made out of God's own substance, must necessarily be good; but Man, in virtue of his reason, has the unique responsibility of moral choice ('Reason also is choice'),[3] which means that man is good only when Reason is in command of the passions. The impulses, though 'naturally' good, are in practice good only when controlled by Reason.

> Reason in man obscur'd, or not obey'd,
> Immediately inordinate desires
> And upstart passions catch the government
> From Reason.[4]

Herein lies the radical or 'original' sinfulness of man, as well as his prerogative. Milton believed in the Fall, but he also believed in the power and freedom of the human will to stand firm, or to recover itself after a lapse.

In many passages Milton, like the Cambridge Platonists, exalts 'Reason' as the godlike principle in man, meaning by this term, again like them, the principle of moral control rather than of intellectual enlightenment. Here are a few examples from the *De doctrina christiana*:

1. It should be remembered that Milton is here actually in agreement with Hobbes. (Cf. p. 98 above.)
2. *De doctrina christiana*, Ch. 30, Bohn, IV, p. 449. (Cf. pp. 70–1 and 205 above.)
3. *Paradise Lost*, III, 108   4. *Paradise Lost*, XII, 86.

The Deity has imprinted upon the human mind so many unquestionable tokens of himself, and so many traces of him are apparent throughout the whole of nature, that no one in his senses can remain ignorant of the truth.[1]

Man was originally made in the image of God, and had the whole 'law of Nature' implanted and innate in him. And even after the Fall, with the 'spiritual death' which followed,

The existence of God is further proved by that feeling, whether we term it conscience, or right reason, which even in the worst of characters, is not altogether extinguished.[2]

Man's 'Renovation' is defined as a change whereby

some remnants of the divine image still exist in us, not wholly extinguished by this spiritual death. . . . These vestiges of original excellence are visible, first in the *understanding* . . . Secondly, the *will* is clearly not altogether inefficient in respect of good works, or at any rate of good endeavours. . . .[3] the natural mind and will of man being partially renewed by a divine impulse, are led to seek the knowledge of God, and for the time, at least, undergo an alteration for the better.[4]

The Law of God is both written *and* unwritten: the unwritten being

no other than that law of nature given originally to Adam, and of which a certain remnant, or imperfect illumination, still dwells in the hearts of all mankind; which in the regenerate, under the influence of the Holy Spirit, is *daily tending towards a renewal of its primitive brightness*.[5]

This is the language of one who is trying to reconstruct protestant doctrine in terms of a humanistic ethic. Milton has so far emancipated himself from Calvinistic theology, as to believe that there is a godlike principle in Man, and that that principle is to be found in the Reason or Understanding, and the Will. Whatever feeds the Understanding, therefore, and procures true knowledge and wisdom is for him of the highest value; hence the importance of study and education. We know that, for his own part, he took 'labour and

---

1. Bohn, IV, p. 14. 2. ibid., p. 15.
3. ibid., p. 266 (italics mine, here and below).
4. ibid., p. 323. 5. ibid., p. 378.

intense study'[1] to be his portion in this life. And the purpose of education he conceived to be 'to repair the ruins of our first parents by regaining to know God aright'.[2]

God himself is truth; in propagating which, as men display a greater integrity and zeal, they approach nearer to the similitude of God, and possess a greater portion of his love. We cannot suppose the Deity envious of truth, or unwilling that it should be freely communicated to mankind.[3]

It was believed of old that Tiresias had been deprived of his sight as a punishment for divulging Jove's secrets to Man, but Milton, now blind himself as a result of study and labour for human enlightenment, disdains the imputation:

The loss of sight, therefore, which this inspired sage, who was so eager in promoting knowledge among men, sustained cannot be considered as a judicial punishment.[4]

Rather the blindness of such as Tiresias and Milton is a condition of prophetic insight into

> things invisible to mortal sight.

The argument of the *Areopagitica* in favour of unrestricted reading is, of course, familiar:

'To the pure all things are pure;' not only meats and drinks, but *all kinds of knowledge, whether of good or evil*: the knowledge cannot defile, nor consequently the books, if the will and conscience be not defiled.

The famous passage about the knowledge of good and evil in this treatise has been as much quoted as anything in Milton's prose, but its bearing upon what I have to say is so close that I must quote it once again:

Good and evil we know in the field of this world grow up together almost inseparably; and the knowledge of good is so involved and interwoven

1. *Reason of Church Government*, Bohn, II, p. 477–8
2. *Tractate on Education*, Bohn, III, p. 464.
3. *Second Defence*, Bohn, I, p. 236.
4. ibid., p. 237.

with the knowledge of evil, and in so many cunning resemblances hardly to be discerned, that those confused seeds which were imposed upon Psyche as an incessant labour to cull out, and sort asunder, were not more intermixed. It was from out the rind of one apple tasted, that the knowledge of good and evil, as two twins cleaving together, leaped forth into the world. And perhaps this is that doom which Adam fell into of knowing good and evil; that is to say, of knowing good by evil.

As therefore the state of man now is; what wisdom can there be to choose, what continence to forbear, without the knowledge of evil? He that can apprehend and consider vice with all her baits and seeming pleasures, and yet abstain, and yet distinguish, and yet prefer that which is truly better, he is the true wayfaring Christian. I cannot praise a fugitive and cloistered virtue unexercised and unbreathed, that never sallies out and seeks her adversary, but slinks out of the race, where that immortal garland is to be run for, not without dust and heat. Assuredly we bring not innocence into the world, we bring impurity much rather; that which purifies us is trial, and trial is by what is contrary. That virtue therefore which is but a youngling in the contemplation of evil, and knows not the utmost that vice promises to her followers, and rejects it, is but a blank virtue, not a pure; her whiteness is but an excremental whiteness; which was the reason why our sage and serious poet Spenser (whom I dare be known to think a better teacher than Scotus or Aquinas), describing true temperance under the person of Guion, brings him in with his palmer through the cave of Mammon, and the bower of earthly bliss, that he might see and know, and yet abstain.

Since therefore the knowledge and survey of vice is in this world so necessary to the constituting of human virtue, and the scanning of error to the confirmation of truth, how can we more safely, and with less danger, scout into the regions of sin and falsity, than by reading all manner of tractates, and hearing all manner of reason?[1]

'Virtue' for Milton, then, 'consists in the will doing what is right in full knowledge of the issues'.[2] And of moral knowledge (to close this array of examples) Milton writes elsewhere that he who has arrived

to know anything distinctly of God, and of his true worship, and what is

1. *Areopagitica*, Bohn, ii, p. 67–8.
2. Tillyard, op. cit., p. 54.

infallibly good and happy in the state of man's life, what in itself evil and miserable, though vulgarly not so esteemed.

has obtained the 'only high valuable wisdom indeed'.[1]

We must now consider the main problem towards which this discussion has been leading, namely, what, holding these brave humanist views of man and of knowledge, would be Milton's view of the Fall, and how would he treat it as the central event of his great poem? My reason for discussing this matter here is that in my view Milton's handling of this theme furnishes an illustration of the conflict, in the seventeenth century, between pictorial and conceptual thinking.

I have already stated that Milton believed in a 'Fall' in some sense. No true humanist has ever doubted that there is in man a radical tendency to err. Aristotle said that it was hard to be good, even though virtue was the realization of man's true 'nature'; and modern humanists can find in human futility, perversity, and laziness ample equivalents for the 'original sin' of theology. From the humanist standpoint the Fall may be conceptualized as the sad condition of mankind, whereby '*video meliora proboque, deteriora sequor*'; or any one such surrender to impulse might be described as a 'Fall'. It might be supposed that the Fall would be one of those doctrines which Milton would re-state for himself in terms of humanist morality; and in fact there is evidence enough that he did so. The Fall was the surrender of Reason to upstart passions, and its effect was 'spiritual death', or the loss of the will's freedom to choose rightly.

> Reason in Man obscur'd, or not obey'd,
> Immediately inordinate desires
> And upstart passions catch the government
> From Reason.

Here Milton, through the mouth of Michael, is speaking of the Fall as a fact of experience which he has known in his own life, and perhaps still more glaringly in his contacts with Man as a political animal. He is speaking of the same thing, and in the same mode of

1. *Reason of Church Government*, Bohn, II, p. 473.

thought, when he writes in the *De doctrina christiana* of 'spiritual death' as the punishment of sin. It consists, he says, in

the loss, or at least in the obscuration to a great extent of that right reason which enabled men to discern the chief good, and in which consisted as it were the life of the understanding. . . . It consists, secondly, in that deprivation of righteousness and liberty to do good, and in that slavish submission to sin and the devil, which constitutes, as it were, the death of the will.[1]

It was also a characteristic part of Milton's doctrine on this point that this loss of inward liberty was inevitably accompanied by, and punished by, loss of political liberty. True liberty dwells ever with Right Reason; but 'fallen' man is deservedly subject to tyranny. 'Redemption' meant the process, possible by God's grace, by which the will recovered once again its liberty to do good.

So much, then, for 'The Fall' considered as expressive of a fact in spiritual psychology. But now, what of the *historical* 'Fall' of Genesis? what of man's first disobedience, and the fruit of that forbidden tree? Milton has to speak of this as an expounder of Christian doctrine; as the poet of Paradise Lost he has to sing of this above all. Once again we are in face of the characteristic seventeenth-century situation, in which a picture confronts a concept; and here, as in all cases where the pictorial account was the scriptural one, it must at all costs be retained; the Fall as a historical fact must be reconciled with the Fall as a condition. This perhaps might have presented no particular difficulty but for the fact that Genesis, to which Milton must needs adhere, represented the Fall as due to, or as consisting of, the acquisition by Man of that very knowledge, the Knowledge of good and evil, by the possession of which alone Milton the humanist believed man could be truly virtuous. Here indeed was a strange situation: Milton, believing, as we have seen, in 'Knowledge', and in 'Reason' as choice of good by a free agent cognizant of evil, selects as the subject of his greatest poem a fable which represents the acquisition of these very things as the source of all our woe. It may be said that it is only in our fallen state that moral knowledge has become essential – that it is only 'as therefore the state of man now

1. Bohn, IV, p. 265.

is' that there can be no 'wisdom to choose', no 'continence to for-bear', without the knowledge of evil; that, in a word, innocence would have been better than morality. But Milton does not really believe this, as is clearly shown by his failure to convince us that the prelapsarian life of Adam and Eve in the 'happy garden' was genu-inely happy. 'Assuredly we bring not innocence into the world, we bring impurity much rather': this is what Milton knew and be-lieved; yet his adherence to Genesis involved him in the neccesity of representing man's true and primal happiness as the innocence of Eden. Milton's treatment of the ancient Hebrew myth (or more probably, amalgam of myths) is somewhat analogous to Bacon's elucidation of pagan fables; it illustrates the plight of a seventeenth-century moralist, scholarly and earnest but unhistorically-minded, when faced with ancient material which anthropology has only recently begun to unravel. I am not competent to expound the original meaning, or meanings, of the myth of the Tree of Know-ledge; nor is this necessary for the present argument. It is suggested by a competent biblical critic[1] that the story in Genesis is of the kind known as 'aetiological', that is, that it attempts to account in terms of myth, not for the origin of sin, but for the facts of the human situation. Here is man, civilized and knowing above the rest of creation, yet gaining his bread in the sweat of his brow; while woman brings forth her children in sorrow. Why should this be so? And why must mankind be clothed while the beasts go naked? Alas, this knowledge which has brought civilization and power, this self-consciousness which has come upon us, has produced more misery than happiness. Perhaps the gods were jealous of man's knowledge, as in the stories of Prometheus and Tiresias, and revenged them-selves for his encroachment on their prerogative by bringing all this woe upon him. Or perhaps, to take a more charitable (and pious) view, they were anxious to spare man the pain of truth. In either case the story would be a pessimistic interpretation of evolution. Man was driven from the 'Eden of the Unconscious'[2] when he began to reason.

1. Prof. A. S. Peake, *Commentary on the Bible*, p. 139.
2. The phrase is Mr Middleton Murry's.

Our concern, however, is not so much with the original meaning of the myth as with how Milton faced up to the issues which it seemed to him to raise. This much seems clear, that in the Genesis myth the trees of knowledge and of life were unlike all the rest of the vegetation of Eden in that they were magical trees: they really did contain the 'virtues' implied in their names; man did acquire his distinctive knowledge, for better or for worse (apparently the ancient mythologist thought it was for worse), by eating of the Tree of Knowledge, neither could the gods prevent this from being the result; and the prohibition was laid upon the fruit *because* of its magical properties. These meanings must have seemed to Milton to lie clearly upon the surface of the biblical narrative, and they were highly unacceptable to him. He must, moreover, have supposed 'knowledge of good and evil' to mean knowledge of moral distinctions, and not, what Professor Peake tells us it means, scientific 'knowledge of things so far as they are useful or harmful'. Now what could Milton, with his belief in Right Reason, make of all this material? What had the eating of a magic sciential apple to do with the Fall that he knew – the usurpation of the passions upon Reason? It was clearly necessary for him to explain much away, to re-state the biblical account and interpret it in the light of that Spirit within which is 'a more certain guide than Scripture'. Let us see, first, how Milton attempts this in the prose of *De doctrina christiana*:[1]

Man was made in the image of God, and

had the whole law of nature so implanted and innate in him, that he needed no precept to enforce its observance.

It follows that if Adam

received any additional commands whether respecting the tree of know-ledge, or the institution of marriage, these commands formed no part of the law of nature, which is sufficient of itself to teach whatever is agreeable to right reason, that is to say, whatever is intrinsically good.

The 'laws of God' are thus rationalized as equivalent to the laws of nature and reason, the view being the same as that held by the

1. The extracts are from Chap. 10.

Cambridge Platonists, that God does not constitute right and wrong by the absolute fiat of his despotic will, but that he wills and commands what as a matter of fact *is* right, and *because* it is so. This is practically to supersede the image of a personal God and to deify instead the concept 'right', since the latter becomes in this view antecedent to God. But because God desired the service of free agents, and not of automata, he deliberately introduced amongst the laws of nature another law of a wholly different kind, the taboo upon the Tree of Knowledge. This intrusive law was not a law of nature like the rest of God's commands. What law of nature forbade the acquisition of knowledge, moral or scientific – still less the mere eating of an apple? It was a 'positive law', that is, the prohibited act became wrong because forbidden; it was not prohibited because intrinsically wrong. We now come to the most significant point of all, the point at which Milton deals most high-handedly with the myth. It was wrong to eat the fruit, according to him, because it was prohibited, and only because of this. He represents the taboo as imposed simply as a test of man's obedience:

It was necessary that something should be forbidden or commanded as a test of fidelity, *and that an act of its own nature indifferent*, in order that man's obedience might be thereby manifested.[1]

It was in this direction alone that the unfallen Adam could practise free choice, and the choice lay simply between obedience and disobedience. But – 'an act of its own nature indifferent?' The eating of the fruit can only be so regarded by ignoring the magical nature of the tree in the original myth, and this is precisely what Milton, because he believed in virtue as conscious moral choice, is here compelled to do. No 'knowledge' was in fact derived from the fruit; Man was disobedient, and disobedience against God implies the commission of all possible sins. The tree was only named of good and evil, he assures us, *'from the event'*; not because it taught man the difference between right and wrong, but because through the *disobedience* with which the tree was associated man came to know 'good lost, and evil got'. Milton does not try to explain why, if the

1. Bohn, IV, p. 221 (my italics).

act was in its own nature indifferent, the taboo was laid upon that particular tree, so significantly distinguished by God himself, *before* 'the event', as the tree of knowledge of good and evil. That part of the myth's meaning was irreconcilable with Milton's real beliefs. The 'real' Miltonic Fall, the obscuration of Reason and the loss of liberty, has to be represented as the *result* of this purely legal transgression; the actual eating of the fruit Milton can only rationalize as disobedience.

It remains to point out certain relevant aspects of Milton's poetic treatment of the same theme in *Paradise Lost*. As a poet Milton has, of course, to speak pictorially; he has to dramatize, to narrate, to portray, the persons and events of the story. In making a *poem* at all of Paradise Lost, he is in a sense running counter both to the temper of the age, and to a strong impulse in his own mind, which was moving towards the rationalization of religious imagery. That he was able to believe in his own subject-matter as 'real' as well as 'typical' was due, as I have suggested, to his sharing the protestant confidence in the authority of Scripture. That he did so believe in his own high argument is evident, I think, from the fact that the poem as a whole does not read like allegory. The persons have the solidity of real persons; the events have the air of having really happened. Satan would not be what he is if he were merely the translation into picture-language of the abstract idea of evil, or of passion. The few appearances of genuine allegory (all of them non-scriptural in origin) are at once felt to be on a different plane of reality from their context: the characters of Sin and Death, for example; the causeway they build across Chaos; and the Limbo of Vanity on the outer edge of the world. Nevertheless some of the difficulties of the Christian epic, indicated by Boileau and Dryden,[1] were inevitably present to Milton. Certain parts of his machinery were necessarily less real to him than others; in particular, of course, God as an epic personage was less real than Satan. The whole effort of theology for centuries, and particularly in the seventeenth century, had been to avoid the contradictions which result from conceiving of God pictorially as a magnified human potentate. But this is how Milton

1. Cf. above, pp. 210–11.

had to represent him if he were to appear as a character in a heroic poem. Milton's own insight, like that of the Platonists and many other thinkers of the time, led him, in his inmost cogitation, to translate 'God' as the eternal Law of Right, whose service is perfect freedom. But the whole theme of *Paradise Lost* implies a much less conceptualized God, one, in fact, whose very existence as a 'person' causes most of the difficulties of the story. The inferiority of Milton's God to his Satan, both poetically and morally, has often been pointed out,[1] and need not be further emphasized here. God had to be *deemed* omnipresent, omniscient, omnipotent, and benevolent, yet *portrayed* as localized in Heaven, subject to gross attacks from his enemies, and administering the universe in a manner which it taxed Milton's utmost energies to 'justify'. The weakness of this part of the machinery may be attributed to this: that it collapses into fragments at once if Milton's own best theological insight is applied to it. As is well known, Milton bases his justification of God's ways entirely on the fact that Adam fell of his own 'free' will.

> So without least impulse or shadow of fate,
> Or aught by me immutably foreseen,
> They trespass; authors to themselves in all
> Both what they judge and what they choose; for so
> I form'd them free, and free they must remain
> Till they enthral themselves. . . .[2]

'Free' here means 'not constrained', exempt from the rigour of the divine 'decrees' which otherwise bound nature fast in fate. It has, that is to say, the negative sense of 'freedom *from*' external coercion. But Milton is also in the habit of using 'freedom' in a profounder, more conceptualized sense, and the two planes of meaning sometimes intersect bewilderingly. This second meaning is seen in a passage I have already cited in part more than once:

> Since thy original lapse, true Liberty
> Is lost, which always with Right Reason dwells

1. Cf., for example, Shelley's *Defence of Poetry*.
2. From God's speech, *Paradise Lost*, III, 120

> Twinn'd, and from her hath no dividual being:
> Reason in Man obscur'd, or not obey'd,
> Immediately inordinate desires
> And upstart passions catch the government
> From Reason, and to servitude reduce
> Man, till then free.[1]

'Freedom' in this sense is *the service of reason*, or voluntary submission to the law which preserves the stars from wrong. This meaning even creeps into the last words of the first-quoted extract:

> free they must remain
> Till they enthral themselves –

'free' here meaning not the 'unconstrained' of the earlier lines, but 'reason-serving'. The same sense appears in Adam's remark to Eve:

> But God left free the will, *for what obeys*
> *Reason, is free, and Reason he made right.*[2]

According to this view, 'freedom' is only attained when 'constraint' is absolute, constraint, however, by the Law of Reason. Meaning is also found, within this view, for the negative sense; it becomes 'freedom from' the solicitations of unreason. Now it happens that it is 'freedom' in the negative sense – 'freedom from constraint' – that Milton wishes to claim for Adam before his Fall. This was necessary in order to exonerate God from the charge of unjust behaviour, and might serve well enough as long as Milton was thinking pictorially. But difficulty arises directly we remember that as it is from God, not from Charles I, that Adam is to be 'free', his freedom is only a freedom-to-lose-freedom, a freedom-to-become-enslaved: real freedom being precisely submission to God (Right Reason). Adam is free when he is most God-constrained; directly he exercises his unconstrained choice he departs from God, and automatically ceases to be 'free'. It is only as long as God is being conceived pictorially that 'freedom from' him can be supposed to be desirable; substitute the idea-God (Right Reason) for the picture-God, and you produce the contradiction 'freedom-from

1. *Paradise Lost*, XII, 83.   2. *Paradise Lost*, IX, 351.

freedom'. There remains, however, a further complication. Adam, though free before his fall, had not the full spiritual liberty which consists in the voluntary submission of a rational being to the law of reason. With the exception of his one vulnerable point, his paradoxical capacity to lose his freedom, he was really God-constrained, not in the manner of a responsible moral being, but in the manner of the animals and the rest of nature. He could not but will what was right until, having disobeyed, he had become capable of sin. Only a being capable of sin could know the meaning which Milton really attached to the notion of spiritual freedom; thus the Fall was logically a necessary stage in the evolution of man. It may be said that Adam and Eve were capable of moral choice, and hence of sin, before they ate the fruit, otherwise they could not have chosen to disobey God's express command; and Milton, in his endeavour to make his epic narrative humanly convincing, certainly has to attribute to them some of the frailties of fallen humanity in order to make their behaviour plausible. But this limited freedom of choice, and its arbitrary connexion with an inexplicable taboo, did not constitute the full 'liberty' of Milton's own ripest thought. A man must *know good and evil* much more intimately than prelapsarian Adam could before he can submit with his whole being to the control of that divine law in whose service is perfect freedom. Milton is thus caught in the tangle of his biblical imagery. He is bound to represent the unfallen Adam as perfect, made in the image of God; and he is bound to represent the act of disobedience as a calamity engineered by the devil. And yet that act represented the liberation of man from the beneficent determinism of Jehovah, and the birth – accompanied, indeed, by the throes of sin and suffering – of his capacity for true 'liberty'. Milton was a Promethean, a Renaissance humanist, in the toils of a myth of quite contrary import, a myth which yearned, as no Milton could, for the blank innocence and effortlessness of a golden age. He must, of course, have intended us to applaud when God says, with unpleasant irony:

> O Sons, like one of us Man is become
> To know both good and evil, since his taste
> Of that defended fruit; but let him boast

His knowledge of good lost, and evil got;
Happier, had it suffic'd him to have known
Good by itself, and evil not at all.[1]

But we do not believe it; and it is hard to conceive that Milton did.
His own thought is better expressed by the Son, where he prophesies
to the Father that repentant Man will at length bring forth

Fruits of more pleasing savour from thy seed
Sown with contrition in his heart, than those
Which his own hand *manuring all the trees*
Of Paradise could have produc't, ere fall'n
From innocence – [2]

and by Michael, when he comforts Adam with the assurance:

Then wilt thou not be loath
To leave this Paradise, but shalt possess
A Paradise within thee, happier far.[3]

THE TREE OF KNOWLEDGE IN 'PARADISE LOST'

There is a significant difference between Milton's poetic handling
of this subject in *Paradise Lost* and his prose exposition in *De doctrina
christiana*. In the poem he is of necessity tied closely to the biblical
story, and he cannot therefore ignore the magical properties of the
forbidden tree as he could when he was rationalizing the whole
myth in prose. In fact, almost every possible objection to the myth
in its literal acceptation is to be found expressed in the poem, and it
is therefore clear that Milton had fully pondered all its implications.
But it is to be observed that all the analysis of the tree-allegory is
attributed to Satan. It is Satan who is made to represent the tree as

1. *Paradise Lost*, XI, 84 (my italics).   2. *Paradise Lost*, XI, 26.
3. *Paradise Lost*, XII, 585. Cf. *De doctrina christiana*, Ch. 14, in which Milton
says that through Christ man is 'raised to a far more excellent state of grace
and glory than that from which he had fallen.'

really knowledge-bringing. Milton, in putting into the mouth of Satan all his own criticisms of the myth as it stands, is virtually rejecting its original meaning and preparing the ground for the rationalization which he preferred. For Milton it was Satanic to suppose that the myth meant what it said; therefore it must mean something else.

The moment Satan hears of the Tree of Knowledge he makes the relevant criticism:

> Knowledge forbidd'n?
> Suspicious, reasonless. Why should their Lord
> Envy them that? Can it be sin to know,
> Can it be death? And do they only stand
> By ignorance, is that their happy state,
> The proof of their obedience and their faith?
>
> . . .
>
> Envious commands, invented with design
> To keep them low whom knowledge might exalt.[1]

It is instructive to compare Satan's reasoning with Milton's own in *Areopagitica*.[2] Their close parallel shows that if Milton had not managed to find a meaning for the Tree-myth more acceptable to him than its surface (and probably real) meaning, he would have agreed with Satan. If the myth, plainly interpreted, were divine Truth, then Milton's highest wisdom was Satanic sophistry. But of course the plain interpretation was wrong, so Satan (and Milton) could be allowed to pulverize it to his heart's content. As early as *Areopagitica* Milton had settled upon his own explanation; Adam *learnt* nothing from the tree, he merely fell into the fate of 'knowing good by evil', that is, of experiencing sin and misery and contrasting them with past innocence. And this is represented as the true theory of the tree throughout *Paradise Lost*:

> Knowledge of good bought dear by knowing ill.[3]

The *easiness* of God's sole charge is several times mentioned:

1. *Paradise Lost*, IV, 515.   2. Cf. above, p. 220.   3. *Paradise Lost*, IV, 222.

> This one, this easy charge, of all the trees
> In Paradise that bear delicious fruit
> So various, not to taste that only tree
> Of Knowledge . . .[1]

> that sole command
> So easily obey'd.[2]

This view implies the theory of the *De doctrina christiana*, that the prohibition was applied to an act 'indifferent in itself'. It would *not* have been 'easy' to abstain from knowledge freely to be grasped and in fact it was by insisting upon the magic virtue of the fruit that Satan successfully tempted Eve. The loquacious Serpent answers her astonished inquiries, it will be recalled, by explaining that he is able to speak because he has already tasted the fruit himself; it produced, he says,

> Strange alteration in me, to degree
> Of Reason in my inward powers, and speech
> Wanted not long, though to this shape retain'd.
> Thenceforth to speculations high or deep
> I turn'd my thoughts, and with capacious mind
> Consider'd all things visible in Heav'n,
> Or Earth, or middle. . . .[3]

The Tempter attributes to the fruit powers of universal enlightenment; it can give scientific knowledge –

> O sacred, wise, and wisdom-giving Plant!
> Mother of science! now I feel thy power
> Within me clear, not only to discern
> Things in their causes, but to trace the ways
> Of highest agents. . . .[4]

– and, of course, it imparts its own specific gift of moral knowledge:

> knowledge of good and evil;
> Of good, how just? Of evil, if what is evil
> Be real, why not known, since easier shunn'd?

1. *Paradise Lost*, IV, 420 (Adam to Eve).   2. *Paradise Lost*, VII, 46.
3. *Paradise Lost*, IX, 599.   4. *Paradise Lost*, IX, 679.

> Why then was this forbid? Why but to awe,
> Why but to keep you low and ignorant,
> His worshippers; he knows that in the day
> You eat thereof, your eyes that seem so clear
> Yet are but dim, shall perfectly be then
> Open'd and clear'd; and ye shall be as Gods,
> Knowing both good and evil as they know.[1]

Satan, applying to the myth the equipment of a seventeenth-century rational theologian, easily exposes its weaknesses; he questions if 'the Gods' (note the pagan implication) really produced all things:

> if they all things, who enclos'd
> Knowledge of good and evil in this tree,
> That whoso eats thereof, forthwith attains
> Wisdom without their leave?

On the other hand,

> What can your knowledge hurt him, or this tree
> Impart against his will if all be his?

All these reasonings of Satan show that Milton had considered all the consequences of supposing the Tree to have been really the mother of science and of morality. He averts these consequences by making the Tree *deceiving* tree; it does not really contain, magically enclosed within it, the knowledge promised by its title. No sooner is the fatal act accomplished than the fruit turns out to be 'false fruit', 'fallacious fruit',[2] engendering, not godlike knowledge, but intoxication and sensuality. All they had 'gained', they found, was sexual self-consciousness. Thus their 'knowledge of good and evil', the name given by God himself to the tree, turns out to mean merely that

> We know
> Both good and evil, good lost and evil got.[3]

1. See the whole speech, *Paradise Lost*, IX, 679 ff.
2. *Paradise Lost*, IX, 1011 and 1046.
3. *Paradise Lost*, IX, 1070.

After sensuality, the other passions are awakened:

> anger, hate,
> Mistrust, suspicion, discord; and shook sore
> Their inward state of mind, calm region once
> And full of peace, now tost and turbulent:
> For Understanding rul'd not, and the Will
> Heard not her lore; both in subjection now
> To sensual Appetite, who from beneath
> Usurping over sovran Reason claim'd
> Superior sway. . . .[1]

The psychological Fall, the result of disobedience not of knowledge, was now complete.

One further question must be raised: What of the Tree of Life? Even Milton cannot ignore the awkward fact that in Genesis Adam is expelled from the Garden of Eden, lest, having become as one of the gods by knowing good and evil, he now 'put forth his hand, and take also of the tree of life, and eat, and live for ever: therefore the Lord God sent him forth from the garden of Eden.'[2] If this tree really conferred immortality against God's will, so Milton-Satan might have argued, where was God's omnipotence? Or if it, too, was a false, fallacious tree, why need it matter if Adam ate of it (it had not been tabooed previously)? Milton's evasion of this difficulty is characteristic. He was not interested in the Tree of Life, so he dismisses the offending text with a nonchalant sophism. I will present it in italics without further comment. God says, in his speech after the Fall:

> Lest therefore his now bolder hand
> Reach also of the tree of Life, and eat,
> And live for ever, *dream at least to live*
> *For ever*, to remove him I decree.

Although Milton thus seems clearly to have thought it a Satanic suggestion to suppose that God desired to withhold any vital knowledge from man – 'we cannot suppose the Deity envious of truth, or unwilling that it should be communicated to man,' he wrote in

1. *Paradise Lost*, IX, 1123.   2. Genesis, 3: 22.

the *Defensio Secunda*, a work probably contemporary[1] with the actual planning of *Paradise Lost* – he was yet prepared to use a portion of the significance of the original myth. For there were kinds of 'knowledge' which even Milton considered pernicious and 'forbidden', and he is willing to believe that the sin of our first parents included aspiring after these. For Milton, as for Bacon and all the anti-scholastics of the seventeenth century this forbidden knowledge was connected with the speculative *hubris* which presumed to pry into the why as well as the how of natural and divine laws, in a real sense 'affecting Godhead'. The angel Raphael, answering Adam's legitimate inquiries about the Creation – questions which

> we not to explore the secrets ask
> Of his eternal empire, but the more
> To magnify his works, the more we know

replies that he has received commission

> to answer thy desire
> Of knowledge within bounds; beyond abstain
> To ask, nor let thine own inventions hope
> Things not revealed. . . .
> Enough is left besides to search and know.[2]

There is, I think, a glance at scholasticism in 'thine own inventions'. Adam further expresses curiosity about the system of the heavens, and wonders that the celestial bodies should be so tasked for the sake of the sedentary earth. Raphael in reply uses one of Galileo's arguments against the scholastic assumption about the 'perfection' of heavenly bodies (though in a different connexion): consider, he says,

> that great
> Or bright infers not excellence: the Earth

1. 1654. Dr Tillyard says it is 'the one prose work that sprang directly from the mood which first conceived *Paradise Lost*'. op. cit., p. 193. (Cf. above, p. 218.)
2. *Paradise Lost*, VII, 95 and 119.

> Though in comparison of Heav'n, so small,
> Nor glistering, may of solid good contain
> More plenty than the sun that barren shines.[1]

But, after non-committally propounding to Adam both the Ptolemaic and the Copernican systems – though I think with a preference for that sponsored by the Tuscan artist; it was not *his* theories, but the 'epicycles' of medieval astronomy, which might move God's laughter – Raphael exhorts Adam to desist from such inquiries:

> Solicit not thy thoughts with matters hid,
> Leave them to God above . . .
> . . . be lowly wise:
> Think only what concerns thee and thy being.

And Adam dutifully agrees that the proper study of mankind is man –

> That not to know at large of things remote
> From use, obscure and subtle, but to know
> That which before us lies in daily life,
> Is the prime wisdom; what is more, is fume,
> Or emptiness, or fond impertinence,
> And renders us in things that most concern
> Unpractis'd, unprepar'd, and still to seek.

It may be that in his later disillusioned years, and especially in his blindness, Milton underwent a bitter reaction against the much reading of his youth. In these words of Adam we have an anticipation of the much more sweeping, and more petulantly worded, rejection of learning in *Paradise Regained*.[2] But education, for Milton, had always been education for life – 'that which fits a man to perform justly, skilfully, and magnanimously all the offices, both private and public, of peace and war';[3] and the Milton who condemned the 'intellective abstractions of logic and metaphysics' offered to tender youth at Cambridge as an 'asinine feast of sow-

---

1. *Paradise Lost*, VIII, 90.   2. Bk IV, 286 ff.
3. *On Education*, Bohn, III, p. 467.

thistles and brambles' would have no difficulty in associating this sort of knowledge with the Fall of Man. We are told that the sin of Eve included

> expectation high
> Of knowledge, nor was Godhead from her thought.[1]

And Adam, though his first thought is simply to share Eve's fate, begins to conjecture the same as he approaches his own fall. In speaking to Michael afterwards, Adam twice[2] ascribes his fall to seeking forbidden knowledge, although this is certainly not made to appear his real motive in Book ix. The fact is, I think, that Milton, having emptied the myth of Genesis of most of its original meaning, was not unwilling to put back into it, by way of compensation, something of his own dislike of scholasticism. In somewhat similar fashion he enlarges the significance of Adam's disobedience by making it a capital instance of surrender to 'female charm'; and in this manner he is able not only to harmonize the historical fall with the psychological fall, but also to vent much of his personal resentment against womankind.

1. *Paradise Lost*, ix, 789. 2. Bk xii, 278 and 560.

CHAPTER II

John Locke

Why need I name thy Boyle, whose pious search
Amid the dark recesses of his works
The great Creator sought? And why thy Locke,
Who made the whole internal world his own?

(Thomson's *Seasons*)

THERE was every reason why Thomson, apostrophizing happy Britannia as the home of Liberty and Plenty, and celebrating her many glorious sons from King Alfred to Newton, should mention the name of John Locke, and there are also good reasons why our present studies should terminate with him. Locke stands at the end of the seventeenth century, and at the beginning of the eighteenth; his work is at once a summing-up of seventeenth-century conclusions and the starting-point for eighteenth-century inquiries. The early eighteenth century did not, like the early seventeenth, witness a great intellectual revolution; it merely inherited the results and consolidated the certainties of the previous century. Addison's England was fortunate in having behind it not only the Glorious Revolution of 1688, but such a poet as Milton, such a physicist as Newton, and such a philosopher as Locke. All the dearest ambitions of men and of Britons had been realized; the Constitution had been established and 'freedom' secured; Homer and Vergil had been equalled if not outdone; the law which preserves the stars from wrong had been made manifest; and the true workings of the mind had been revealed. All these things had been done not only by Englishmen, but by Christians. The brilliant explanations of Newton and Locke had not only removed the strain of living in a mysterious universe, but confirmed the principles of religion. The sense of being at last in possession of the Truth, which gladdened this enviable age, shines clearly throughout the passage of Thomson from which I have quoted, and its satisfaction at finding this Truth so conformable to Faith as well as to Reason is seen in the poet's apostrophe to the True Philosophy as

> Daughter of Heaven! that slow-ascending still,
> Investigating sure the chain of things,
> With radiant finger points to Heaven again.

We need not wonder that Addison, the mouthpiece of the age, should have regarded it as his appointed task to 'engage my Reader to consider the World in its most agreeable Lights'.[1]

The Newtonian world-picture, and Locke's picture of the mind, came to be, in the eighteenth century, the normal possession of the educated and enlightened of Europe. Locke, in particular, has been described as 'the writer whose influence pervades the eighteenth century with an almost scriptural authority'.[2] This remark is doubtless truer of Locke's political writings than of his philosophy, for as a recent editor of the *Essay Concerning Human Understanding* has said, 'the subsequent course of European philosophy consists largely of a series of attempts to clear up the ambiguities of Locke's terminology and to surmount the difficulties created for him by his presuppositions'.[3] Nevertheless it was Locke who determined the direction of this 'subsequent course', and he may truly be called, after Descartes, the founder of modern philosophy. For Addison, and the men of letters in general, he was 'the philosopher', somewhat as Aristotle had been for the schoolmen. The supremacy which Milton held in heroic poetry, and Newton in physics, belonged in philosophy to Locke. Moreover, his authority was not confined to this one sphere; indeed, the prestige of his philosophical work was itself ascribable to the wide acceptance of his views on political liberty and religious toleration. As the philosophic vindicator of the Glorious Revolution he was, unlike Hobbes, in the position to supply his generation with precisely the doctrine most congenial to them. In celebrating the

1. *Spectator*, No. 387.
2. Cobban, *Edmund Burke and the Revolt against the Eighteenth Century*, p. 16.
3. Pringle-Pattison, Introduction to his edition of Locke's *Essay*, p. xlvi.

final triumph of Whig principles over the Stuarts, Locke founded the 'liberal' tradition of political thought which was vigorous in the eighteenth century, and inspired both the American and the French Revolutions. Locke's authority was behind the eighteenth-century belief in the inalienable rights of the human individual as such, and in the 'natural' and 'original' liberties of man.

Man being born ... with a title to perfect freedom and uncontrolled enjoyment of all the rights and privileges of the law of nature ... no one can be put out of this estate and subjected to the political power of another, without his own consent.[1]

The 'State of Nature', in Locke, is so far from resembling the 'ill condition' described by Hobbes, that it approximates rather to the Eden of the religious tradition, or the golden age of the poets. After Locke, this conception becomes an expression of the current faith that, on the whole, *things if left to themselves* are more likely to work together for good than if interfered with by meddling man. To this conception of 'Nature' as a system of divine laws whose workings, if unimpeded by governmental or other interference, will produce the greatest happiness of the greatest number, must be ascribed the *laissez-faire* economics of later times, and the confidence in the virtues of unrestricted competition in industry. In Locke's political theory the thing to be explained was, not by what fortunate device men escaped from the State of Nature, but what motives could ever have induced them to desert their Eden. The explanation he gives is highly characteristic. In the state of nature, in spite of all its advantages, *Property* was insecure, and it was to remedy this defect that men entered into the Social Contract. Locke is never more completely the spokesman of the Whig oligarchy than in his insistence on the protection of property as the characteristic function of government. The 'Rights of Man', as yet, are the rights of Proprietors. Locke is the father of nineteenth-century as well as eighteenth-century 'liberalism'.

In his religious writings, too, as we shall see more fully presently,[2]

1. *Treatise of Civil Government*, Bk II, sects. 87 and 95.
2. Cf. below, pp. 251-2.

he gave his age just what it was ready to receive, a reasoned plea for toleration and a demonstration of the Reasonableness of Christianity. It was Locke's appointed task to work up into a system all the assumptions about God, Nature, and Man which, as the seventeenth century storm-clouds drew off, seemed to most men to stand firm and unquestionable in the light of common day. Locke is like Milton in numerous ways – in his Puritan upbringing, in his passion for liberty, in his rational piety, in his feeling for human dignity, in his views on education, in his sense of the limits of human knowledge, in his acceptance of Scripture;[1] but he is a Milton without the garland and the singing-robes. It is wholly in the cool element of prose that Locke lives and moves. The passionate sense of life as perilous, glorious, or tragic which inspired Milton to prophecy, whether in prose or in verse, has all departed; instead, there is a feeling of security, of confidence in the rationality of the universe, in the virtuousness of man, in the stability of society, and in the deliverances of enlightened common sense; while underneath are the everlasting arms. The things that were most real to Locke were also the things that were most real to the majority of his readers for several generations. The very limitations of his mind fitted him to be the accepted thinker of an age which had lost the taste for spiritual exploration. There is a safeness in Locke's mental habits which made him a fit guide for readers of the *Spectator*; when he comes to a speculative precipice he does not peer over it with dread or fascination, but gives it a glance and returns promptly to the path of common sense.

Locke's prose style is the best index of his mind, and the mind of his age as well. Like Wren's architecture, it is harmonious, lucid, and severe, rising occasionally into a dome of manly eloquence. The prose of Browne, Milton, or even Hobbes looks Gothic by the side of it. In reading Locke we are conscious of being in the presence of a mind which has come to rest in the 'philosophic' world-view. There is no more of the metaphysical flicker from world to world, none of the old imagery struck out in the heat of struggle or in the

1. And not least, perhaps, in 'long choosing and beginning late'. Locke was well over fifty when his first published work appeared.

ardour of discovery. Locke writes philosophy in the tone of well-bred conversation, and makes it his boast to have discarded the uncouth and pedantic jargon of the schools. His air is that of a gentleman who, along with a group of like-minded friends, proposes to conduct a disinterested inquiry into truth. The very ease of his prose betokens a mind at rest in its own assumptions, and reveals how fully Locke could count on these being also the assumptions of his readers. His vocabulary is almost wholly abstract and uncoloured; what he offers us is always the reasoning of a grave and sober man, not the visions of enthusiasm or the fictions of poetry. Compare, for example, his comment on *credo quia impossibile* with Browne's:

> As for those wingy Mysteries in Divinity, and airy subtleties in Religion, which have unhing'd the brains of better heads, they never stretched the *Pia Mater* of mine. . . . I love to lose myself in a mystery, to pursue my Reason to an *O altitudo*! . . . I can answer all the Objections of Satan and my rebellious reason with that odd resolution I learned of Tertullian, *Certum est quia impossibile est.* (*Religio medici*, I, 9.)

Locke writes:

> Religion, which should most distinguish us from beasts, and ought most peculiarly to elevate us as rational creatures above brutes, is that wherein men often appear most irrational, and more senseless than beasts themselves. *Credo quia impossibile est:* 'I believe because it is impossible', might, in a good man, pass for a sally of zeal, but would prove a very ill rule for men to choose their opinions or religion by. (*Human Understanding*, IV, 18, sect. II.)

In order to illustrate Locke's use, in stating a philosophical point, of purely abstract language, stripped of rhetorical colouring, one might juxtapose Glanvill's above-quoted[1] passage about the union of soul and body with a deliverance of Locke on the same topic:

> How the purer Spirit is united to this Clod, is a knot too hard for fallen Humanity to unty. . . . The freezing of the words in the air in the northern climes, is as conceivable as this strange union. . . . And to hang weights on the wings of the winde seems far more intelligible. (*Vanity of Dogmatizing*, p. 20.)

1. pp. 81 and 159.

As the ideas of sensible Secondary qualities which we have in our minds can by us be no way deduced from bodily causes, nor any correspondence or connexion be found between them and those primary qualities which . . . produce them in us; so, on the other side, the operation of our minds upon our bodies is as inconceivable. How any thought should produce a motion in body, is as remote from the nature of our ideas, as how any body should produce any thought in the mind. (*Human Understanding*, IV, 3, sect. 28.)

The man who writes 'remote from the nature of our ideas' where his predecessor wrote 'a knot too hard for fallen humanity to unty' is one who has tacitly agreed with his readers to keep the 'pure glass of the understanding' as free as possible from the 'gross dew'[1] of imagination. Truly, as John Smith wrote (quoting Plutarch), 'God hath now taken away from his Oracles Poetrie, and the variety of dialect and circumlocution, and obscuritie',[2] and has bidden them speak, instead, in the most 'intelligible' language exclusively.

I have ventured to compare Locke with Milton; but a comparison say, of their respective essays on Education reveals, together with many ideas held in common, an instructive difference in tone and aim – the difference, one might perhaps say, between Renaissance and Augustan ethics. Both believe in education for life and not for learning's sake only; and both believe that an incredible syllabus may be got through 'between twelve and twenty, less time than is now bestowed in pure trifling at grammar and sophistry.'[3] But whereas Milton aims at inspiring his pupils with 'high hopes of living to be brave men, and worthy patriots, dear to God and famous to all ages', and 'infusing into their young breasts such an ingenuous and noble ardour, as would not fail to make many of them renowned and matchless men', Locke, with the general aim of producing a 'sound mind in a sound body', has more particularly in view the 'breeding' of a 'gentleman's son' rather than the rearing of heroes or saints. He discourses of the things that are 'convenient and necessary to be known by a gentleman'; and we feel that we are nearer to Lord Chesterfield than to Milton when Locke tells us that 'it is

1. Cf. above, p. 130.   2. Cf. above, p. 141.
3. Milton's tractate *On Education*, Bohn, Vol. III, p. 467.

necessary in this learned age' for a gentleman to study natural philosophy 'to fit himself for conversation', and when he prescribes dancing-lessons as the cure for clownishness. Milton's heroic tone is absent; and it will suffice for Locke's ideal pupil, whose lot is cast in a less warlike age, to conduct himself in accordance with the dictates of Reason, Religion, and Good Breeding.[1]

When Voltaire visited England in 1726 he found to his joy that it was the land of liberty and philosophy, and as Locke was the recognized exponent of both these things, Voltaire not unnaturally regarded him with enthusiastic admiration. In his *Lettres philosophiques* on the subject of England, Voltaire helped to make both Locke and Newton better known in France, and his account of Locke may serve here to show what the eighteenth century considered Locke to have achieved in philosophy, and why his thought was so acceptable to them. 'Our *Des Cartes*,' says Voltaire, concluding an ironic survey of the course of philosophic speculation from Greece onwards,

> Our *Des Cartes*, born to discover the Errors of Antiquity, and at the same Time to substitute his own; and hurried away by that systematic Spirit which throws a Cloud over the Minds of the greatest Men, thought he had demonstrated that the Soul is the same Thing as Thought, in the same Manner as Matter, in his Opinion, is the same as Extension. He asserted, that Man thinks eternally, and that the Soul, at its coming into the Body, is inform'd with the whole Series of metaphysical Notions; knowing God, infinite Space, possessing all abstract Ideas; in a Word, completely endued with the most sublime Lights, which it unhappily forgets at its issuing from the Womb. ... *Such a Multitude of Reasoners having written the Romance of the Soul, a Sage at last arose, who gave, with an Air of the Greatest Modesty, the History of it.*[2]

Locke himself has described the genesis of the *Essay Concerning Human Understanding*. Five or six friends met in his room[3] to dis-

---

1. An actual and not unworthy product of Locke's system was the 3rd Earl of Shaftesbury, author of *Characteristics*, whose education Locke superintended.

2. *Letters Concerning the English Nation* (London, 1733), p. 97 (my italics).

3. Presumably about the year 1670. Locke spent twenty years in meditating the *Essay*, which first appeared in its complete form in 1690.

cuss the principles of morality and revealed religion, and found themselves 'quickly at a stand by the difficulties that rose on every side'.

> After we had a while puzzled ourselves, without coming any nearer a resolution of those doubts which perplexed us, it came into my thoughts, that we took a wrong course; and that, before we set ourselves upon inquiries of that nature, it was necessary *to examine our own abilities, and see what objects our understandings were or were not fitted to deal with*.[1]

The commonwealth of learning has its master-builders, such as Boyle, Huygenius, and 'the incomparable Mr Newton'; Locke for his part will modestly content himself with the office of 'clearing away some of the rubbish that lies in the way to Knowledge'. We are reminded of Sprat when Locke tells us that he means, in particular, the 'learned but frivolous use of uncouth, affected, or unintelligible terms', whereby philosophy has incurred the reputation of being unfit 'to be brought into well-bred company and polite conversation'. Locke begins, then, characteristically, by deliberately limiting the field of discourse. Not only the Baconian and the Augustan, but also the Milton who speaks through the angel Raphael,[2] are united in Locke when he assures us that 'our business here is not to know all things, but those which concern our conduct'.

> We shall not have much reason to complain of the narrowness of our minds, if we will but employ them about what may be of use to us; for of that they are very capable; and it will be an unpardonable as well as childish peevishness, if we undervalue the advantages of our knowledge, and neglect to improve it to the ends for which it was given us, because there are some things that are set out of the reach of it.[3]

The true procedure, and the method Locke follows himself, is first 'to take a survey of our own understandings, examine our own powers, and see to what things they were adapted'. It is in vain for us to 'let loose our thoughts into the vast ocean of Being'; are not the empty and presumptuous logomachies of scholasticism there to warn us of this? It is for us to be lowly wise, and solicit not our

1. *Essay*, Epistle to the Reader (my italics).   2. Cf. above, pp. 235–6.
3. *Essay*, I, I, sects. 4–7.

thoughts with matters hid;[1] or, to use Locke's own words, which are singularly close to Milton's, to seek 'for satisfaction in a quiet and secure possession of truths that most concern[ed] us'. The proper study of mankind is man, though, as we shall see shortly, God may and must be scanned in Revelation. Locke, again like Milton, retained to the end the Puritan reverence for Scripture.

It is not my purpose here to offer a critical summary of the argument of Locke's most celebrated work; this has many times been done already, and by writers far better qualified for the task. I will merely try, in what follows, to disengage the fundamental certainties of this representative thinker of the late seventeenth century, and to indicate their significance for religion and for poetry.

Locke's Theory of Knowledge

In the first part of the *Essay* Locke, employing the 'historical, plain method' so highly approved of by Voltaire, inquires into 'the ways whereby our understandings come to attain those notions of things we have'. It is well known that Locke derives all our ideas from Experience, which in turn is made up of Sensation and Reflection.

All those sublime thoughts which tower above the clouds, and reach as high as heaven itself, take their rise and footing here: in all that great extent wherein the mind wanders in those remote speculations it may seem to be elevated with, it stirs not one jot beyond those ideas which *sense* **or** *reflection* have offered for its contemplation.

It must undoubtedly be mentioned first amongst Locke's assumptions, that our minds become furnished in the course of actual contact with reality; that it is only by drinking in the soul of things that we become wise. The whole force of Locke's polemic against 'innate' ideas and principles springs from his presupposition that we must each one of us build up our own being for ourselves out of our own dealings with the universe, not relying upon 'common

1. Cf. *Paradise Lost*, VIII, 167, and cf. above, p. 236.

notions' which are said to be from God, but are really the received opinions of country or of party, or the sacrosanct dogmas of tradition. God has not 'stamped' any 'truths' upon the mind; but he has furnished us with faculties which sufficiently serve for the discovery of all we need to know. He gives us powers of sensation and reflection, not information ready-made, just as he gives us, not bridges or houses, but hands and materials. We should seek our knowledge, then, in the consideration of 'things themselves' (our minds are themselves included amongst these 'things'), and use our own, not other men's thoughts.

We shall have to return to Locke's account of sensation afterwards in speaking of his significance for poetic theory. For the moment our concern is with his views on the relative validity of our various ideas when acquired rather than with their sources, and I propose therefore to deal first with the material of Book IV of the *Essay*, which treats of what knowledge we have by our ideas, and the degrees of its certainty.

Locke's theory of knowledge reveals that quality which his philosophy shares with the Church of England and perhaps other English things, its power to comprehend in a vague synthesis principles really belonging to opposite schools of thought. He begins by laying down that

since the mind, in all its thoughts and reasonings, hath no other immediate object but its own ideas, which it alone does or can contemplate, it is evident that our knowledge is only conversant about them.[1]

Thus knowledge is defined as the perception of the agreement or disagreement of ideas with each other; we perceive, for instance, first, that one idea is different from another (white is not black); secondly, we perceive the particular relation one idea holds to another, as of greater or less, before and after, etc.; thirdly, we perceive the co-existence of certain ideas, as of yellowness, weight, solubility in *aqua regia*, and the rest, which make up the complex idea 'gold'. So far all these kinds of knowledge are confined within

1. *Essay*, IV, I, sect. I.

the closed circle of the mind and relate solely to its contents. But then Locke immediately proceeds to enumerate a fourth kind, which is knowledge of 'real existence', that is to say, of real 'things' agreeing to the ideas we have 'of' them. It is clear that this is not the perception of any relation 'between ideas' at all, but involves two assumptions, first the existence of objective 'things', and secondly, the possibility of a relationship between these things and the ideas we have of them. Locke does, however, place our knowledge of things by sensation in the lowest of his three degrees of certainty. These three degrees are:

1. Intuition
2. Demonstration
3. Sensation

Intuition is the perception of self-evident truths, and has the highest degree of certainty. Demonstration aims at showing the connexion between ideas which, owing to their distance from each other, cannot be compared by simple intuition. It proceeds by constructing a bridge of intermediate ideas between those to be compared, and thus revealing the nature of their connexion. Demonstration can produce certainty, though inevitably not with the same immediacy as intuition. Lastly, there are 'the ideas we receive from an external object' by Sensation. It is indeed an intuitive certainty that when we have such an idea, *the idea is in our minds*; but

whether there be anything more than barely that idea in our minds, whether we can thence certainly infer the existence of anything without us which corresponds to that idea, is that whereof some men think there may be a question made.[1]

But this was precisely the sort of speculative possibility from which Locke's common sense recoiled. He admits that it theoretically renders our knowledge of external things less certain than the two former degrees of knowledge, but it is clear that in practice Locke is as certain of this as he is of anything. His replies to the supposed sceptic are significant; let him 'please to dream that I make him this

---

1. *Essay*, IV, 2, sect. 14.

answer' – that there is a manifest difference between dreaming of being in a fire, and being actually in it; and that as we indubitably find that pleasure and pain follow

upon the application of certain objects to us, whose existence we perceive, or dream that we perceive, by our senses; *this certainty is as great as our happiness and misery, beyond which we have no concernment to know or to be.*[1]

There are three kinds of realities or 'existences' of which Locke was certain, and these correspond again to the three degrees of knowledge just mentioned. These are (1) Our own existence, which we know by Intuition; (2) God's existence, which we know by Demonstration; (3) Other Things, which we know by Sensation. I will speak of these in the same order, taking occasion to discuss Locke's general religious views under the second heading, and the significance of his sensationalism for poetry under the third.

OUR OWN EXISTENCE

Locke agrees with Descartes in regarding our own existence as the first of all certainties.

I think, I reason, I feel pleasure and pain: can any of these be more evident to me than my own existence?[2]

Locke assumes, that is to say, that these immediately intuited experiences presuppose a 'substance', the *ego*, in which they inhere, and of which they are in a sense modifications. But he characteristically blurs the sharp outline of Descartes' definitions. He will not allow, for instance, that 'thought' is the 'essence' of the soul, but makes it rather its *function*, or activity, which may at one time be in operation and at another quiescent.

I confess myself to have one of those dull souls that doth not perceive itself always to contemplate ideas; nor can conceive it any more necessary for the soul always to think, than for the body always to move: the perception of ideas being, as I conceive, to the soul, what motion is to the body, not its essence, but one of its operations. [3]

1. *Essay*, IV, (my italics).   2. ibid., IV, 9, sect. 3.   3. ibid., II, 1, sect. 10.

Voltaire, commenting upon this subject, observes that he has 'the Honour to be as stupid in this Particular as Mr *Locke*'.[1] Only thought at the conscious level was of course recognized at that time or for long afterwards. But, what was more startling, and gave Locke's critics occasion to blaspheme, was his permitting himself to wonder whether the 'I', the thinking thing, must necessarily be an *incorporeal* substance. Undoubtedly matter could not of itself generate life and consciousness, but why may not God have imparted to 'some systems of matter, fitly disposed, a power to perceive and think?'[2] It is no more inconceivable than what we all admit, that God has given matter the power to move. Locke has no desire, however, to prove the materiality of the soul. Indeed he considers it 'the more probable opinion' that the consciousness of personal identity is 'annexed to, and the affection of, one individual immaterial substance'.[3] He regards the question of the materiality or immateriality of the soul, a point so vital to the orthodox, with the same indifference as Milton felt towards the Ptolemaic and Copernican systems. We are simply not informed on this subject; 'it is a point which seems to me to be put out of the reach of our knowledge'. Locke quotes it merely as an example of the limited extent of human knowledge: 'I say not this that I would any way lessen the belief of the soul's immateriality.' For him this dispute was unconnected with the really important question of the soul's *immortality*. Corporeal or incorporeal, the soul would meet with its appropriate reward or punishment in a future state; as Voltaire expresses it, ''tis of little Importance to Religion, which only requires the Soul to be virtuous, what Substance it may be made of'.

THE EXISTENCE OF GOD[4]

(1) Our knowledge of the existence of 'a God' (Locke's use of the indefinite article seems significant) is, he holds, 'the most obvious truth that reason discovers', its evidence being 'equal to mathe-

1. op. cit., p. 99.   2. *Essay*, IV, 3, sect. 6.
3. Cf. ibid., IV, 10.   4. ibid., II, 27, sect. 25.

matical certainty'. 'We more certainly know that there is a God than that there is anything else without us.' Locke's proof is not the same as Descartes'; indeed, he expressly states that he will not determine how far *the idea of a most perfect being* which a man may frame in his mind does or does not prove the existence of a God', adding that it is unwise, in his view, to depend exclusively upon this one type of argument.[1] But like Descartes he sets out from our certainty of our own existence. We know that we are ourselves *something*, and it is self-evident ('an intuitive certainty') that 'bare nothing can no more produce any real being, than it can be equal to two right angles'. Further, as all the qualities of a thing produced must be present in the cause, an *intelligent being* alone could have produced us. Nonentity could not have generated matter, neither could matter have generated life, sense, and intelligence unaided, although, as we have seen, God might have *endowed* it with these attributes. Similarly, arguing in the manner of the time from the 'order, harmony, and beauty, which is to be found in nature', Locke urges (quoting St Paul) that 'the invisible things of God are clearly seen from the creation of the world, being understood by the things that are made, even his eternal power and Godhead'.[2]

Locke's Deity, in a word, is that of the contemporary reconcilers of science and religion, such as Glanvill or Boyle, and that of the eighteenth century as a whole – a Deity to be approached by demonstration, and whose existence, proclaimed by the spacious firmament on high, is as well attested as any proof in Euclid. This phase of religious thought, with which the term 'Deism' is often associated, was rendered possible largely by the completeness with which the findings of seventeenth-century science, up to that date, could be made to fuse with the inherited religious certainties. Newton's Great Machine needed a Mechanic, and religion was prepared ahead with that which could serve this purpose. Everywhere what science had so far disclosed was nothing but 'order, harmony, and beauty'; and finally the incomparable Newton had linked the infinitely great

1. Later he definitely rejected the ontological proof. (Cf. Pringle-Pattison, op. cit., p. 313, note.)
2. *Essay*, IV, 10, sect. 7.

and the infinitely little in one inspired synthesis. The mighty maze
was not without a plan, and Locke could declare with perfect can-
dour that 'the works of nature in every part of them sufficiently
evidence a Deity'.[1] Such a statement as this was then scientific as well
as pious. Had not Newton conjectured that Absolute Space was
constituted by God's omnipresence, and Time by his eternal duration? and was not God still in a variety of other ways an indispen-
sable hypothesis? In this way a belief like the belief in God, arising
in reality from depths of time and consciousness undreamed of by
this unhistorical and over-rational age, could be made to seem as if
it rested entirely upon intellectual 'evidence'. The Cambridge
Platonists, as we have seen, were great rationalizers of religious
imagery, and strove to keep their understanding clear of the gross
phantasms of the imagination. But if we compare, say, Smith's
Discourses with the *Reasonableness of Christianity*, and still more if we
compare them with Toland's *Christianity not Mysterious*, the immediate offspring of Locke's book, we notice an immense difference in
real content, a difference which can perhaps be expressed by simply
saying that Smith's work is a contribution to religion and Locke's is
not. I suggested above[2] that the Platonists, for all their 'modernism',
did not contribute to the decline of religion which was undoubtedly
taking place in the latter half of the century. They seem always to
have grasped, what their deistic and scientific successors lost sight
of, that religious belief is founded not upon 'evidence' but upon
'experience'. By insisting that God must be known, not by demonstration, but by spiritual sensation, and by teaching that this experience is given only to purified and disciplined souls, Smith kept his
modernism at once mystical and poetical. Locke admired Whichcote's sermons and was intimate with the family of Cudworth; he
is connected by many a thread, both intellectual and personal, with
the Latitudinarians. But when we turn from Smith or Whichcote
to Locke's writings on religion, we feel that we have left both religion and poetry behind, and entered wholly into the 'cooler element
of prose'. It is noticeable that Locke habitually speaks of *mathematical*

---

1. *Reasonableness of Christianity*, Works (12th edition), Vol. VI, p. 135.
2. Cf. p. 139.

certainty as the perfect type of the certainties reached by demonstration; and the highest testimonial he can give to a religious belief
is that it has the same degree of evidence as a geometrical proof. It
was this belief in the unique claims of mathematics, shared by him
with Hobbes and the Cartesians, which led Locke to believe that
morality, which he took to be 'the proper science and business of
mankind in general', was capable of mathematical demonstration.[1]

(2) Locke certainly conceived himself to be, at least as far as
beliefs were concerned, a devout and orthodox Christian; and
we must now inquire a little into his views on the subject of
Revealed Religion. It must be clearly grasped that Locke did
not base the whole of religious belief upon demonstration. For
him, as fully as for Milton or for Stillingfleet, it was an unquestioned fact that a 'positive revelation' had been communicated
by God in addition to the light of reason. What was the relation,
in his view, between the deliverances of revelation and those of
reason?

'The bare testimony of revelation', he writes, 'is the highest
certainty ... whether the thing proposed agree or disagree
with common experience and the ordinary course of things or
no,'[2] because in this case the testimony is that of God himself.
Faith, then, is definable as 'assent to revelation'. Only, he adds
significantly,

we must be sure that it be a divine revelation, and that we understand it
right:

and this brings us back immediately to the office of Reason in
religion.

Whatever God hath revealed is certainly true; no doubt can be made of it.
This is the proper object of faith: but *whether it be a divine revelation or no,
reason must judge.*[3]

1. *Essay*, IV, 12, sect. 11, and IV, 3, sect. 18.
2. ibid., IV, 16, sect. 14.   3. ibid., IV, 18, sect. 4.

Reason itself he calls 'natural revelation', whereby God communicates to us as much truth as lies within the reach of our natural faculties. Revelation is

natural reason enlarged by a new set of discoveries communicated by God immediately, which reason vouches the truth of by the testimony and proofs it gives that they come from God.[1]

Locke, like a true son of his age, is so convinced that 'Reason must be our last judge and guide in everything',[2] that he writes sometimes as if revelation were, by comparison, untrustworthy or superfluous. For instance, if God by revelation proclaimed the truth of a proposition in Euclid, our certainty that this revelation really came from God could never be so absolute as our certainty of the truth of the proposition by reason. By the same principle,

no proposition can be received for divine revelation, or obtain the assent due to such, if it be contrary to our clear intuitive knowledge.[3]

In other words, we do not need revelation to tell us what we already know, and when it contradicts what we know we must reject it. It seems clear, however, that these arguments are not directed against believing the Scriptures to be of divine origin, for this Locke repeatedly affirms. He is aiming rather at superstition (including, and mainly consisting of, the special doctrines of Popery) and at enthusiasm, or the pseudo-revelations of the Protestant fanatics. Reason must judge, for instance, that transubstantiation is not a truth proceeding from God, and that the 'illuminations' of the sectaries are but 'the ungrounded fancies of a man's own brain'. But Locke does not think it necessary to show cause why he or anyone should believe the Scriptures to be 'from God'. This was a traditional certainty too deeply rooted for Locke to question. But he could and did question other men's interpretations of Scripture, and in the *Reasonableness of Christianity* he undertook to show what it was, in his opinion, that the Gospels did reveal to us.

1. *Essay*, IV, 19, sect. 4.   2. ibid., sect. 14.
3. ibid., VI, 18, sects. 4–11.

Locke's main object in writing this treatise[1] seems to have been to show how few and how simple were the credal demands made upon us by Christianity, and how consonant with 'natural revelation' were its moral injunctions. In a sense the treatise is an inquiry into the credentials of Christian doctrine, and a proof of its divine origin from its reasonableness. He postulates at the outset that the Bible is

a collection of writings, designed by God, for the instruction of the illiterate bulk of mankind, in the way to salvation,[2]

and that consequently in all 'necessary points' it is to be understood 'in the plain direct meaning of its words and phrases'. Now the Christian doctrine of redemption, and therefore the Gospel, is founded upon 'the supposition of Adam's fall'. What did Adam lose, and to what does Christ restore us? Locke's reply is, in brief, that Adam lost bliss and immortality. Adam bequeathed to his posterity, not the dire fate of necessarily sinning in every action of their lives, as alleged by some theologians, but simply mortality, and exposure to the toils and sufferings of earthly life. And as in Adam all die, so the mission of Christ, the second Adam (whose miraculous birth constitutes him, like Adam, in a special sense the Son of God), is to 'bring life and immortality to light'. To those who believe in him Christ restores what Adam lost, not here and now, but in the Kingdom of Heaven after the Resurrection. In order to attain this salvation only two things are necessary: first, to believe that Jesus really was the Messiah, the Christ sent by God for our redemption; and secondly, to repent and live thenceforth a righteous life. The first and greater part of Locke's argument is devoted to showing that this was in fact what Jesus expected of his own followers, and commanded them to preach after his death. The miracles, teachings, and actions of Jesus were designed to prove that he was the Messiah, while giving no occasion to the Jews or to the Roman government for suspecting him of plotting a political uprising. No other belief than this was required by Christ himself or his apostles as necessary for justification. But it was further required that

1. It was published in 1695.   2. *Reasonableness*, Works, Vol. VI, p. 5.

believers should bring forth fruits meet for repentance; and Locke therefore proceeds to show that, in his teaching, Jesus Christ confirmed the moral laws which reason had already discovered, clarified them from the corrupt glosses of scribes and pharisees, and commanded certain new ones.

> There is not, I think, any one of the duties of morality, which he has not, somewhere or other, by himself and his apostles, inculcated over and over again to his followers in express terms.[1]

Than these simple requirements, Locke constantly implies, what could be more 'reasonable'? Yet certain objections had to be met, and with a brief account of Locke's treatment of these I will conclude my summary. First there was the old question – what of the worthies of Old Testament times who, however well they may have kept the law, ceremonial and moral, could not have had the saving faith? Locke disposes of this easily – all that was expected of them, and necessary for their justification, was that they should trust in God's promise to send the Messiah. Was not Abraham's faith in God's promises counted to him for righteousness? But there is the more weighty objection still to be raised – what shall become of the rest of mankind, who never heard of Christ at all? In the charity of his heart, and in the strength of his confidence in Reason as the 'candle of the Lord',[2] Locke allows himself such latitude when answering this objection, that he almost gives away the case for Christianity. The light of nature, he says, revealed to the Gentiles the main articles of the moral law, and

> the same spark of the divine nature and knowledge in man, which making him a man, showed him the law he was under, as a man, showed him also the way of atoning the merciful, kind, compassionate Author and Father of him and his being, when he had transgressed that law.[3]

The Gentiles, then, may be safely left 'to stand and fall to their own Father and Master, whose goodness and mercy is over all his works'.

1. *Reasonableness*, p. 122.
2. Locke several times quotes this favourite text of Whichcote's.
3. ibid., p. 133.

But having admitted so much, Locke cannot now avoid the further question: What need was there, then, of the Christian scheme of redemption? Locke's replies to this question are illuminating, for this was no mere rhetorical objection set up in the course of argument simply to be overturned. It was the main problem confronting Christian apologists in Locke's day and for many years following. Where nature and reason supply us with such clear evidence, what need have we of revelation? Locke's reply, made in perfect good faith and, I think, quite without the cynicism of a Voltaire, a Hume, or a Gibbon, was that although for the wise and the virtuous nature and reason 'sufficiently evidence a deity', natural religion 'had never authority enough to prevail on the multitude', and a special revelational sanction was therefore required, which should be 'suited to vulgar capacities'. Not only vice and ignorance had prevented the voice of reason from being heard by the 'illiterate bulk of mankind', but also the craft of priests, who, 'to secure their empire', had everywhere 'excluded reason from having anything to do in religion'. We may infer from Locke's tone here that in his opinion this priestly activity had not been confined to the period before the appearance of Christ. But Locke claims a wider necessity for revelation. Although, as we have seen, he surmised that morality might turn out some day to be mathematically demonstrable, he admitted that it had hitherto proved 'too hard a task for unassisted reason to establish morality in all its parts'.

Experience shows, that the knowledge of morality, by mere natural light (how agreeable soever it be to it) makes but a slow progress, and little advance in the world.[1]

It was necessary that the divine imprimatur should be stamped upon the laws of reason, and this Christ effected. Further, the Christian revelation teaches certain important truths which unaided reason could never have reached, in particular the doctrine of a future life. True, the heathens had had their dim conjectures about such a possibility; they had had the names of 'Styx and Acheron, of

1. For all this discussion cf. *Reasonableness*, pp. 134–58.

Elysian fields and seats of the blessed', but these were mere fables,

more like the inventions of wit, and ornament of poetry, than the serious persuasions of the wise and sober.[1]

That virtue is her own reward is therefore 'not all that can now be said of her'.

In this way Locke managed to fit 'Revelation' on to his philosophic world-scheme. However disastrously Popery had re-paganized Christianity with its ceremonies and its sacerdotalism, however wildly the enthusiasts might rear their baseless fabrics, it was still possible, thank Heaven, for an Englishman and a philosopher to hold a sober and rational faith. Bishops might raise a suspicious eyebrow at the credal tenuity of Locke's Christianity; and Toland's *Christianity Not Mysterious*,[2] appearing so soon after Locke's treatise, and so evidently inspired by it, might indicate the direction in which his influence would afterwards move. To us, however, Locke's religious writings are of interest because in them is revealed, with unusual clarity, the nature of the compromise reached at the close of our period between traditional beliefs and the new philosophy. Locke's solution here, as in most departments of thought, served the eighteenth century as a veritable Act of Settlement.

THE EXISTENCE OF OTHER THINGS

As we have seen, the existence of a real external world, though not intuitively or demonstratively known, was as certain to Locke as 'our happiness and misery'. He never allowed himself, as Berkeley afterwards did, to accept the whole implication of his own statement that the mind has 'no other immediate object but its own ideas'. No other *immediate* object, perhaps, but in Locke's view no reasonable man could doubt that our knowledge 'goes a little farther than bare imagination'; there is 'something farther intended'. The mind

1. *Reasonableness*, p. 149. The implied estimate of 'poetry' is significant (cf. below, pp. 261 ff.)
2. 1696.

indeed 'knows not things immediately, but only by the intervention of the ideas it has of them'; yet our ideas must point to something real if we are to preserve the distinction – surely a valid distinction? – between the 'visions of an enthusiast' and the 'reasonings of a sober man'. Our knowledge is 'real', Locke teaches, when there is 'a conformity between our ideas and the reality of things'. But what, he very properly asks, 'shall here be our criterion? How shall the mind, when it perceives nothing but its own ideas, know that they agree with things themselves?'[1] Locke's reply is an appeal to the principle of our passivity in sensation:

> The eye – it cannot choose but see;
> We cannot bid the ear be still;
> Our bodies feel, where'er they be,
> Against or with our will.[2]

As everybody knows, Locke believed the human mind to begin its career as a sheet of 'white paper, void of all characters, without any ideas'[3]. Whence, then, come the simple ideas which soon get inscribed upon it, and are afterwards elaborated, together with the ideas of reflection, into all the complexity of our mature knowledge? The facts, he holds, force upon us the belief that there are powers which of themselves our minds impress. These powers are the attributes or qualities of matter, the real substance of which the physical world is composed. 'In bare, naked perception the mind is, for the most part, merely passive,'[4] Locke repeatedly insists. Our simple ideas therefore attest the existence of a real substance with power to produce them in us. As to what this substance is, Locke expresses the frankest agnosticism. Neither sensation nor reflection, which Locke has told us are the only sources of our ideas, give us any idea of 'substance', and we therefore have no conception of it. It is merely the something, 'we know not what',[5] which underlies or supports the sensible qualities of things; the 'supposed, but

1. The phrases quoted are from the *Essay*, IV, 4.
2. Wordsworth's *Expostulation and Reply*.
3. *Essay*, II, I, sect. 2.
4. ibid., II, 9, sect. I.　　　5. ibid., I, 4, sect. 19.

unknown, support of those qualities we find existing';[1] the 'something besides' the extension, figure, solidity, and motion of sensible things. Similarly, 'spirit' is the substratum underlying the operations of the mind. But whereas of spirit we are intuitively certain, of matter we merely 'suppose' the reality.

Actually Locke was confirmed in this somewhat paradoxical certainty by the fact that he habitually pictured matter in his mind, according to the prevalent 'corpuscularian' theory, as a collection of invisible atoms varying in their figure and motion. This to him, as to Hobbes, Descartes, and the Cartesians, was the real world; and when he pondered the phenomena of sensation it was always this that he visualized as acting upon our senses. This consideration helps also to explain his belief in the reality of our ideas of the 'primary qualities' of things, by which he understood the qualities just mentioned: extension, figure, solidity, and mobility. Because the real world was made up, for him, of bodies to which only these mathematical qualities could with certainty be attributed, our ideas of these qualities seemed to him to have a degree of reality denied to our ideas of 'secondary' qualities. They were 'resemblances' of 'the thing as it is in itself', whereas the ideas of secondary qualities (colour, sound, temperature, etc.) were merely the mental picturings set up in us by the varying bulk, figure, and texture of the minute parts of the object. In all our ideas of 'things', then, there is a strange mingling of ignorance, reality, and fancy. We are ignorant of the supporting substance, but our ideas of objects, when stripped of subjective accretions, and reduced to their mathematical skeletons, are resemblances of real or primary qualities in the objects. The other ingredients in our ideas of objects – such as round, red, cold, smooth, and the like – are the mind's reaction to certain 'powers' in the material particles of the object, and are therefore not resemblances of real things. What is real in every case is some primary quality, some feature in the configuration or motion of the material particles, which our mind registers as a 'secondary' quality. Locke more than once assures us that if we possessed an ultra-microscopic eye, such as perhaps the angels have, we should then have a direct

1. *Essay*, II, 23, sect. 2.

view of the inner constitution of things, and should perceive, in all their nakedness, the shapes and the movements which now masquerade in our imaginations as colours and sounds, tastes and smells. But, like Swift, Locke reflects that perhaps it behoves us to be content with beautiful surfaces, and not hanker after a direct gaze into this alleged real world of jostling geometrical shapes. Our faculties are suited to our state, he concludes (in a passage suggestive of the *Essay on Man*[1]); we must rest satisfied with the assurance that all we know on earth is all we need to know, and that our ideas of 'Other Things', if inadequate, are such as an all-wise Contriver has fitted our faculties to receive. Thus, as usual, Locke gives his speculations a happy ending, and like an indulgent schoolmaster allows us the reward, after the toil of following his lessons, of running out and playing unconcernedly again in the open air of common sense.

Locke and Poetry

Lastly, it remains to be asked, what, if anything, did this influential philosophy mean for poetry? Most of us today consider the arts to hold something of a central position amongst the activities of human existence, and it is hardly to be supposed that a system of thought which affected the outlook of several generations can have had no relevance whatever for poetry. Locke himself seems to have taken no interest in art, and the few references he makes to poetry are of a disparaging kind. This fact alone is significant, and suggests part of the answer to our question. Philosophers of earlier and of later ages, particularly those of the nineteenth century, have thought it necessary to find a place in their systems for the 'imaginative' way of approaching truth, and some have given it the very highest credentials. But seventeenth-century philosophers as a whole, and Locke above all, did not feel this necessity. It has been one of the main purposes of this book to show how inevitably the whole philosophic movement of the century told against poetry, and I need not

1. *Essay*, II, 23, sects. 11 and 12.

repeat here what has already been said on this subject. Locke summed up in his work the doctrines and assumptions of the seventeenth century, and his great influence imposed them bodily upon the eighteenth as unquestionable truths. That the things which were most real to Locke – his metaphysically-certified God, his outer world of geometrical atoms, and his inner world of mathematical ideas – were not the realities of poetry, will perhaps be generally allowed, suspicious though we rightly are of all romantic presuppositions about what is poetic. Locke's philosophy is the philosophy of an age whose whole effort had been to arrive at 'truth' by exorcising the phantasms of the imagination, and the truth-standards which the eighteenth century inherited through him involved the relegation of the mind's shaping-power to an inferior status. What Locke himself thought of 'the imagination', and of 'poetry', as he understood these terms, can be illustrated from his remarks on 'wit' and 'judgement'. The mind, though passive in perception, becomes active in all the subsequent processes of reflection, which include compounding, comparing, and abstracting from the ideas that sensation has impressed upon it. Our complex ideas so formed are 'real' when they correspond to an actual state of affairs in the 'real' world; or again, they are real if they are mathematical, that is to say, if they are *wholly* the 'workmanship of the mind', and are thus exempted, by their abstract nature, from having any reference to external 'things'. Other mental compounds are 'fantastic', 'chimerical' fictions of our fancies. These may indeed be allowed for purposes of pleasure, but no philosopher can regard them as having any serious importance. 'Wit', for Locke, as for Hobbes and Dryden, consists in a certain 'quickness of parts', whereby the contents of memory – the storehouse of impressions – are readily available when needed. Men who have 'a great deal of wit and prompt memories', however, are not usually distinguished for the 'clearest judgement' or 'deepest reason'. For wit consists in a facility for assembling or combining any ideas which may seem to have some congruity with each other,

thereby to make up pleasant pictures and agreeable visions in the fancy.[1]

1. *Essay*, II, 11, sect. 3 (my italics).

Wit is completely irresponsible, concerning itself not a jot with the 'truth' or 'reality' of its conceits. Judgement, on the other hand, proceeds by a method exactly contrary – by the method, in fact, which it is Locke's whole purpose to recommend. It carefully distinguishes one idea from another, wherever the least difference is discernible, so as to avoid being 'misled by similitude' into mistaking one thing for another. Locke emphasizes the radical opposition between this method and that of 'wit'; it is evidently a matter of importance to him to 'place' poetry as unambiguously as he can:

This is a way of proceeding quite contrary to metaphor and allusion, wherein for the most part lies that *entertainment and pleasantry of wit* which strikes so lively on the fancy, and therefore so acceptable to all people, because its beauty appears at first sight, and there is required *no labour of thought to examine what truth or reason there is in it.*[1]

The mind is content to be amused with 'the agreeableness of the picture', and the 'gaiety of the fancy'; its pleasure would be spoiled by the application of the 'severe rules of *truth and good reason*, whereby it appears that *it consists in something that is not perfectly conformable to them*'.[2] And for what was not conformable to 'truth and good reason' Locke could not be expected to have a very high regard. We get a glimpse of his true feelings about poetry in his *Thoughts Concerning Education*, where he declares that if a child has a poetic vein, the parents, so far from cherishing it, 'should labour to have it stifled and suppressed as much as may be'. The air of Parnassus may be pleasant, but its soil is barren.[3]

Thus do all charms fly 'at the touch of cold philosophy'.[4] I do not wish to suggest, however, that the ascendancy of Locke, or the wide acceptance of his standards of truth, made every sort of poetry impossible. We of this generation have less cause than our predecessors to undervalue the poetic output of the eighteenth century.

1. ibid.   2. ibid.
3. Locke is here urging the drawbacks of poetry as a *career*. (Cf. 'Poetry and gaming, which usually go together, are alike in this too, that they seldom bring any advantage, but to those who have nothing else to live on.' Works, Vol. VIII, p. 167). But the implications remain.
4. Cf. Keats's *Lamia*.

Conformity to truth and good reason is never a wholly bad principle, even for poets; and we owe to it much first-rate satire, as well as a work like the *Essay on Man*. What the cold philosophy did destroy was the union of heart and head, the synthesis of thought and feeling, out of which major poetry seems to be born. There were, it is true, elements in Locke's oddly-composite system which later proved of unexpected service to poetry. The doctrine which derived all our knowledge from the senses was capable of serving Wordsworth, who imbibed it through Hartley, as a philosophic sanction for his own most deep-rooted instincts, and furnished him with at least a foundation for his conscious poetic theory. Wordsworth was working in the spirit and tradition of Locke when he rejected gaudy and inane phraseology and devoted his powers to the task of making verse 'deal boldly with substantial things'. And in a sense, moreover, Locke's 'new way of knowing by ideas', his insistence that all we can contemplate is mind-stuff, contained the implication (though Locke would not have welcomed it) that 'mind is incorrigibly poetical'.[1] But all that this could as yet mean to the average intelligent man of letters is illustrated by Addison in one of his papers on 'Chearfulness'.[2] Concerned, as always, to put a favourable interpretation upon everything, Addison finds in the limitation of our knowledge to 'ideas' a source of satisfaction rather than of humiliation. If the material world, he says, had appeared to us 'endow'd only with *those real Qualities which it actually possesses*, it would have made but a very joyless and uncomfortable Figure'. A kindly Providence, therefore, has given matter the power of producing in us a whole series of delightful 'imaginary' qualities, to the end that man might 'have his Mind cheared and delighted with agreeable Sensations'. In indulging in the Pleasures of the Imagination, therefore, we are doing something not unworthy of a rational being, and something, moreover, which has the approval of Heaven.

But, of course, much more than this was required before there could arise a theory of the imagination adequate to the dignity of

1. Santayana, *Five Essays* (1933), p. 22.
2. *Spectator*, No. 387. (The italics in the ensuing quotations are mine.)

poetry, and much had to be added to Locke's sensationalism before it could be pressed into the service of the creative power. Above all, there was required the conviction that the 'inanimate cold world' of the mechanical philosophy was not the whole reality, that there was a closer bond between the mind and nature than the old dualism could conceive, and that 'Truth' was not given to the naked Reason, but was constituted, in moments of impassioned vigilance, by the whole soul of man

> Working but in alliance with the works
> Which it beholds.

CHAPTER 12

Wordsworth and the Locke Tradition

THE manner in which the triumph of the mechanical philosophy affected poetry can be illustrated, I think, by comparing a representative serious poem of the earlier eighteenth century, Pope's *Essay on Man*, with *Paradise Lost* as representing the previous century. It has been pointed out that there is no Satan in Pope's poem. From one standpoint this fact merely exemplifies Pope's optimistic 'philosophy'. With the characteristic desire of his time to explain, and to explain favourably, Pope unquestioningly makes his poem a theodicy, a vindication of an order of things in which evil appears, but only appears, to exist. To 'explain' evil is almost necessarily to explain it away. But, taking a more general view, one is struck by the absence, in Pope's poem, of any sort of mythological machinery. In giving pointed expression to the real beliefs of his time, Pope instinctively adopts an explanatory method. It would have been unthinkable in Pope's time that a serious poet should have used any such machinery, or even an allegorical convention, for such a purpose. Mythologies, including the Christian, were now felt to be exploded; what may have been 'true' in them is that part which can be conceptually or intellectually stated. Milton, as we have seen, although himself a considerable rationalizer, could still employ the concrete symbols of the faith without feeling that he was deliberately utilizing what was fictitious. God and Satan were real beings to him, as well as 'principles'. But though Pope and his contemporaries were debarred by their intellectual climate from using any great system of commonly-accepted symbols, as Dante and Milton could, they could still employ mythological material for other purposes, as Pope did in the *Rape of the Lock*, for example. They could use it consciously, for technical convenience and for purposes of 'delight'. It is in this manner that the mythologies of the ancient world are generally used by eighteenth-century poets. These poets employ their personifications and their other mythological apparatus in full awareness that they are 'fiction'. They are 'fictions' of proved evocative power and of long association with poetic experience, and they can thus still be made use of to assist in producing poetry out of the dead-matter of modernity. But fictions they are still felt to be, and they cannot therefore be used with full conviction. Their employment involves the deliberate exploitation of obsolete modes of feeling, a conscious disregard of contemporary truth-standards. It was, one may suppose, his sense of this situation which made Johnson dislike *Lycidas* and Gray's *Odes*.

As a consequence of these developments it was inevitable that when a major poet again appeared he should be 'left alone, seeking the visible world'. No existing mythology would express the 'real', as the 'real' was now felt to be. A final effort had been made, by Erasmus Darwin, to enlist poetry under the banner of science by describing the Loves of the Plants with all the apparatus of 'poetical machinery', but of this unholy alliance it would be hard to say whether it was more degrading to science or to poetry. The new poet must therefore either make poetry out of the direct dealings of his mind and heart with the visible universe, or he must fabricate a genuine new mythology of his own (not necessarily rejecting all old material in so doing). Keats and Shelley often follow the second of these methods; Wordsworth typically follows the first.

Wordsworth's relation to the 'scientific' tradition is not quite simple. In a sense he is in violent reaction against it, and yet it conditioned much of his poetic experience. What he owed to it was his instinctive repudiation of any concrete mythology. His poetry was 'scientific' in that his interest lay in the free relations between the mind of man and the universe to which, he believes, it is 'so exquisitely fitted'. According to him, we 'build up the being that we are' by 'deeply drinking-in the soul of things'. That is, there must be no abstractions, no symbols, no myths, to stand between the mind and its true object. In so far as it was the abstract world-picture (the world as 'machine') of the seventeenth-century natural philosophers which had exploded the mythologies, Wordsworth may be said to have owed to them (as well as to his own temperament) his root-assumption that truth could only be achieved by 'making verse deal boldly with substantial things'. Wordsworth was the kind of poet who could only have appeared at the end of the eighteenth century, when mythologies were exploded, and a belief in the visible universe as the body of which God was the soul alone remained. In this sense his beliefs can be viewed as data furnished to him by a tradition; in this sense he, as well as Dante, may be said to have employed his sensibility within a framework of received beliefs. But his debt to tradition, unlike Dante's, was a negative one; he owed to it his *deprivation* of mythology, his aloneness with the universe. His more positive beliefs, those by which he appears in reaction against the scientific tradition, were built up by him out of his own poetic experiences, and it is this which makes him representative of the modern situation – the situation in which beliefs are made out of poetry rather than poetry out of beliefs. To animize the 'real' world, the 'universe of death' that the 'mechanical' system of philosophy had produced, but to do so without either using an exploded mythology or fabricating a new one, this was the special task and mission of Wordsworth. Wordsworth's conviction that the human mind was capable of this task was the most important of his 'positive' beliefs, and this belief he owed chiefly to his own experiences. It is this which distinguishes his 'deism' from that of, for instance, Thomson's *Seasons*, to which it bears an obvious superficial resemblance. For Thomson, as for Pope, mythologies were almost as 'unreal' as for Wordsworth, but their positive belief, their Deism (in so far as they genuinely held it), was 'intellectually' held, and it consequently appears in poetry mainly as rhetoric. The poetry exists to decorate, to render agreeable, a set of abstract notions; and these abstractions have been taken over, as truth, from the natural philosophers – from Descartes, Newton, Locke, or Leibnitz. Wordsworth's beliefs, on the other hand, were largely the formulation of his own dealings with 'substantial things'; they were held intellectually only because they had first been 'proved upon the pulses'. That the result of his 'dealings' was not a *Divine Comedy* or a *Paradise Lost* was due, we may say, to the scientific movement and the sensationalist philosophy of Locke and Hartley; that the result was not an *Essay on Man*, a *Seasons*, or a *Botanic Garden* was due to himself. For it was the 'visible world', no abstract machine, that Wordsworth sought; and he felt that mechanical materialism had substituted a 'universe of death for that which moves with light and life instinct, actual, divine, and true'.[1] The belief that Wordsworth constructed out of his experiences was a belief in the capacity of the mind to cooperate with this 'active universe', to contribute something of its own to it in perceiving it, and not, as sensationalism taught, merely to receive, passively, impressions from without. It was this belief, or the experiences upon which the belief was based, which encouraged him to hope that poetry might be delivered from the fetters of the mechanical tradition without being allowed to fall into disrepute as 'unreal' or 'fanciful'.

Of this belief, as intellectually formulated, there are many explicit statements in Wordsworth's poetry, especially in the *Prelude*, as well as in his prose. There is, for example, the passage on the child (the 'inmate of this active universe'):

> For feeling has to him imparted power
> That through the growing faculties of sense
> Doth like an agent of the one great Mind
> Create, creator and receiver both,
> Working but in alliance with the works
> Which it beholds.[2]

In a later passage of the same Book he distinguishes the true creative power from arbitrary fancy:

> A plastic power
> Abode with me, a forming hand, at times
> Rebellious, acting in a devious mood,
> A local spirit of his own, at war
> With general tendency, but, for the most,
> Subservient strictly to external things
> With which it communed.[3]

The classic 'locus' is in the Preface to the *Excursion*, where in

1. *Prelude*, XIV, 160.   2. ibid., II, 254.   3. ibid., 362.

deliberately Miltonic language he has been claiming more than epic dignity for his own subject-matter:[1]

> Paradise, and groves
> Elysian, Fortunate Fields – *why should they be*
> *A history only of departed things,*
> *Or a mere fiction of what never was?*
> *For the discerning intellect of Man,*
> *When wedded to this goodly universe*
> *In love and holy passion, shall find these*
> *A simple produce of the common day.*
> – I, long before the blissful hour arrives,
> Would chant in lonely peace the spousal verse
> Of this great consummation: – and, *by words*
> *Which speak of nothing more than what we are,*
> Would I arouse the sensual from their sleep
> Of Death, and win the vacant and the vain
> To noble raptures; while my voice proclaims
> How exquisitely the individual Mind
>   to the external World
> Is fitted, and how exquisitely too –
> Theme this but little heard of among men –
> The external World is fitted to the Mind;
> *And the Creation* (by no lower name
> Can it be called) *which they with blended might*
> *Accomplish.*

The famous 'Fancy-Imagination' distinction of Wordsworth and Coleridge, and their followers, may best be understood as arising from the existence in them of the particular 'belief-state' I have tried to indicate. The fact-world of modern scientific consciousness was the primary datum. In this 'inanimate cold world' 'objects, *as* objects, are essentially fixed and dead'.[2] But just as a 'known and familiar landscape' may be transmuted by moonlight or 'accidents of light and shade',[3] so, owing to the bond between nature and the soul of man, this dead world may be brought to life by the modify-

1. The italics are mine.
2. Coleridge, *Biographia Literaria*, Ch. 13 (Vol. I, p. 202 in Shawcross).
3. Phrases from the opening of Ch. 14 of *Biographia Literaria*.

ing colours of the 'imagination'. Of the *imagination*, for this is the faculty which works the required magic without producing what is now felt to be 'fictitious'. Where there is consciousness of fiction, it is the *fancy* that has been at work. The test of the 'imaginative', as distinct from the 'imaginary', is that external objects shall have been coloured by the poet's own mood, or made the symbol of it; that the plastic power shall have been exercised, but kept 'subservient strictly to external things'. Modifications *so* wrought, values *so* ascribed to the fact-world, have a reality-status which is unassailable, because they are psychological in origin; they spring, that is, from states of mind, of which the 'reality' cannot be questioned.

Wordsworth's belief in the possibility of this creation which the mind and the universe may 'with blended might accomplish' was, I have suggested, largely built up out of his own poetic experience. One need only consider a number of passages in which Wordsworth has commemorated those of his experiences which he felt to be most significant, to see that they are generally occasions on which he had (for the most part unconsciously at the time) exerted the 'visionary', the 'plastic' power upon some external object. In the celebrated 'spots of time' passage at the end of Book XII of the *Prelude*,[1] he says explicitly that of all the recollections which hold for him a 'renovating virtue', he values most those which record moments of the greatest self-activity, those which 'give knowledge to what point, and how, the mind is lord and master, outward sense the obedient servant of her will'; recollections, that is, which show the mind 'not prostrate, overborne, as if the mind herself were nothing, a mere pensioner on outward forms –' (as in sensationalist philosophy), but in its native dignity, creating significance in alliance with external things. It is unfortunately true that Wordsworth frequently *discusses* his experiences, and states the results which his intellect has extracted from them, instead of communicating them to us. The modern reader demands the experience, and cares little or nothing what metaphysical or psychological principle they are supposed to exemplify. This criticism is perhaps applicable to the passage in

1. Lines 208–86.

Book XII to which I have referred, for Wordsworth there avows his inability to communicate the 'visionary dreariness' which then invested the moor, the lonely pool, and the woman with the pitcher, although the knowledge that his imagination had been strong enough to impart the visionary quality to the scene was his reason for valuing the recollection. But he has given enough examples of his sensibility in action for us to see that its workings were independent of, and antecedent to, the formulation of the belief. When (to take a few illustrations at random):

> a gentle shock of mild surprise
> Has carried far into his heart the voice
> Of mountain torrent;[1]

when he saw the Leech-Gatherer pace

> About the weary moors continually,
> Wandering about alone and silently;[2]

when the Highland woman's greeting seemed

> a sound
> Of something without place or bound;[3]

when

> the high spear-grass on that wall
> By mist and silent rain-drops silvered o'er,
> As once I passed, into my heart conveyed
> So still an image of tranquillity,
> So calm and still, and looked so beautiful
> Among the uneasy thoughts which filled my mind,[4]

these experiences, and many another that could be collected from his best poetry, depended upon no special beliefs (and of course no beliefs are needed by the reader in order to share them to the full). It was out of the repetition of these imaginative moments that the belief arose; the belief itself was the intellectual formulation of what

1. *Prelude*, v, 382.   2. *Resolution and Independence*, stanza xix.
3. *Stepping Westward*, verse 2.   4. *Excursion*, I, 943.

they seemed to mean. It must be recognized, nevertheless, that the formulation, once made (no doubt with Coleridge's assistance), gave added importance to the recollected 'moments', the 'spots of time', and that Wordsworth would probably not have conducted his *recherche du temps perdu* with such eagerness and such conviction if he had not so formulated it.

Wordsworth's poetic activity, then, was largely conditioned by the 'reality-standards' of his time, which left him alone with the visible universe. But this 'creative sensibility' had taught him that he was not alone with an 'inanimate cold world', but with an 'active universe', a universe capable of being moulded and modified by the 'plastic power' which abode within himself. As long as he could be a poet, this belief in the bond between man and nature was valid. Poetry becomes, with Wordsworth, the record of moments of 'ennobling interchange of action from within and from without';[1] it takes on, in fine, a *psychological* aspect. 'There is scarcely one of my poems', Wordsworth wrote to Lady Beaumont, 'which does not aim to direct the attention to some moral sentiment, or to some general principle, or law of thought, or of our intellectual constitution.'[2]

I have emphasized this 'aloneness' of Wordsworth with the universe, because I think it marks his position in the history of 'poetry and beliefs', and because it seems to determine the quality of much of his work. Centuries of intellectual development had now brought matters to this, that if poetry were still to be made, it must be made by the sheer unaided power of the individual poet. And what was it that he must make? A record of successes; of successful imaginative dealings with the world of eye and ear. And what was to be the criterion of success? That plastic power shall have been exerted upon the 'vulgar forms of every day', but in such a way that there shall be no departure from 'nature's living images'. The midnight storm may grow darker in presence of the poet's eye, the visionary dreariness, the consecration, may be spread

1. *Prelude*, XIII, 375.
2. In *Wordsworth's Literary Criticism*, p. 51.

over sea or land, but the transforming power must work 'subservient strictly to external things'; there must be intensification without distortion. Fact and value were to be combined in this 'fine balance of truth in observing, with the imaginative faculty in modifying, the object observed'. But what sort of 'truth' may be claimed for the creation which world and mind 'with blended might accomplish'? – for, that poetry is 'the most philosophic of all writing', that 'its object is truth', is Wordsworth's profound conviction.[1] I suppose the answer would be, 'psychological' truth; that is to say, the poetry is faithfully expressive of certain states of consciousness. Of the two elements of which these states are composed, fact and value, Wordsworth is equally sure of both. He is sure of the fact, because he knows no man has observed it more intently; he is sure of the value, because this was intuitively apprehended in himself, it came from within. He is no less sure of the truth of the resulting creation, because it had been experienced as a modification of his own consciousness. But it was only as long as his mind was dealing thus nakedly with observed fact that Wordsworth could feel this conviction of truthfulness. Any translation of his experience into myth, personification, or fable, though not necessarily always culpable, is inevitably a lapse towards a lower level of truth, a fall, in fact, from imagination to fancy. Poetry exists to transform, to make this muchloved earth more lovely; and in former times men could express their sense of fact, without misgivings, in mythologies. But since the coming of the enlightened age this was becoming almost impossible. The efforts of eighteenth-century poets to vitalize the dead matter of the Cartesian universe by using the symbols of an outworn mythology had ended in fiasco, and the abandonment of the symbols, at any rate for a time, became a necessity.

But this abandonment threw upon Wordsworth, as it throws still more emphatically upon the contemporary poet, an enormous burden, no less, in fact, than 'the weight of all this unintelligible world'. He must be continually giving proofs of strength in order to maintain his belief that the load *could* be lightened. To keep the vast encompassing world from becoming 'cold and inanimate' by

1. *Lyrical Ballads*, Preface, p. 25 in *Wordsworth's Literary Criticism*.

transferring to it a 'human and intellectual life' from the poet's own spirit; to 'dissolve, diffuse, and dissipate in order to re-create'; to 'idealize, and to unify'; to 'shoot one's being through earth, air, and sea' – what a stupendous task for the unaided spirit of man. Is it to be wondered at that Wordsworth, after bearing the heavy and the weary weight, Atlas-like, for many years, should at last, like Atlas, have turned into a mountain of stone? Youth, and Coleridge, and Dorothy, and the moonlight of Alfoxden – these could and did lighten the burden for him for a while. But there are many signs that after this his material began to resist him more and more stubbornly. Was there not something in the very nature of the poetic task he had set himself which made this inevitable? 'To spread the tone, the atmosphere, and with it the depth and height of the ideal world around forms, incidents, and situations, of which, for the common view, custom had bedimmed all the lustre, had dried up the sparkle and the dew-drops'[1] – this is probably the special prerogative of youth. In youth the imagination poured the modifying colours prodigally over all things, and only when its vitality began to sink did the man discover how much virtue had been going out of him. With the realization that 'objects *as* objects, are essentially fixed and dead', comes the disturbing sense that 'in our life alone does nature live'. That Wordsworth had reached this point at about the age of thirty-five is fairly clear from the passage in Book XII of the *Prelude*, where, echoing Coleridge, he declares

> That from thyself it comes, that thou must give,
> Else never canst receive.[2]

The whole context from which these words are taken shows also how habitually, by this time, Wordsworth had come to find in *memory* his chief reservoir of strength. Certain memories are the 'hiding-places of man's power'; memories, that is, of former successful exertions of imaginative strength. In the *Prelude* pre-eminently, though elsewhere as well, Wordsworth, now fighting a

1. Coleridge, *Biographia Literaria*, Ch. 5, Vol. I, p. 59. The other quoted phrases on this and the former page are also Coleridge's.
2. XII, 276.

losing battle with *das Gemeine*, supported his strength for a while by drawing upon the past. But he was living upon capital, and when that was spent, what was to remain?

Poetry, as we have since learnt, has other tasks than that of imparting psychological values to the visible world. Had Wordsworth turned his attention towards these, his genius might not have atrophied so soon. It remains to indicate briefly, in conclusion, what gave Wordsworth his initial direction towards 'Nature' as the inevitable raw material for his creative sensibility. Here we meet, I think, with two other groups of beliefs current in his age, which may be said to have conditioned his poetic experience: postulates ('doctrines-felt-as-facts') without which his poetry would not have been what it actually is. The first was the product of the deistic tradition of the seventeenth and eighteenth centuries, to which I have already alluded in passing. Ever since the Renaissance the Creation had been steadily gaining in prestige as the 'art of God', the universal divine Scripture which 'lies expans'd unto the eyes of all'.[1] The emotion of the 'numinous', formerly associated with super-nature, had become attached to Nature itself; and by the end of the eighteenth century the divinity, the sacredness of nature was, to those affected by this tradition, almost a first datum of consciousness. Wordsworth, then, did not have to construct this belief wholly out of his experience; much of it was given to him.

Much the same is true of the second of these fundamental beliefs, the belief in the grandeur and dignity of man, and the holiness of the heart's affections. This, too, was the product of forces originating (for our purposes) in the Renaissance; it had arisen out of the ruins of the theological view of man. As the 'Fall' receded further and further into the region of fable, man was increasingly regarded as a creature not only made in, but retaining, God's image; and Wordsworth could acknowledge, without misgiving, 'a grandeur in the beatings of the heart', and speak in good faith of 'man and his noble nature'. In Wordsworth's lifetime this humanism had taken a colouring from Rousseau, and the special nobility of man was

1. Sir T. Browne, *Religio medici*, I, sect. xvi.

therefore only to be looked for 'in huts where poor men lie'. The 'higher' grades of society, in which the culture of the Renaissance had been exclusively fostered, were now

> A light, a cruel, and vain world, cut off
> From the natural inlets of just sentiment,
> From lowly sympathy, and chastening truth.[1]

The blend of these two closely-related beliefs resulted, with Wordsworth, in his typical celebration of figures like the Leech-Gatherer, Michael, or 'Nature's Lady'; beings whose humanity is ennobled by close association with 'mute insensate things'. Wordsworth is indebted to the traditions I have mentioned for his pre-conception that humanity is in closest touch with 'reality', as well as in its healthiest, most wisely tranquil, state when it is most intimately blended with the cosmic processes.

Many and great changes have taken place since Wordsworth's time, changes which have involved the evaporation of most of his characteristic beliefs, both inherited and self-wrought. Few now have any faith in 'nature', or in 'man', or in the bond between man and nature. Most readers seem to find it harder to yield 'imaginative assent' to these doctrines than to others more remote from our present habits of mind. The poetic tradition founded by Wordsworth is probably now dead and superseded. Yet as he is the first, so he remains the type, of the 'modern' poets who, 'left alone' with a vaster material than his, must bear as best they can, unaided by any universally-held mythology, the 'weight of all this unintelligible world'.

1. *Prelude*, IX, 349.

Index

280

MORE ABOUT PENGUINS
AND PELICANS

Penguinews, which appears every month, contains details of all the new books issued by Penguins as they are published. From time to time it is supplemented by *Penguins in Print*, which is a complete list of all available books published by Penguins. (There are well over three thousand of these.)

A specimen copy of *Penguinews* will be sent to you free on request, and you can become a subscriber for the price of the postage. For a year's issues (including the complete lists) please send 30p if you live in the United Kingdom, or 60p if you live elsewhere. Just write to Dept. EP, Penguin Books Ltd, Harmondsworth, Middlesex, enclosing a cheque or postal order, and your name will be added to the mailing list.

Note: *Penguinews* and *Penguins in Print* are not available in the U.S.A. or Canada

BASIL WILLEY

The Eighteenth-Century Background

What key word suggests itself as a 'way in' to eighteenth-century thought – to Shaftesbury, Butler, Swift, Hume, Hartley, Holbach, and Priestley? To Professor Willey that word is 'nature', and he traces the various stages in the divinization of the idea of nature that led to the Romantic Revival. In doing so he shows the importance of this concept in religion, ethics, philosophy, science, and politics – every sphere, in fact, of the intellectual activity of the eighteenth century.

Like Professor Willey's seventeenth-century studies, *The Eighteenth-Century Background* is based on lectures delivered in the English faculty at Cambridge. Originally addressed to the literary student looking for extra-literary associations and explanations, it will appeal to all who are interested in the history of ideas.

'An important contribution to scholarship' – *Oxford Magazine*

NOT FOR SALE IN THE U.S.A.

BASIL WILLEY

Nineteenth-Century Studies

Professor Willey's 'background' books on the eighteenth and nineteenth centuries (both already available in Pelicans) are well-known as lucid expositions of the main intellectual currents of their periods. In writing about the nineteenth century, he again illustrates his profound grasp of the history of ideas. The field is a particularly rich one: the great nineteenth-century debates on religion and ethics form the major theme, and the writers considered are Coleridge, Thomas Arnold, Newman, Carlyle, Bentham, J. S. Mill, Auguste Comte, George Eliot (including the influence on her of Hennell, Strauss, and Feuerbach), and Matthew Arnold.

'A work written with grace and lucidity, based on a profound knowledge of the writers upon whom he focuses his attention' – *The Times Literary Supplement*